Th

The Shadow Cast
15th Anniversary Edition

The Shadow Cast

Published internationally by Torchmark Books

© Mike Broemmel 2020

Dedicated to the memory of my father, Frank Broemmel.

Author's Notes

The Shadow Cast is the second collection of my short fiction to be published internationally. Of all of the writing projects I've undertaken through the years, I believe this book remains my proudest achievement.

The re-release of *The Shadow Cast* on the 15th anniversary of its original publication means a great deal to me personally. My sincere hope is that a whole new generation of readers will be able to get to know the characters that populate this book, characters that have remained close to me through the years.

My life has been described as a rollercoaster of great successes and tremendous failures. On some level, the characters on the pages of this book epitomize the ups and downs that I have experienced through my own time on Earth.

My sincere hope is that a reader of *The Shadow Cast* will be left with the understanding that even in the darkest of times, brighter days always come. I truly know this to be true.

Mike Broemmel

South Beach, Florida USA, 2020

Acknowledgments

Editor's Note: The Acknowledgments were written for the original edition of The Shadow Cast.

The creation of *The Shadow Cast* was far from a solitary act. Without the generous support of numerous people, the words I scribbled by pencil through the creative process onto whatever paper came to hand never would have taken shape in polished book form. Those tatty sheets might always have remained, gathering dust in an attic somewhere, and roughly titled 'Toilet Paper Memoirs'.

I remain forever grateful to my incomparable editor at BeWrite Books, Neil Marr. When it comes to writing, I more often than not feel I am a blacksmith bashing away at an anvil. Neil fashions my roughish hammerings into something altogether more laudable. And to my publisher at BeWrite Books, Caitlin Myers: Thank you. When many others might very well have cast me aside as too troublesome an author to do business with, you've remained fast and firm; your support will always be remembered.

The original title of this collection was *Toilet Paper Memoirs.* Because that's just what the stories originally were – a way of marking creative time without the advantage of proper writing materials – sometimes not even a piece of notepaper, never mind a new-fangled word processor. The stub of a crayon, a scrap of toilet paper was all I had. I was spurred for years by the way this provoking working title focused and then held together my random thoughts. Without that simple but vital stimulation, this work wouldn't have been born, let alone come of age. And this was a gift to me from a friend of twenty years, Karen Staudinger; the friendship that was lives on in the pages of this book.

Without the support and efforts of Frances A. Rove, Jana Beethe, Loretta Simms, Sue Widmann, Kim Streff and Renee DeAlba who diligently assisted with my manuscript, my scratches and dashes never would have seen the light of day.

A special thanks as well to stalwart friends who stood by me and often encouraged me during the toughest, most daunting time of my life: Cheryl Logan, John Holzhuter, Rosemary Holzhuter, Leonard Pickard, Katy Field, Paulette Sober, Lisa O'Day, Patrick DeLapp, Susie Hoffmann, Christopher Chapman, Nancy Weber, Margaret Stoehr, Regina Nieberding, Herbert Tegler, Winston Alexander, Margie Simms, Mike Widmann, James Simms, Dave Simms, Steve Lehman, Patti Winocur, Fred Winocur, Steve Simms, Debbie Simms and Stamie Minor and the men and women of the Phoenix Project.

Finally, as always, all my thanks and love to my dear family: Frank, Thelma and Jill Broemmel.

Contents

Introduction

Editor's Note: The Introduction was written for the original edition of The Shadow Cast *by the book's initial editor, Neil Marr. Marr worked with Mike Broemmel on his first two internationally published books. Marr passed away in 2014.*

The Shadow Cast is a collection of twenty-two short stories … but a book debunking any claim that a whole cannot be greater than the sum of its parts.

Each tale in Mike Broemmel's new anthology can proudly stand alone in the greatest tradition of story-telling; but read in sequence his painstakingly ordered works pack the punch of an epic novel. They present an unbroken saga of stark, simple truth that is all but unique in the annals of fiction.

People, places, periods develop and seamlessly intertwine, story-by-story.

The Shadow Cast is an insightful record of a reality we never realized existed before Broemmel. The shadow may sometimes represent shelter and escape, sometimes the umbrella that obscures so many of our quiet doings. The cast? The cast is you … you and that guy down the road apiece. It's about how you manage to share this world with him and her as earth bound companions, fellow mortals.

The Shadow Cast

Broemmel penned *The Shadow Cast* during a particularly challenging point in his own life. When there was nothing but a stub of a pencil and a few squares of toilet paper to turn his thoughts into shades of black and white, that's what he used.

The result is this book with its humble clarity and the act of contrition of a human being whose heart might be outweighed only by his talent.

But don't leap to the flawed conclusion that what you are about to read reflects bitterness or numbingly agonizing memoir of Broemmel's trials and tribulations. Nothing could be further from the truth. Gritty and honest as these stories are, they are nothing if not a celebration of the indomitable human spirit. The spirit of the fading actress, the hapless lover, the forgotten inventor, the heartless businessman, the crippled, the crazed, the clumsy, the dastardly and the destitute all find a home here where nobodies become somebodies in the hands of a master of literature.

Because, you see, Mike Broemmel has discovered a vital truth – the harder you gaze from the shelter of an umbrella, the more likely you are to see the clouds break … and those first shafts of sunlight that dry the rain – and the tears.

Neil Marr
Editor
Monaco – 2004

Special thanks to Frances Rove, without whose assistance this book would never have been possible.

ix

Miss Trent Plays the Jayhawk

Pam Ella Trent breezed into the ornate lobby of the Hotel Savoy in downtown Kansas City, Missouri at noon on the dot. She planned her appearance to coincide with the rush and bustle of luncheon diners who made their treks through the lobby at that time en route to the hotel's elegant eatery. Scribbling her signature on napkins, scraps of paper, and porter cards, Miss Trent received her fans, women and men, who recognized her instantly.

Spending nearly half an hour wrapped in the glow of her admirers, Miss Trent finally and reluctantly excused herself to join two men who were waiting for her outside the main entrance to the Savoy. On the sidewalk stood an earnest, rail thin, bespectacled, twenty-something reporter for 'Hollywood Chatterbox,' Handy Weather. Calmly watching the rookie scribe rock back and forth from leg to leg, was the aging chauffeur at Miss Trent's service on that part of the circuit, a sharecropper's son and the grandson of slaves. Currently called Clyde, the old fellow used various monikers at different junctures in his life.

A full hour earlier, Clyde had double-parked a bluegray Packard in front of the hotel's entrance, during which time he simply ignored the blooming wrath engendered by the hefty motorcar blocking the trafficway.

Quite like a peppy mongrel pup, Handy Weather was on Pam Ella Trent's heels the moment she set foot onto the sidewalk fronting the Savoy.

"Miss Trent?" Handy blathered.

Spinning around to face Handy, Miss Trent prepared to autograph another paper scrap for a fan.

"I am," she boasted, batting her heavily made up eyes.

"Oh, Miss Trent, I'm Handy Weather."

Pursing her lips, Miss Trent did not understand what the reporter said, unable to hear over the din of yet another horn of a passing auto bearing still one more driver delayed by the offending Packard.

"The weather? Is what?" she asked, plainly irritated.

Cupping his hands over his mouth to form a makeshift bullhorn, Handy Weather repeated his introduction.

Improvidently screaming when the passing motorist ceased laying on the horn, Handy Weather bellowed: "I'm a reporter from 'Hollywood Chatterbox'."

Pam Ella Trent's eyes popped wide open, her face looking quite like a quickly uprighted ceramic doll with movable lids.

"Reporter?" Miss Trent cooed.

"Yes, ma'am. I'm to go with you to Topeka today."

"Oh my, yes," she replied, having no idea what Handy Weather was talking about.

No longer particularly listening to the cub reporter she asked: "'Hollywood Chatterbox', then?"

"Yes, ma'am."

"Delicious," she exclaimed, turning to Clyde the chauffeur. "Floyd, let's be off."

Clyde courteously tipped his driving cap, ignoring the misnomer, used to being called many names.

The Shadow Cast

Handy followed Miss Trent into the broad, leather rear seat of the Packard. Clyde wasted little time in maneuvering the auto into the flow of traffic. "Now, tell me, Randy ..." "Handy," he corrected.

Miss Trent believed he referred to the ever-ready reporter's notepad that he held rather than correcting her abuse of his name.

"Oh, yes, handy," she replied. "Now, Randy, tell me, will this be a cover story?"

"It's Handy," he repeated.

"Yes, love. It's a handy little pad you have there. So Randy, will this be a cover story?"

Resigned, Handy advised the actress that the piece on her was intended for the cover.

"Delicious," she enthused as Clyde pointed the automobile west towards Topeka.

"My editor and your manager agreed that I can stay with you through your show tonight, backstage, even."

"Of course," Miss Trent firmly responded despite lacking any prior recollection of anything Handy discussed.

The mid-July afternoon was a scorcher. The plains' inferno took a toll on the corn crops. As the Packard sped towards the Kansas capital city, fields on each side of the roadway featured weather weary sentinels: drooping, drying, stalks of corn.

Handy scribbled here and there on his narrow notepad as he chatted with the actress during the seventy-mile motor trek to Topeka.

"So, Miss Trent, you began the circuit in New York?"

"Yes, Andy, we did. We began at the Apollo. It was a delicious start."

3

The Shadow Cast

"And, you end in Hollywood?"

"Yes. And that will also be delicious."

"And you play thirty cities in between?"

"That's right, Andy."

Miss Trent diverted her attention from the reporter and on towards Clyde in the front seat. "Bradley," she sounded, not getting the driver's attention immediately because of the error in name. She patted on the front car seat to get Clyde's attention.

"Bradley, how long 'til Topeka?"

"About forty-five minutes, Miss Trent," Clyde replied.

"Your show is a revue?" Handy asked.

"Yes, a delightful revue. A revue of Broadway tunes from '27, '28, and '29."

"But not this year?" he asked.

"None from 1930, that's right. But all the divine show tunes from '27, '28, and '29." Miss Trent bubbled in her seat, sounding more like a teenage schoolgirl than a sixty-year-old songstress.

"Will you do any films anytime soon?" Handy earnestly inquired of the actress.

With pursed lips, nearly a frown, Miss Trent responded with a terse, "Films?"

"Yes, ma'am."

"Films?"

"Yes, ma'am. Any new films coming up?"

Miss Trent sat motionless, as if a brittle frost had infiltrated the auto and chilled her stony solid. "No," she replied, hardly over a whisper.

"I love your films," Handy noted, with a glowing smile.

4

Warming up promptly, Miss Trent grabbed onto one of the reporter's hands with both of her own. "You do?" she beamed.

"Oh, yes, Miss Trent. I've seen them all, every one."

"Oh, my, Andy, that's so kind." She feigned embarrassment, held her breath hoping her cheeks would flush.

"You're my favorite, Miss Trent."

"Oh, you're a divine young man."

"I bet your revue is packing them in, Miss Trent."

"Packing … them in," she hesitated. "Well, yes."

Pam Ella Trent and Handy Weather continued to chat. Handy occasionally scribbling a note or thought on his reporter's pad. Within what seemed like little time to the Packard's passengers, they reached the outskirts of Topeka.

"You know, Randy, the Governor will be at my performance tonight."

"The Governor?"

"Yes, Alf Landon, the Governor. You know, in nearly every state I've performed, the Governor has come."

"I'm not surprised," Handy fawned. "You're just the best"

"Randy, you're so lovely."

Clyde interrupted the conversation between Miss Trent and the reporter for the first time since the auto trip commenced. "We'll be at your hotel in a few minutes, Miss Trent."

"Marvelous. I could use a nap." Turning to Handy, she fluffed her hair and added, "Beauty sleep, you know."

Handy bowed his head, like a shy schoolboy laying an apple on the teacher's desk. "Aw, Miss Trent, you'd be beautiful with no sleep at all."

"You're spoiling me, Andy," she swooned. "I'll never be able to sit for another interview again. Not ever, ever."

"Rupert!" Miss Trent called out to the driver. "Rupert!" she repeated.

"Oh, yes ma'am," Clyde finally replied, realizing he was being called upon.

"Rupert, how far is the hotel from the theater?"

"Right next door, ma'am. Actually connected. Plus, the theater has refrigerated air."

She giggled with delight. "And they say everything's up to date in New York City."

Within a few minutes, the Packard pulled up to the Hotel Jayhawk.

Clyde hurried to open Miss Trent's door and then that of her ride-along guest. She strutted into the lobby with Handy shuffling behind, Clyde hoisting her luggage out of the trunk.

Pam Ella Trent looked obviously disappointed to find the lobby empty except for a bald reservation clerk and a bellman sound asleep on a chair near the main entrance. She snorted, clearly displeased.

"Franklin!" she shouted, again for Clyde. He was quicker on his feet in that instance.

"Ma'am?" he replied, weighed down with the lady's luggage.

"There's no one here," she snapped.

Clyde scoured the lobby, spotting the desk clerk and the dozing bellman. He wondered who else would be

6

necessary. He only wished the bellman was alert and not snoozing. He needed help with Miss Trent's traveling packs.

Handy knew to what Miss Trent referred and shuttled up to her side. "Miss Trent, the folks here obviously didn't know when you were scheduled to arrive or this lobby, this whole city block, would be filled with your people ... your fans."

Handy's exuberant style made Miss Trent's face beam.

"Oh, Andy," she gushed, shortly stopping and bestowing full attention on the eager reporter. "You're such a dear."

Handy blushed, scraping the tip of his left shoe across the terrazzo tile floor. Clyde, in the meantime, had reached the reservation service desk and advised the clerk of Miss Trent's arrival. The desk clerk fumbled about clearing some loose papers off the counter. He then licked his fingertips and slid them across the wispy ring of hair on each side of his balding head.

Handy and Miss Trent reached the reservation desk at the moment the clerk finished fiddling with his thin mane.

"Miss Trent," he greeted, his nasal, high pitched, nearly whining voice causing Pam Ella Trent and Handy Weather to actually wince.

"Good afternoon," she replied with flourish.

"I'm so excited to have you here," the clerk went on.

Miss Trent raised her arm and bent her hand forward at her wrist: "Go on."

"Really. And I have a ticket for your show. I got a ticket, I did."

7

The Shadow Cast

"How wonderful! I am so glad you will be there."

"Me, too! Me, too!" the desk clerk bounced as he spoke.

The clerk turned his attention towards Handy and frowned.

"Do you have a reservation?" he snapped, acting as if Handy Weather invaded his domain.

Handy nodded, grinning. Miss Trent spoke extolling Handy's praises. "He's a reporter for 'Hollywood Chatterbox.' He's doing a story on me … a cover story."

In a condescending way, the clerk snorted: "Oh, a reporter. The press." He wholly refocused on Miss Trent and told the actress the hotel set aside the best suite for her stay.

"Delightful," she replied.

Looking down his nose, over the top of his glasses, the clerk told Handy he would find a room for the reporter. Once he had Miss Trent registered, he clapped his hands sharply twice, bringing around the dozing bellman who moved to the desk as if waiting a command to service and not as a man lumbering in sleep.

The clerk announced Pam Ella Trent as if boasting of a newly obtained and precious possession. "The Jayhawk Suite," the clerk concluded, after which the bellman placed Miss Trent's luggage on a porter's cart.

"Will you need me any more this afternoon?" Clyde diligently inquired.

"No, Emerson. Be back tomorrow in time for me to get to Kansas City and the airfield." Turning to the clerk, she spouted that her next show was the following night in Denver. Facing Handy, Miss Trent rattled: "Then off to Salt Lake, Boise, Seattle, San Francisco, and Hollywood."

"It's great," Handy enthused.

"Yes!" Miss Trent agreed.

"What about my room?" Handy asked of the clerk. The clerk responded by waving him off.

"Take Miss Trent to her suite," the clerk directed the porter, pointing towards the elevators. "If you need anything at all, Miss Trent, you just ring on down. I'll be on duty until your show."

"Wonderful."

The desk clerk asked for Miss Trent's autograph, which she scribbled on a guest ticket. She started off towards the elevators; two double sets of golden doors, the bellman following closely behind.

"Miss Trent," Handy called after the actress.

She spun around, her dress easily twirling. "Yes, Randy?"

"My interview …" his voice trailed off.

"Oh, of course dear. You meet me here in the lobby, say, at six tonight. Then we'll go off to my dressing room at the theater and you can do your interview there."

"Great," he eagerly agreed.

Miss Trent stepped into the elevator, leaving the clerk and Handy Weather standing in the lobby with longing eyes like two whelping pups. Clyde grinned wryly and slightly shook his head, making for the door and the shiny Packard.

Ensconced in the heavily appointed suite, Miss Trent quickly abandoned her day clothes and slipped into a lavender silk dressing gown. She poured herself a gin with a spritz of tonic and took a seat on an emerald plush chaise.

Handy was ushered to a simple room on the hotel's second floor. He spent the afternoon sketching penciled pictures of cats, dogs and ducks. The reservation clerk spent the afternoon doodling 'Pam Ella Trent' on guest cards and bellman receipts.

Miss Trent's revue's staging director arrived in Topeka nearly two hours behind the star, stuck in Kansas City dealing with a frustrated costumer who needed to be coaxed, cajoled and finally cleanly bribed to continue with the circuit. He was frantic and irritable when he reached the Jayhawk Theater.

The Jayhawk Theater, nearly ten years old, was a graceful venue. The elaborate décor and resplendent lighting created the perfect environment for traveling vaudevillians, play actors, and other sundry performers who trooped across the heartland. When opened, at a festive gala still well recalled in the Midwestern city, the State Theater of Kansas proudly proclaimed its refrigerated air and fine facilities as making the Jayhawk a 'haven for performers and audiences alike'.

By the time Hartford Wayclocks, the staging director, arrived in Topeka, late, he was so disorganized, perturbed, he stormed into the gaily elegant theater barely taking in any of the accoutrements and trappings. The chilled air, however, braced him like an icy splash.

The Jayhawk Theater's manager nervously waited at the main entrance, a post he maintained for over ninety minutes, anxiously expecting the well-overdue director of Pam Ella Trent's revue. He dramatically gasped, with theatrical relish, when Hartford Wayclocks finally appeared at the show palace.

"Where have you been?" the theater manager asked, trying to hide his anger behind a flat, even Midwestern drone.

"Problems," the life-long New Yorker, with matching accent, snapped.

"Follow me," the theater manager, resigned, prompted. He led Hartford Wayclocks through the plush, dimly lit auditorium up to the stage where redfaced and tiring hands busied themselves setting up for the revue. "Things seem to be getting in order," the manager remarked, doing his best not to sound snide.

"Thank God," Hartford exclaimed, relieved. He imagined the stage and house to be in disarray because of his tardy appearance. "Did Miss Trent stop in?"

"No."

"No?" Hartford, somewhat surprised, asked.

"No." The manager's voice remained as level as a Kansas plain, leaving Hartford unable to determine how the chap felt.

"Is she here?" Hartford asked, meaning in Topeka.

"No," the manager replied, an edge of frustration inching into his voice.

"No?"

"I've told you that, Mr Wayclocks."

"I mean, is she in Topeka?" Hartford clarified.

"I don't know."

"You don't know?"

"I don't."

Muttering to himself, Hartford decided to dash next door to the hotel to see if the leading, indeed the show's *only* lady, had arrived. Without saying another word to the manager, Hartford dismounted the stage and started plodding through the empty house. He turned when he reached the back rows and asked how the house looked for the night.

The manager replied by sticking his arm out straight, hand flat, and tipping his hand slightly from side to side. "So-so," he replied.

"Damn!" Hartford shot, slapping his own thigh before exiting the theater.

While Hartford Wayclocks bustled over to the hotel, Pam Ella Trent poured herself another gin with a dinky dash of tonic water. She opened her cosmetic bag, sifting around until she found a vial of lavender bubble bath, the color matching her silken dressing gown. Making her way to the bathroom, tiled in powder blue, she twisted on the tub's faucet to draw herself a steaming bath. Directly before she plunged into the tub, as she dangled her toes in the water, the telephone in her room clanged to life.

"Rats!" she blurted, quickly retreating from the bathroom, snatching the phone.

"Yes?" she answered.

"Miss Trent?" Hartford Wayclocks asked, phoning from the lobby.

"Yes?" She still did not recognize the director's voice even after several months of rehearsals and performances.

"It's Hartford … Wayclocks," he sighed.

"Love, how are you?"

The Shadow Cast

"What's the matter with the costume for the finale?" he bluntly asked, referring to his battle that morning in Kansas City with the seamstress who almost abandoned ship.

"That's correct," she snipped back.

Not understanding, he asked Miss Trent what she meant.

"Hartford," she purred, "it looks like a costume. It should look like … no, no … it should *be* a gown … a delicious, beaded gown."

"Miss Trent," he sighed, tightly shutting his eyes and then jabbing his eyelids with two fingers. "It is the same dress you've worn in every show since we started the circuit. Why now? Why change now?" "Hartford," she cooed.

"But Miss Trent …"

"Hartford …" she interrupted.

"I'll stay on it," he surrendered.

"You're delicious."

At precisely six o'clock, Pam Ella Trent descended on the lift and entered the lobby like a grand dame, gowned in white silk and velvet, bejeweled in dazzling sapphires. Handy Weather stiffly sat on a couch in the lobby, the reservation clerk outside his post scurried across to meet Miss Trent. The bellman, again asleep, lightly snored. A half dozen others, five hotel guests and a lost visiting minister looking for the First Presbyterian Church some five blocks away, idled in the lobby until Pam Ella Trent appeared. They all, including the black clad preacher, swept up to the actress.

13

The Shadow Cast

Miss Trent spent several minutes taking their praise and writing her name on snips and snatches of paper. She caught sight of Handy, smiling, on the sofa.

"Oh, dear," she told her clutch of fans. "I must go. The press is here, you see. A reporter from 'Hollywood Chatterbox' covering my revue."

She sashayed across the lobby to join Handy.

"Randy!" she greeted, beaming ear to ear.

"Miss Trent," he replied, quickly scrambling to his feet. "You look … fantastic."

She giggled like a teenaged girl before a summer cotillion. Together they left the hotel and walked to the theater. "We'll visit in my dressing room," she explained to the earnest scribe.

The theater manager, dutifully flitting about the house, escorted Miss Trent and the young reporter backstage to the actress' designated dressing room. A spray of two dozen white roses sat in a crystal vase on a mahogany table in the center of the smallish room. Miss Trent made a beeline at once for the blooms, inhaling a healthy dose of their fragrance.

"Delicious," she sighed.

At the time she arrived, the room was softly lit; the more garish roundabout of white light bulbs surrounding a large makeup mirror remained unlit. Miss Trent graciously asked Handy to join her, to sit with her on a loveseat-sized sofa of burgundy chintz. He propped his ever-present reporter's notepad on his knee and began to interview the star.

The couple spent over an hour discussing Miss Trent's various films and then drifted into a discussion of her early life.

"I'm from West Virginia, you know," she remarked at one point. Handy, in fact, did not.

"Oh, it's true," she said, her gaze drifting off to the white roses and away from Handy Weather.

"I never heard that before," Handy remarked, suddenly flipping through his pages of notes as if the information on Pam Ella Trent's birth and early life might instantly appear in the midst of his scratchings.

"My father ..." she continued, staring at the roses and in a gentle, mellow tone of voice Handy had not yet heard. "Papa ... he mined coal."

Handy stopped flitting through the sheets of notes, put his pen on the sofa, down at his side.

"Mama ... Mama ..." Handy thought, for a fleeting moment, that Miss Trent's eyes nearly pooled in tears. "She passed ... Mama passed on when I was thirteen. I had six older brothers, Andy, and one younger sister."

Miss Trent smiled, a misty look, as if lost in the tender white rose petals.

"Poor ... we were, of course, poor ... lived in a small house, really only two rooms. We lived not so far from Virginia ... that end of West Virginia, in a small town called Galaxy Falls."

"I've never heard any of this," Handy mumbled. "The studio says ... well, there's nothing of this in what the studio writes about you."

"I imagine not," she knowingly smiled.

"I thought you were from California."

Miss Trent shyly grinned. "For the past twenty years, Randy, I almost believed I was from California myself."

"How'd you get there, Miss Trent?"

Sadly, slowly, she explained that her father was killed in a mine fire when she was fifteen. "My brothers were just old enough to be on their own. My sister was just young enough to be terribly innocent, needy you see. But, there I was … lost, really, in the middle of it all."

In Handy's eyes, Miss Trent – Pam Ella – suddenly appeared differently. She seemed vulnerable, gentle, kindly, soft.

Before either Handy or Miss Trent spoke further, a stern rapping came from the other side of the dressing room door.

"Miss Trent?" the man's voice called out.

Once more not recognizing the voice of her show's director, she panned: "I wonder who that could be?"

Just as quickly as her expression and features had become delicate and fragile, she bloomed fully back into Pam Ella Trent, the indomitable star.

She moved to the door with a flurry that belied the rather tight quarters. Popping the door open, she found Hartford Wayclocks standing in front of her.

"Hartford!" she exclaimed, as if not having set eyes on the man for years, rather than hours.

"Miss Trent," he responded, far more subdued.

"You know," she puffed, "the press is here."

Hartford looked confused. "Here?" he asked.

"Here," she enthused, gesturing at Handy Weather. "Randy Winter," she incorrectly continued, "my director, Hartford Wayclocks."

Hartford moved towards Handy, who stood and flushed crimson.

16

The Shadow Cast

"You're with 'The Tattler?'" Hartford asked, referring to a scandal rag.

Handy meekly shook his head. "No."

Hartford barely paid attention to Handy's response, focusing on Miss Trent, who he believed had concocted a story to cover the young man's presence in her dressing room.

"I thought ..." Hartford said to Miss Trent in a paternal tone. "I thought 'The Tattler' reporter met up with us tomorrow in Denver."

"Oh, no, Love, the press is here now," Miss Trent grandly replied, gesturing magnificently at Handy Weather. "He's with 'Hollywood Chatterbox,' Hartford."

Hartford frowned, displeased. Nonetheless, he carried on and asked if everything in the dressing room was satisfactory.

"Aren't the flowers delicious?" she asked. "I've never seen anything like them."

Hartford rolled his eyes to the ceiling. Miss Trent always insisted on two dozen white roses in her dressing room and the buds and blossoms always looked the same. "Right," he muttered.

"Are we sold out again?" she asked.

Pam Ella Trent's revue had not sold out one night during the circuit, Hartford obviously knew.

"No," he tersely responded.

"Well, fiddle-dee-dee," she replied, waving a hand in front of her face. "I'm sure by show time the house will be filled."

She asked Hartford what the time was for curtain. Throughout the entire circuit, curtain was set for eight o'clock each night. Mouthing "eight" directly to Miss

17

Trent, Hartford exited the dressing room, the door slamming behind him.

"I really must prepare," Miss Trent advised when they were left alone.

Handy looked bruised, hurt like a boy child who misplaced his baseball mitt.

"Can we finish this later?" he meekly asked the star.

"Of course! We'll celebrate the show – with Champagne." She directed Handy to return to her dressing room when the curtain fell.

The doors of the Jayhawk opened to the public at seven o'clock. By show time the house ended up threequarters full, a respectable turnout with unreserved arrivals.

The petite orchestra traveling with the revue struck up the overture directly after eight o'clock. As the curtain rose, a solitary spotlight with a blue gel cast a soft circle of light center stage. There stood Pam Ella Trent, resplendent in a sleek satin gown, rose colored, with a blood red boa wrapping her neck and falling down her front and back.

Accepting the applause of her faithful fans with a regal thrust of both arms, hands upward, she then greeted: "Good evening."

The dutiful orchestra struck up the opening tune, which Miss Trent belted out with vim and flare. Fortyfive minutes later, she wound down the first half of her show with a bluesy medley of songs from a Broadway cabaret of 1928.

The curtain fell as the audience stood in ovation. Miss Trent stood center stage with folded hands and head bowed, a prayerful stance. She remained frozen in that position for over ninety seconds after the curtain fell and the house lights went up. She then whisked off stage to her dressing room, lightly moving between crew and props like a dainty sprite.

Hartford Wayclocks waited for Miss Trent directly outside her dressing room door.

"Isn't it a divine night," she gushed, swirling past Hartford into her space. He had to admit the show progressed well, the audience pleased.

A dressmaker's dummy stood square center in the dressing room with a new, replacement gown hanging neatly.

"Better?" Hartford asked, referring to the gown.

"Delicious," she broadly smiled, waving the stage director off so she could re-garb. She wasted no time in putting on the new gown, a crepe and beaded creation in ivory.

During intermission, the gathered theatergoers milled around the lobby, pleasantly discussing their approval of the show.

"She's so elegant," a plump, merry lady of Topeka society remarked to recognized folk time and time again.

"Her gown … majestic," commented another similarly situated woman.

"Her voice, like an angel. Two angels, in fact," the city's Mayor crooned.

"Time of my life," the bare crowned hotel desk clerk told a handsome couple who attended his church.

Within twenty minutes, the lobby lights flashed, the house lights began to dim. The patrons hurried back to their thickly upholstered seats, cool refrigerated air swirling about the theater despite the mid-summer night and the gaggle of the formally dressed.

The musicians in the pit mounted the overture for the second act, a lightly tuned lead in to Miss Trent's reopening number. The curtain rose with Miss Trent center stage, resplendently illuminated and perfectly poised.

Her performance for the final half of the evening's show was flawlessly made, a perfect presentation in all respects. She rounded out the revue with a finale featuring a rousing showstopper from the hit musical of 1929 on the Great White Way. After the initial curtain call, Miss Trent took three more before the jocular crowd gave way, ending their steady ovation.

Miss Trent retired to her dressing room, awaiting Handy Weather to conclude his interview for the 'Hollywood Chatterbox.' Ten minutes passed before she heard a knock at the door. Expecting the reporter, she instead found Hartford Wayclocks, the Jayhawk Theater manager, and the hotel desk clerk standing beyond the threshold.

Hartford wore a queerly satisfied expression while the manager and the clerk shifted nervously from side to side.

"We have news," Hartford piped up.

"Entrez," Miss Trent graciously invited. "The press will be here soon," she added. Hartford smiled at the remark.

"Your reporter friend …" Hartford said slyly, turning to the theater manager. "What's his name?"

"Weather … Handy Weather."

"Delightful man," Miss Trent interjected. "And a wonderful reporter. Very successful."

The same impish smile swept over Hartford's face. "Yes, well …" he replied. "That's our news."

"Oh, Miss Trent," the reservation clerk from the neighboring Hotel Jayhawk blathered. "It's horrible, just terrible."

A baffled look crossed Miss Trent's face. "Yes?" she asked tentatively.

"Your reporter friend," Hartford stated, with definite relish.

"Is Randy all right?" she asked.

"Your reporter friend," Hartford continued as if Miss Trent had not spoken. "He isn't a reporter at all," he said, savoring the moment.

Miss Trent furrowed her brow, raised a finger to her ruby lips.

"It's just horrible," the clerk muttered his earlier mantra.

Hartford chuckled heartily. "Turns out," he stated, almost in a boast, "turns out your friend the reporter, this Handy Weather … turns out Handy Weather, he walked off from the State Insane Asylum a few days back. Walked away, ended up in Kansas City, ended up playing reporter."

Miss Trent let out a short whimper, quickly covering her mouth fully with the previously poised hand. The desk clerk solemnly shook his head, grieving that the film star had been duped. Trying to boost Miss Trent, he remarked that he "was certain that young fellow was up to no good."

The Shadow Cast

Having almost savagely struck with his news, Hartford casually announced that he and his temporary cohorts would take their leave. Left to herself in the dressing room, Miss Trent methodically changed out of the new gown.

She departed her dressing room, walked across the lonely stage where a man was busy sweeping. Their eyes met and for an instant she brightened like a star. Taking the steps at stage left, she walked through the empty house, through the lobby and out onto the street.

As Pam Ella Trent walked back to the hotel, light rain began to fall.

The Confessor

President Eisenhower had given his farewell speech a few weeks earlier, bemoaning something he called the "Military Industrial Complex." A fresh President, Jack Kennedy, had since moved into the White House far off in Washington, DC, promising that by joining together for the sake of the country, all Americans would lead better lives.

The grim lamentations of the old soldier and the lofty declarations of his suave successor seemed foreign to the residents of Winthrop, although the Iowa town was nestled quietly, snugly in the nation's heartland.

The tiny berg of Winthrop rested fleetingly on a narrow strip of road called Highway 20. Two narrow streets ran from the highway into the town itself, a pea gravel road to the West that the town residents used and an asphalt one to the East favored by visitors to town, mostly relatives of locals from exotic places like Cedar Rapids, Waterloo and Des Moines.

The Mayor of Winthrop, Doc Potter, who was also the local general practitioner, had erected a neat wooden billboard just before the asphalt road into Winthrop on Highway 20. The roadside placard, festooned firmly in Hank White's cornfield, happily proclaimed Winthrop, Iowa to be "the friendliest town for miles around." And generally speaking, the 718 souls residing in the hamlet were friendly and considerate, even to the occasional stranger that happened in their paths because of automobile engine troubles and the like.

Directly at the intersection of Highway 20 and the paved street into town sat the red brick St Patrick's Roman Catholic Church, with a green tiled roof that would please the Irish patron. The master of the church was its ancient looking pastor, Father Goering, who immigrated to the United States and who finally settled with his own parents in northeastern Iowa at the turn of the century. Indeed, the area was awash with the offspring of German immigrants, settling in either Lutheran or Roman Catholic enclaves. Winthrop was well populated with Catholics, St Patrick's being the only church ever built in the town's history.

The early February day was remarkably pleasant. A trace of snow lay about here and there in dirty clumps, but beyond that evidence there existed no other indication on that Saturday that it was wintertime.

At around noon, Father Goering ambled out of the rectory house, a two story square set directly next to the church and made of the same brick and topped with matching emerald tiles. Father Goering was a portly fellow, the result of an unbridled diet of stout foods and rich ales. He had a bulbous nose, riddled a patchy red from broken blood vessels. The old priest had a pair of intense, dark eyes, nearly the color of the rich soil of the Iowan fields.

The most prominent features of the pastor's broad face were his untamed eyebrows. They looked to be a clutch of pipe cleaners absently smashed and twisted, aimlessly poking about in a multitude of directions.

The Shadow Cast

Father Goering had taken his lunch, a thick stew Margaret his housekeeper had prepared for him the day before, which he did not bother to warm on the stove top before eating. When finished, he decided to step out onto the porch of the rectory house to sit a while on the sturdy rocker he had taken with him from one parish assignment to the next. He never had any real property to call his own, but he had the rocker, built when he was a lad by his own father.

After he had been perched on his rocking chair for half an hour, enjoying the warm sun bathing the rectory porch, Father Goering spotted young Wayne Price, perhaps all of fourteen, stepping slowly up the paved road that ran in front of the church and then on to the highway. The Price family lived several blocks down from the church, off of the road on which Wayne slowly plodded, and just before Main Street.

The priest kept his eyes trained on the boy, wondering where he might be off to at the moment. Most often, local folk only headed up the road when leaving town for one excursion or another and to attend Mass at nine on Sunday mornings. They also came, occasionally, for confession, but Father Goering did not start to hear his flock's wrongdoings until four on Saturday afternoons, more than three hours from when he spotted Wayne Price on the street.

Father Goering continued to watch the boy come on, quite like a wily dog nestled in a reed thicket tracking a mallard on a pond hoping the bird might take leave of the water. Perhaps, the priest silently thought, the lad was heading to the church. But, the pastor knew well that boys did not visit his church as a routine on a

25

The Shadow Cast

Saturday afternoon, particularly on a winter day when the weather nicely and so pleasantly mellowed.

As Wayne Price drew within a block of St Patrick's, the church and rectory, Father Goering realized the boy had not noticed him sitting on the porch. At least he appeared to have paid no never mind to the old man in his rocking chair. From the priest's vantage point, the boy appeared to be transfixed on the two silver, aluminum framed front doors of the church.

Reaching the point on the street directly in front of the sidewalk that led up to the six steps to the church's doors, Wayne came to a stop. The boy's full and as yet unyielding attention was tacked on the church, most specifically on the entrance door. If the youth was debating with himself, perhaps about taking the steps and trying the doors to see if they were unlocked, the priest could not tell. The boy's face was stony firm, belying no particular emotion beyond what seemed to be a steely resolve.

After a couple minutes standing still in front of the church, Wayne took a few tentative paces up the sidewalk, to the edge of the steps leading to the doorway. He scratched his head.

The watching priest thought the boy looked every bit like a confused character in the films of the 1940s Father Goering most enjoyed.

For a moment, the priest thought of calling out to the boy, beckoning him to come over to the porch. But he held his tongue knowing more often than not when a person approached his church at an odd and off time, that individual normally wanted time alone with the Lord or the Virgin.

The Shadow Cast

Much like a rabbit caught outside his protective cover of brush, the boy suddenly sprinted up the steps and grasped a hold of the church door. Father Goering always kept the church unlocked from dawn until dusk in the event a parishioner wanted to wander in for a moment or so of reflection or prayer. Wayne Price must not have known this fact as when the door easily pulled open, Father Goering saw the youth's expression change for the first time. The boy looked surprised.

He hesitated for several seconds before plunging into the quiet church that Father Goering had left illuminated only by the columned light streaming in from the stained glass windows and from the flickering glow of votive candles in the stands under a statue of the Virgin to the right and St Joseph to the left.

Father Goering had so intently focused his attention on Wayne Price during the boy's approach and entrance to the church that he did not notice Gladys Gridd walking from the same direction down the street walked previously by the boy. Indeed, the priest was not aware of Gladys' presence until the rotund woman planted her fleshy legs covered in overstretched hose with a runner on each leg directly in front of the rectory.

"Yoo-hoo! Father Goering! It's me! Gladys Gridd." She spoke as if she were materializing out of nothingness and that the pastor was unable to see her as she was still translucent. Many a Saturday, not long after lunch, Gladys Gridd appeared at the rectory. And, failing that, she most definitely would come round for confession at four.

"Gladys," he said, after clearing his voice because he had not yet spoken to a soul that day. He instinctively motioned for Gladys to join him on the porch, which was in fact unnecessary as the woman already lumbered towards him.

Gladys wore a faded house dress which appeared to Father Goering to have once been fashioned with crisp lavender and gay yellow stripes, now faded and over washed to mute tones the priest could not rightly name. She wore a thick woolen sweater, a ratty gray piece, over her dress.

Gladys and her husband, Harold, had spent fortysome odd years farming and moved into town after retiring a couple of years earlier.

Gladys had well-thinned hair that looked more like a scant dust bunny than intended scalp covering. She religiously dyed her hair weekly, more precisely what was left of it, a dire black, which only further exasperated the sparse crop. The raven dye contrasted most starkly with her pale skin.

Near the rocker on the porch Father Goering had long ago set a couple of stationary chairs to allow others to join him in his favored spot should they come calling on a pleasant day.

Gladys plopped down on one of the chairs, well winded from her walk. Father Goering could not guess how much the woman weighed, but he knew it was way more than her five foot frame could effectively manage. Despite himself, the priest could not help but notice that Gladys continued to shake, like a mound of gelatin dessert, for an unseemly bit after seizing a chair.

Gladys pulled a handkerchief out of a sweater pocket and dabbed off her damp brow.

The Shadow Cast

"Oh, my stars and heavens," she moaned. "I had quite the walk Father. Quite the walk. I think I may have gone a mile or so, I'd imagine."

Father Goering smiled kindly, imagining Gladys in fact plodded only from her home which was four or five blocks away at most.

"Well, very good, Gladys," he said, completely obscuring any doubts he may have had regarding the woman's afternoon trek.

"Was that the Price boy, the younger one, I saw going inside the church?" she asked.

Father Goering hesitated a moment before answering, feeling somewhat indiscreet about confirming the comings and goings of a parishioner. But he realized in the instant that if he dodged the query, Gladys would later concoct some wild tale about the boy being in church and the good priest having to cover up for the child for some outlandish purpose.

"Yes, Gladys, I believe that was the younger Price boy," he answered.

As if imparting a grave revelation, Gladys stated, as she tucked her hankie away: "That'd be Wayne. He's a good boy. You know, both those Price boys are good boys. The Prices, they live one block over from me and Harold. Wayne, the younger one, and the older one, Ken, they both come around and shovel our snow in the winter and help out with the leaves in the fall. Ever since Harold and I moved to town, those good boys have come around."

"They are good boys," the priest answered.

"Not like the Haglin twins, those demons. The Haglin twins, Jerry and Johnny, they're not good ones, good boys, like those Price boys. They live on our street, the Haglin twins. But, they never once come around to shovel our snow, Harold's and mine, or help out with the leaves in the fall."

"I see," Father Goering said, not knowing what else to say in response to Gladys. He knew she was building up a full head of steam and might very well keep prattling on until confession time at four. Despite her knack to talk insistently on all occasions – after Sunday Mass, on holy days of obligation, following funerals, at women's auxiliary covered dishes as well as on sleepy Saturday afternoons – Father Goering quite liked Gladys Gridd.

"I was at McElroy's this morning," Gladys said, changing subjects the priest imagined. McElroy's was the nicely tended grocery market at the corner of the asphalt covered roadway leading into town and Main Street, perhaps half a mile from St Patrick's and catty corner to the Winthrop Grain Elevator. "Frances Waterman was there, like she is most Saturdays. But, she hadn't been coming in for three Saturdays now on account of Dick, her husband. You know he had a heart attack? Of course you know that, the Watermans going to church here and all. Well, of course, she didn't come to McElroy's on Saturday the last three weeks because of Dick being at the hospital in Waterloo."

"I visited Dick at the hospital," Father Goering volunteered.

"Oh, my, of course. You know all about Dick and all that. Poor man. Not fifty and he's got that bum ticker, just like Fred Hoyt, who died last year."

30

The Shadow Cast

Father Goering failed to make the connection. Dick Waterman, forty-eight, survived a heart attack. Fred Hoyt, twenty-six, was crushed to death in a silo full of corn. But, the priest merely nodded.

After Gladys spent nearly an hour on the rectory porch, Father Goering realized that Wayne Price had not exited from the church. Sixty plus minutes was an awfully long time for a teenaged boy to spend in church when it was not a Sunday Mass. He thought better of mentioning anything about the length of time Wayne had spent inside the church to Gladys. The woman apparently had forgotten about the boy and Father Goering wanted to leave well enough alone in that regard. He decided if the boy did not exit fairly soon, he would excuse himself from Gladys for a moment or two to check up on Wayne under the plausible pretense that he needed to make certain everything was in order for that afternoon's confession.

Gladys forged ahead on her visiting all the while Father Goering contemplated the boy in his church. He had no idea what his guest was speaking of when he returned his attention back to her.

"And that's what I told her, flat out. Right there in the check out line at McElroy's. Heaven knows you can't do something like that with a pork cutlet. It would be sinful."

Father Goering dared not imagine what Gladys was discussing at that juncture.

Off in the distance, the priest heard the whistle of a train approaching town. An average of three locomotives pulled through Winthrop on any given day. The priest decided to use the whistle and growing rumble of the train as an excuse to break into his conversation with Gladys for a bit to stroll over to the church under the pretense of readying for confessions at four.

"Gladys, will you excuse me for a couple of minutes so I can go over to the church and make sure I have everything ready for confession?"

"Oh, of course, Father. A priest's work is never done, that's what I always tell Harold. Speaking of that, did I tell you about John and Mary Proctor's new car? An Oldsmobile?"

Father Goering politely interrupted, not understanding a possible connection between busy priests and two thousand pound automobiles. He gently told Gladys to sit tight and keep her thoughts while he checked on the readiness of the church for confession.

He hurried off to the church, moving across the lawn that separated the place of worship from the rectory. Had he dawdled, he was certain Gladys would carry on discussing the hectic life of a priest in relationship to the better appointments of an Oldsmobile motor car.

Reaching the church doors, he went in, stopping a moment in the vestibule to allow himself the chance to adjust to the dim illumination inside. After spending nearly two hours outside on the bright winter day, the priest could make out very little in the church nave upon first entering.

In a minute, perhaps two, Father Goering was finally capable of making out the small human form of a boy seated in the forward pew to the right, in front of the statue of the Virgin. From where the priest stood, the dancing flickers of the votive candles in the stand under the Virgin's statue made it look for the instant as if Mary

32

was tenderly gazing down at the young Iowa child. The priest smiled, pleased with the scene.

He slowly walked up the main aisle, clearing his throat purposefully midway to the altar so that Wayne Price would not be startled by his approach. After the priest rasped, the boy shifted in the pew as if he heard the man but did not turn around. Father Goering imagined the boy to be intent on something, likely prayer or youthful contemplation considering the location.

Nearing the occupied pew, Father Goering softly stated the boy's name. With that, Wayne did pivot about in his seat to face the priest.

"May I?" Father Goering asked, gesturing towards the pew and meaning to take a seat. Wayne nodded, his pale blue eyes, nearly a shade of gray, wide open. The priest noticed the whites of the boy's eyes were rimmed in red as if the child had been crying.

Wayne Price was called a 'darling boy' by more than a few Winthrop matrons. He had his mother's fair hair and looked to be a miniaturized version of his father in relation to his stature and bearing.

The boy was polite to a fault and doubly kind. His mother taught at the grade school he attended while his father sold tractors at the John Deere implement store in neighboring Independence, the Buchanan County seat.

"You've been in church a long while, Wayne," the elderly minister stated in a smooth, non-threatening way.

Again, Wayne nodded but did not speak.

The Shadow Cast

"I like coming in here myself when I can be alone and just sit for a while," Father Goering volunteered, feeling such an easy remark was more prudent than a blustery "Why are you here?"

"How is everything going for you?" the priest asked. Wayne fidgeted on his spot in the pew.

"Everything all right with school?" Father Goering gently inquired, prodding the boy ever so slightly.

"Yeah, Father." Wayne finally spoke.

"Very good for that, then," the priest replied.

"And at home? Everything all right there?" Father Goering meant the question as a pure formality because, well knowing the Price family, he could not envision anything askew in that household.

Wayne sat silently, unmoving. For the minute, the child looked to the pastor as firm and as solid as the plaster cast Virgin Mother standing faithful guard over them beyond the flickering votives.

"I need confession," the boy finally blurted, the words dashing from his mouth with unusual urgency for a lad Wayne's age, the priest thought.

"You do?" Father Goering responded in his most nonjudgmental manner. "You came early, Wayne," he added.

Wayne nodded and then asked the priest if he might be able to give his confession early, before the four o'clock call.

"Surely," the priest agreed. "Why don't we go over to the confessional then."

The boy did not budge. He asked his pastor if he might hear the confession just there, seated in the pew.

"If you'd like," Father Goering replied.

The Shadow Cast

Again, the boy bobbed his head slowly, sadly, but affirmatively.

"Are you ready now?" the priest asked.

"Yeah, Father."

Closing his eyes, the priest began the Latin prayers preliminary to receiving the child's confession. When he concluded, he looked over to Wayne and saw that the boy was fumbling about trying to pull something out of his jacket pocket. Although puzzled, Father Goering sat quietly and waited to see what the boy was up to.

After much fidgeting, the boy extracted what he sought from the jacket pocket.

"Good heavens!" the priest exclaimed. The boy held in his hand a tiny, lively mouse.

"It's a mouse," Wayne said, stating the obvious.

"So I see." The priest wanted to say more, obviously ask more, but instead sat quietly waiting for the boy to speak further.

"He's not wild," the boy said, a solid dash of urgency and defensiveness sparking his remark.

"He does seem very tame."

"I got him in Waterloo," Wayne said. "At a store that sells little pets. They had a cage of little mice, pretty much like this one."

"I see."

Father Goering could not relate the procurement of the gray mouse to an occasion of sin. He thought of Gladys and her disjointed conversations.

"Father ..." Wayne looked down, indeed slumped like a withering limb unable to carry its burden of fruit after a long summer.

"Yes, Wayne."

35

The Shadow Cast

In a hushed voice, so softly that the priest wondered if the boy wanted to keep the statue of the Virgin from hearing, Wayne confessed:

"I just took this mouse. I took him from the case. Took him and put him in my pocket, just like I brought him to church today. My parents never would let me have such a thing as a mouse for a pet, you see. So I snuck him out of the store and then snuck him home. I've been keeping him in a shoe box under my bed." Wayne added, resolutely: "I poked holes in the shoe box so he can breathe, and I feed and water him every day."

"I'm sure you do," the priest replied. He noticed that the boy was gently stroking the tiny animal with his nimble fingers.

"You like your mouse?" the priest asked of Wayne.

"I do, Father. Very much, I do."

"But, Wayne, you know it was wrong to take him from the shop?"

"Oh, yes, Father. I know, I know. That's why I came here today. I just got the mouse yesterday when I went to Waterloo with Mom after school."

"I see." The priest paused for almost a minute and then asked Wayne what he thought he should do regarding the purloined mouse.

"Well, Father, I guess I should give him back, take him back to the store. But I really like this mouse, Father. I really like him."

"I can see that you do."

The beautiful child's face took on a pained expression, of the kind Father Goering thought only an adult should make in the worst of circumstances.

36

"I am very sorry … very sorry, Father."

In the instant, the confessor wished all of his parishioners sounded as sincere when receiving the sacrament.

"You say your parents would not let you keep the little fellow at home?"

Glumly, the boy shook his head. "They won't want a mouse in our house," he sighed.

The priest looked up to the statue of the Virgin, rubbing his chin as he thought.

"Perhaps," the priest finally said, "perhaps you and I can go to the shop in Waterloo and take care of all this."

Tears pooled up in each of the sorry lad's pale blue eyes, heart wrenching drops that almost brought the same to the priest. "And give the mouse back?" he asked, barely above a whisper.

The priest patted Wayne on his knee.

"I was thinking, Wayne, that if I went with you to the shop, we might be able to square this all away."

Father Goering looked down at his charge and saw that the boy was perplexed, all the while looking sad.

"What I mean, Wayne," Father Goering gently explained, "what I mean is you and I can go to the shop and get this little fellow paid for …"

Instantly the boy's face brightened but then, just as quickly, his beam slipped away.

"My folks, they won't let me keep the mouse even if I had bought him with cash money."

"Well, Wayne, yes, I do know that. I think you could keep the little fellow with me at the rectory. I can look after the little fellow and you can come over whenever you can. And, in turn for your penance, you can help

37

me out in the yard from time to time. How does that sound?"

"Oh, Father!" the boy exclaimed with relief and joy, throwing his arms tightly around the old pastor.

The priest finished the sacrament, absolved the young boy of his sins and then led him out of the church across the lawn and to the rectory. Gladys Gridd remained seated on the porch, patting her brow with her tattered hankie.

"Oh, Father, is everything set for confession?" she asked with intense seriousness.

"It is," Father Goering replied.

As the priest and the boy mounted the porch, Gladys caught sight of the gray mouse in Wayne's hands.

"Oh, my stars and heavens!" Gladys sputtered. "Are there mice in the church?"

Calmly, serenely, the priest replied: "Well, at least one in the rectory."

The Pony Patch

Ma died, 1928. I was ten. We lost the farm, 1931.

I was thirteen then. I turned fourteen in November of that year; a month later Pa, my little brother, Zack, and my little sister, Sarah, Zack's twin, celebrated Christmas with Nanna and Pappa, Pa's folks. With Ma and the farm gone, Pa moved us to live with Nanna and Pappa in their three-bedroom house in Cedar Flats, Iowa.

The Depression hit Iowa like a burglar in the night. None of the folk in the county saw it coming. But when it hit, the Depression shattered homes and ripped through lives like a midnight bandit.

We were left with nothing. Our neighbors were left with nothing.

Folk lost city jobs, sure. But when the Depression broke in on us farm families, our pas lost work, but our families also lost our homes.

No Ma. No work, really, for Pa. No home.

But, Pa, Zack, Sarah and I were lucky – blessed to have Nanna and Pappa.

They didn't just take us in, they invited us home.

Plus, Pa landed some spot jobs; a day here, another somewhere else.

Nanna and Pappa, in their seventies, had no real savings to speak of. That may have worked out best for them as the Cedar Flats First Bank shut its doors for good way before most other banks. Pappa, like Pa, had farmed, retiring a few years before Ma passed.

The Shadow Cast

Nanna taught school up until Pappa retired.

When they moved off the farm, they rented the place to the neighboring family, a ten-year deal. The monthly rent payments, that's what we lived on, all of us.

Pappa wished he could have held on to the farm a bit longer, he said that often.

Then, he would say, when the Cedar Flats First Bank took our farm, our home (before it shut its doors), we could have moved onto Pappa's and Nanna's farm and carried forth.

The twins, Zack and Sarah, turned nine on December 15, 1931, just before our first Christmas at Nanna's and Pappa's house in town.

Nanna, finding some fabric remnants somewhere, made a dress for Sarah and a shirt and britches for Zack. Birthday presents. With the sewing done, Nanna wrapped the garments in butcher paper she got from Hank's Beef Locker in town. She made ribbons out of corn husks. She made cards, one for Zack, one for Sarah, out of poster board, signing the handmade pieces: "Love Pa."

On the fifteenth, we celebrated the twins' birthday; they thought their swell new clothes, gifts from Pa, came from the big clothing store in Waterloo. Zack felt jaunty, Sarah a regal princess, as they tried on their seemingly store-bought outfits.

I noticed that Pa really did not smile much during the twins' birthday celebration around the kitchen table at Nanna's and Pappa's. I figured, at first, that he was stewing because the gifts for Zack and Sarah really were not from him, but were stitched up creations from

The Shadow Cast

Pa's mother. Then I figured he was worried about something else: Christmas was ten days down the pike.

I was sure he was wondering how he would get presents for the family. Although Santa was no longer a reality for me, Sarah and Zack were expecting a visit from St Nick. And how could Santa not pay a visit? The twins were good, very good, all year.

A few hours after the birthday party, we all turned in for the night. I shared a room with Pa since I was the oldest. Pa slept on one little bed, I took the other. Pappa tracked down the racks from somewhere, after we moved in, Pa, Sarah, Zack and me.

I was pretty certain Pa fell asleep before long, his breathing getting heavy. But, he did not sleep easy, tossing and turning from almost the minute he crawled into his bed. I imagined he was dreaming, probably about Christmas and Zack and Sarah and Santa. He knew I was thirteen, his "little man" as he said. So, surely, he was not knotted up about me, too.

I closed my eyes, but no sleep came. I rolled over and over and over again, but I did not sleep.

"Christmas was ten days away," I thought. Still awake, I heard 'Pappa's clock', an old-fashioned grandfather clock, chime the midnight hour, each gong an effort for the ancient timer. Then, I thought: "Christmas is nine – only nine – days away."

Sometime after midnight, I drifted, finally, to sleep. I wondered if Pa and I had the same dream. Perhaps we did, we slept close enough to each other.

My dream of Christmas day was sad indeed, no visit from Santa and the twins could not understand why.

The Shadow Cast

They were good, very good, all year long. But St Nick did not come with gifts or candy or anything nice and good. Nothing.

Pa woke at five, a habit from the farm with a dairy herd. I heard him crawl out of bed, his feet dropping to the floor, not hitting the boards with the same confidence I knew before we left the farm.

I stayed in bed a while longer until I heard Nanna join Pa in the kitchen, the sound of her dropping the old, iron skillet on a stove burner. In no time, I knew I would hear the sizzle and smell the scent of bacon and eggs frying.

Dressed in long-johns and a pair of huge wool socks, Pappa's, I walked into the kitchen, Nanna at work in front of the stove, Pa staring out the kitchen window. Maybe he looked at the glaze of frost coating the winter brown lawn. Perhaps he looked right at nothing at all. I could not tell for certain.

Taking a chair next to Pa, I said: "Frost, huh?"

He said: "Huh?"

He was not looking at the frozen dust.

"Frost. Outside," I said.

Pa tilted his head a bit, training his eyes directly to the ground.

"Uh-huh," he said.

We sat still and quiet for a few minutes more when Nanna put plates in front of us, bacon, eggs and biscuits.

Eating breakfast at Nanna's was how I imagined dining in a grand, uptown restaurant in the city, Waterloo. People came in to eat when they pleased,

42

served up heaping portions of hot, tasty food. And then more folk would come in, get fresh plates, happily dine.

In the same way, Pappa and the twins came into the kitchen as Pa and I finished our bacon and eggs, Nanna prepared and ready to go.

On a school holiday for Christmas, I did not have to bundle up and troop off to the schoolhouse with the twins in tow. I decided to spend the morning reading a book, an adventure story. The twins dashed outside to play in the backyard. Nanna cleaned up after breakfast, Pappa and Pa sat with me in the parlor reading over yesterday's newspaper.

Every now and then, I looked up from my book, glancing from Pappa to Pa. Pappa, engrossed in the news, seemed oblivious. Pa at first appeared to be reading the portion of the paper he purloined from Pappa, and seemed intent on a particular story.

Eventually, I realized that while Pappa was going from page to page, taking in his section of the 'Waterloo Gazette,' Pa never turned a single sheet. Peering over the top of my book, casting my gaze directly at Pa, I soon saw that his eyes were not moving. He was not reading at all, only staring. He seemed to be holding the newspaper up as a shield, not as something to be read and absorbed.

"St Nick," I thought. "Pa's worried about there being no Santa Claus."

I tried to turn back to my book, the adventure story. But I could not keep my focus. I kept looking back up at Pa.

Finally, I set the book aside, put on my worn winter coat, a hand-me-down, and headed out the front door.

The Shadow Cast

Since moving to town, I liked to walk to the very end of Pappa's and Nanna's street when I needed to think. The road dead-ended at a place with a large house with peeling paint and many trees. But, most special of all, fronting the house was a little pasture and a little shed where the owner kept Shetland ponies.

I had never seen a beast like one of these ponies out on our farm. Cows, plenty. Horses, a few. But nothing like these little fellows.

Before moving into Pappa's and Nanna's house, we did pay regular visits. But I never explored the neighborhood until I ended up a real resident, a townie.

Reaching the pony patch, as I came to call the pasture point, I scrambled up to the top of the threeplank wooden fence, taking a seat. I don't know how long I watched the ponies walk about the yard, meandering in and out of their stable, when I realized someone was standing next to me on the roadway side of the fence. The man, older than Pappa even, finally cleared his throat to snag my attention. Startled, I nearly flipped off the fence and into the pony patch itself.

The old man reached out and snared me by the arm, probably keeping me from a fall.

"Whoa, there," he said, gripping my arm.

I turned to face the man, to thank him for keeping me in place. Before I could speak, my eyes met the old man's. He had green eyes like no color I had ever seen in a person's face. A Christmas-tree-green, deep, rich and large.

He was all bundled up in a thick woolen coat and a lambskin cap, leather gloves covering his hands.

The Shadow Cast

He had a neat white beard, the color of downy, fresh snow. Most of all, the old man had a gentle, kind smile – how I imagined a fawn might look at his mother, the doe.

"Be careful, young man," the old man warned.

"I'm okay," I shot back, boyish defensiveness jagging my reply.

"Looking at the ponies?" the old man asked.

"Yep," I said, explaining that I often visited the pasture and the ponies.

"Good enough," the old man replied. "As do I," he added.

We talked a bit about this pony or that pony and I could tell that he really did spend time at the pasture. He knew at least as much about the characteristics of each animal as did I.

Before much time passed, I found myself telling the old chap about my family, our life on the farm and our move to town. I even went so far as to tell the man at my side about my Christmas worries, about Pa not being able to come up with Santa gifts for my little brother and little sister. I told the fellow that Sarah and Zack were good little kids and deserved a Christmas visit from St Nick.

The old man nodded as I spoke; I could tell he well understood. Finally, he said: "Always think the best thoughts and the best will come to you."

Like the man had done while I spoke, I nodded my head in turn, believing I understood what he said.

Shortly, the man bid his leave and walked off down the road in the direction of my grandparents' home. I returned my attention to the ponies, remaining on the fence for nearly another hour.

I went back home in plenty of time for lunch. The twins were pooped out from a morning spent at play in the yard.

We all spent the rest of the day inside together, Pa still distracted and distant. Before Pa and I turned in for the night, I told him of the man I met at the pony patch that morning. I told Pa what the man said, thinking it would cheer him up: "Always think the best thoughts and the best will come to you."

Pa smiled, tousled my hair and tucked me into bed.

The next week passed pretty quickly, Pa still sad looking throughout. During the week, I made a few more walks down to the pony patch, running into the old chap each time. I began to wonder if the fellow was watching for me to come see the ponies. I thought that perhaps the man lived in the house with peeling paint across the pasture from where I sat on the fence top to think.

He did not walk from the house when he came to me while I sat on the fence. And, I never saw the man walk to the house.

Through the whole week, I never learned the man's name, never thinking to ask.

I continued to share with the stranger with the soft white beard my concerns about Christmas, the twins and St Nick. Each time I explained my heavy heart, the old man listened, keeping the gentle smile on his face as if he understood exactly how I felt.

By the time Christmas Eve rolled around, Pappa had chopped down a hearty evergreen that Nanna had decorated in the parlor. During the afternoon of

The Shadow Cast

Christmas Eve, I overheard Pa and my grandparents talking in hushed tones in the parlor, standing by the tinsel covered tree. Like with the twins' birthday, Nanna said she had made some outfits for the twins, and me.

Nanna tried to convince Pa that the hand-tailored clothes would be enough of a gift from Santa for the children, considering the Depression and all. Pa was unconvinced and, based on the tone of his tired voice, very sad.

The conversation broke up when Pa ended up walking out the parlor door where he smoked a Prince Albert he rolled earlier. I joined Nanna and Pappa in the parlor. From the expression on my face, Nanna knew I'd overheard the discussion between the adults.

Nanna smiled at me and put her arm around my shoulders, with a fast squeeze; she bent over and kissed my cheek.

Pa stayed in the yard for what seemed like forever. A good part of the time he barely moved, looking like a wax statue I once saw at the Black Hawk County Fair.

All the while, the twins happily played in the backyard, jabbering cheerily about Santa's imminent visitation. I ended up taking a walk down to the pony patch, where I once more met up with the friendly gent.

"Good afternoon, young man," he greeted. As always, I did not hear the fellow approach. He just sort of seemed to materialize, appear from nowhere.

"Hi," I replied, happy to see him.

"How is your day?" he asked of me.

I shrugged.

"Still worried about your brother and sister and Santa?" he asked.

The Shadow Cast

"Yeah," I said, looking down at the ground, feeling almost defeated, helpless.

"Remember what I told you?" he asked.

At the same time, the old man and I said: "Always think the best thoughts and the best will come to you." We both laughed at our simultaneous pronouncement, my heart suddenly feeling lighter, happy.

The old chap and I visited a while longer and then I returned home. Pa and the twins were back inside the house by the time I returned, Nanna hard at work getting Christmas Eve supper prepared. The twins were sitting, Indian style, in the center of the parlor floor making out a note for Santa that they would leave out with milk and cookies before going off to bed.

Pa actually looked a bit lighter; however, I could tell his lack of St Nick gifts still weighed heavily on him.

Just at six we gathered around the dining table and feasted on Nanna's glazed ham, marshmallow garnished yams, and peas with sweet onions. Plates cleared, Nanna served piping hot slices of pecan pie with fresh whipping cream.

After our meal, we went into the parlor, Pappa lighting a cozy Christmas fire. At first the twins objected to flaming out Santa's port of entry, but Pappa explained the chimney and fireplace would be well cool before the good fellow arrived.

Together we sang some carols and then Nanna told us the story of the first Christmas, Jesus' birth. Before she finished, before the Magi arrived, the twins were fast asleep on the sofa, one to the right and one to the left side of Pa.

The Shadow Cast

Pa and Pappa carried the twins off to their beds. Although I wanted to stay with the adults a while longer, my eyes were heavy. Nanna prodded me off to my own room while Pa and Pappa tucked in Sarah and Zack for the night.

I slept sound and steady all night, waking just after dawn. Nanna was already at her morning post in the kitchen, I heard her moving about. Pa, out of his bed and out of the room, likely rose more than an hour earlier.

Unexpected, however, was the gleeful trill of the twins, happy in the parlor. Sitting up in my bed, I was surprised to hear the twins sound so merry, knowing that our Christmas gifts from Santa were going to be thin.

In an instant, I heard the sound of the quick patter of the twins' tiny feet speeding towards my bedroom. Popping through the door, Zack exclaimed: "Come quick!"

And Sarah added: "Santa's come!"

Each of the twins grabbed one of my hands, pulling me out from under my covers. Wasting no time in pulling through the kitchen and into the parlor, the twins positioned me to face the front window and the brightly adorned holiday tree. I focused on the tree, and the three small parcels underneath, one for me, one for Zack and the third for Sarah. I was puzzled by their excitement over the little, yet to be opened gifts.

"Not there, silly!" Sarah snapped, directing my attention away from the base of the evergreen.

"There!" beamed Zack, pointing out the parlor window into the front yard. Glancing about the room just

The Shadow Cast

before I took a look out the window, I saw that everyone was looking out to the lawn in front of the house.

Outside, safely hitched to the trunk of a bare oak tree in the yard, was a little pony with a rich red Christmas bow tied about his neck.

"Santa came!" exclaimed Zack.

"Santa came!" Sarah echoed, happily.

Nodding his head, as if in disbelief, but with a broad smile on his face, Pa whispered, "Santa came ..."

We ended up keeping the Christmas pony in the pasture at the end of the road, which turned out to belong to a widow woman named Mary Claire Windsor.

We named the pony Penny and in the spring she gave birth to twins so each of us ended up with our very own pet.

No matter how often I ventured down to the pony patch, I never again saw the kind man with the downy white beard and the Christmas green eyes. I missed seeing the old soul. But, I knew in my heart, on that Christmas so long ago, St Nick paid a visit that I would never forget.

"Always think the best thoughts and the best will come to you."

The Fitter Family

The Wayclocks Institute for the Feeble Minded sat between two gentle rises in the Massanutten Range of the Blue Ridge Mountains in Virginia's Shenandoah Valley. The Institute was housed in a nearly onehundred-year-old stone building with twin spires to the north and south end of the building. The whole structure appeared more like a wicked queen's castle of fairy tale lore than a hospital of sorts in the early twentieth century.

The Wayclocks Institute for the Feeble Minded was home to over three hundred souls, from the mentally infirm to a handful of youthful orphans with no other place to live since they were too young for the Shenandoah County Poor Farm.

The Institute was run by its namesake and founder, Dr Hiram Wayclocks. Hiram Wayclocks, a physician in his early seventies, was a spindly looking man with patrician airs and a prominent, hooked nose.

At Hiram Wayclocks' right hand was his daughter Priscella, a nurse by training and a tight, dour administrator by nature.

Midafternoon on the second of May, 1927, Priscella hurried from her office towards her father's, hustling to the Institute director because she had good news.

The Hazlett family never missed attending the annual Kansas Free Fair at the fairgrounds a mile south of the Statehouse in Topeka. Stanley Hazlett was a pig farmer

51

from the Carbondale area, a sliver of a town some fifteen miles from the Kansas Capital City. Many imagined that spindly Stanley and his corpulent wife Anabeth were the couple from nursery rhyme fame, one eating only lean, the other feasting on fat.

The Hazlett's had five children in stair steps from fifteen to ten. Although Anabeth insisted on bathing at regular intervals, the family always carried with them a vague scent of fetid swine waste.

Frankie, the Hazlett's youngest child, pointed towards the 'Fitter Family' exhibition tent.

"Hey, Pa, can we go there?" he asked.

"What's that boy?"

"Can we go there?" Frankie jabbed his forefinger in the direction of the 'Fitter Family' tent.

Outside the dull brown tent, a canvas square the color of Kansas dirt, stood a marquee which advertized the feature inside.

In big red letters, the sign asked the question: "Is yours a Fitter Family?"

Garish yellow lights flashed on and off around the crimson query.

Directly underneath the illuminated question ran vertically a series of smaller, clear light bulbs, each blinking off and on at different rates of speed. Beside each blinking bulb was a neatly lettered statement, on the human condition.

The Shadow Cast

"Every fifteen seconds a feeble minded person is born."

"Every twenty seconds, a physically deformed person is born."

"Every thirty seconds a person is born who will end up a criminal."

"Every minute, a child is left an orphan."

By the time Priscella reached Dr Hiram Wayclocks' office, she was out of breath.

"Yes?" he asked, not looking up from the paper he was reading at his desk.

"Good news," she managed, while gasping to regain her breath.

"Yes?" Dr Wayclocks repeated.

"The Supreme Court, they've made a decision."

Dr Wayclocks looked up from the document that otherwise held his attention.

"Yes?" his voice resounded in an expectant tone. "That Buck versus Bell case," Priscella added. Dr Wayclocks nodded.

"The law ... the Supreme Court said the law ... it's okay."

A thin smile stitched across Dr Wayclocks narrow lips.

"Excellent," he said, forming a steeple with his bony fingers, his elbows resting on his desk.

"I'll have the girl ready," Priscella advised the doctor, an edge of enthusiasm entering her own otherwise staid voice.

Drawn into the tent, the Hazlett clan took the examination of sorts to determine if they were indeed a Fitter Family. The questioner, perched behind a chipped wooden desk, asked a series of queries designed to discover whether the Hazlett family might have a closeted skeleton or another that might prevent them from being deemed 'Fitter.'

Stanley, with his sixth grade education, did the question answering for his family. He was glad that they asked if any one in his family was *currently* in jail, since he knew some of his kin had been in the past and some maybe should be but hadn't gotten caught. Stanley was pleased to say that all of his kin had been born with all their limbs. He did not add that one of his cousins had lost a hand in a farming accident while he was drunk. When the last query was dashed off regarding the Hazlett family's religious affiliation, the examiner broadly beamed and pronounced Stanley's kin 'Fitter.'

Each of the Hazletts, having been given a blue ribbon to pin to their chest, strutted rather like the top sow at the Agricultural Hall a matter of a dozen yards north of the 'Fitter Family' tent.

May third dawned in a drizzle across the Shenandoah Valley. Eight-year-old Caroline Quinn was rousted out of bed by Priscella Wayclocks a full hour before the sun broke the horizon.

The little girl was stripped bare and prodded through the chilly, dark corridors of the Wayclocks Institute to the surgical suite. Priscella Wayclocks ordered the nude child to crawl up and lie down on the steel The Shadow Cast

examination table centered in the sterile looking room. Nurse Wayclocks instructed the timid girl to put her feet into a pair of leather stirrups.

A couple of times, Caroline started to ask the severe looking nurse a question regarding what was going on, why she was naked, why she was strapped to a cold table. Each time, Priscella Wayclocks snapped: "Be quiet."

Just after dawn, Hiram Wayclocks entered the surgical room to commence the rather simple procedure of removing the young girl's uterus and ovaries.

Dr Wayclocks decided to sterilize Caroline Quinn shortly after the girl arrived on the steps of the Institute. He elected to sterilize the girl simply because she was an orphan. Caroline Quinn was a perfectly healthy, bright child.

"No need passing on those genes," he explained to Priscella at the time of the girl's admission into the Wayclocks Institute. "No need at all."

A moment or two after entering into the surgical room, Hiram Wayclocks looked into the eyes of the stripped, confused girl and said only: "Excellent."

Author's Note:

In 1927, the United States Supreme Court handed down a decision upholding the Virginia eugenics sterilization law, which became model legislation across the United States. Under the eugenics laws, up to 60,000 Americans were forcibly sterilized from 1924 through 1979 for "conditions" such as mental illness, epilepsy, alcoholism … or because a child selected to be sterilized was an orphan.

Caroline Quinn is a fictional character although her plight describes that of hundreds of girls who fell to the scalpel because of eugenics laws. The Kansas Free Fair and its 'Fitter Family' exhibition are historical facts.

The Gleaning

I pumped the peddles on my bicycle, a year-old fire engine red Schwinn, as hard and as fast as possible. I did not manage to wheel down the drive leading up to my family's farmhouse until a few minutes after seven in the morning. I was to be at Hank's place by that time and even though I was just a few minutes late, I knew my school chum would be irritated.

The late August day was hot, unseasonably so, and I beaded up with sweat before I reached Hank's farm, one quarter section down the road from my family's place. Hank and his family lived on the farmstead directly north from our own while our classmate, Al, and his family lived just to the south. The three of us boys were to start the sixth grade that autumn in 1964.

As expected, when I reached Hank's house, he was pacing on the porch, obviously displeased. Before I dismounted from my bike, he blustered: "I*th* path *the*ven already. You're late."

Hank spoke with a bit of an impediment that never seemed to inhibit him from speaking his mind. In fact, I was only a few minutes behind schedule and Al had not yet arrived. But, I elected to keep my trap shut.

For his part, Al peddled onto Hank's drive at 7:15, being greeted by Hank in the same stern tone I received.

"I*th* way path *the*ven. You're late," Hank pounced.

The Shadow Cast

Al rolled his eyes and shot back, "Bite me!" Hank, in turn, whined about us having work to get done and a limited amount of time.

We lived on farms outside a tiny Iowa town christened Otterville. Otterville was a general store, a service station and the Ruby Rose Dining Café. The main, indeed only, street in Otterville was a rutted and pitted dirt and pea gravel road. The Otterville Creek ran along the west edge of town, a rusty iron bridge separating the hamlet from the seemingly unending expanse of black soil farms that extended westward.

Each harvest time for the past three years, Hank, Al and I gleaned corn as a team and at each of our home places. After the combines rumbled through the fields reaping the bulk of the corn crop, we three boys would walk the fields collecting errant ears of corn. We would get paid a pittance for each bushel we gleaned.

Despite the small amount of change we garnered for each filled basket, taken together the cash fruit of our efforts gave us enough money to enjoy regular Saturday matinees at the Regal Bijou Theater in Waterloo, the big city about forty minutes from Otterville. We even made enough dough to get malts at Johnny's across the street from the Regal Bijou after the picture show.

In addition to collecting cash for picture shows and malteds, we pulled in enough money to take our mothers and fathers to the Ruby Rose Dining Café for supper. We started a tradition three years ago of taking our folks out to supper with some of our hard earnings.

Folks on farms around Otterville were not regularly accustomed to dining out. Certainly daily meals, and

58

The Shadow Cast

most special occasions, were taken at home or at a neighbor's place. But, once in a while, including after gleaning, we would find ourselves at the Ruby Rose Dining Café. And, unlike the other rare instances of meals away from home, our brothers and sisters did not come along to our after-gleaning supper. The occasion, and it became a true occasion, was a special gathering just for Hank, Al and me with our folks.

After accosting Al for his tardiness, Hank stomped down the porch steps off in the direction of the cornfield. Bushel baskets in hand, Al and I followed behind at some distance, wanting to allow our friend room to cool.

We made decent progress in gathering errant ears throughout the morning, breaking finally when Hank's Ma rang the dinnerbell straight up at noon.

As was the norm, dinner was full blown: fried chicken, whipped potatoes with newly churned butter, piping hot biscuits and fresh berry pie, still warm from the oven.

"How are you boys coming along?" Hank's Ma asked.

Before Al or I could respond, Hank mumbled something about us getting a late start that morning.

"Oh, pa-shaw," Hank's mother quipped, obviously well used to her son's carrying-on.

Despite the greatness of the meal, we made short shrift of dinner and returned to the cornfield before one that afternoon. After about half an hour into the afternoon shift, Hank spotted something or other in the tangled mess of combined corn stalks.

The Shadow Cast

"Looky here," he called over to Al and I as he pointed ahead of where he stood. We went to Hank's side. His finger directed our gaze to a shiny patent leather shoe – a boy's shoe, about the same size one of the three of us might wear.

"Lose your shoe, Hanky?" Al immediately teased.

"It'*th* not my *th*oe," Hank protested. Indeed, not one of the three of us was much suited towards glossy patent leather. Such was the footwear of city folk.

"What were you doin', Hank? Out here in your Sunday dress all frilly an' havin' a tea party for you an' your pissin' dollies?" Al would not let loose.

"It'*th* not my *th*oe, Al White, and you know it." Hank scowled, turned away from Al and picked up the stray shoe to examine it more closely.

"Wonder how it got out here?" I asked.

Before Al piped up with another rake about girly parties and plastic dolls, Hank blurted once more that the shoe did not belong to him.

After we discussed the shoe and its appearance in the cornfield for a few more minutes, Hank tossed it in his basket quite like another ear of corn.

We all but forgot the new looking dress shoe by the time Al announced we should go fishing.

"Fi*th*ing?" Hank whined, perturbed.

"Yep." Al nodded.

"But we haf' a lot of work," Hank moaned.

In the end Hank relented. We deposited our baskets next to the corncrib, gathered fishing poles and our bicycles and rode off to the bridge over the Otterville Creek at the edge of town. We dropped our lines until about 5:30, each catching a couple of catfish and then hurried to our own homes in time for supper.

The next morning, Al and I made certain we arrived at Hank's place just before the appointed hour. We did not want to endure a second day of Hank dithering over our promptness. Al and I reached Hank's at the same time, meeting up on the road when we were both en route. We gathered in the kitchen at Hank's, while his mother busied herself packing a picnic basket for our noon meal. She thought we would like eating a picnic in the small woods at the edge of the cornfield.

"Doesn't a picnic sound nice?" Hank's ma asked me after I arrived that morning.

"Yes Ma'am, it does," I dutifully replied.

"Ma, hurry up. We're going to be late," Hank prodded, becoming agitated.

"Oh, pa-shaw," his mother rejoined, continuing to pack the basket at her own pace.

We were off to the cornfield by 7:15, Hank relatively happy with our departure time. At least he did not grouse like the day before. The morning was a little cloudy, leaving us to hope that we might be in for a cooler, overcast day. As it turned out, by midmorning the clouds burnt off and we were roasting.

A little before noon, Al started griping about being hungry.

"We haf' to keep working," Hank replied.

"I'm hungry," Al maintained.

"We haf' a lot of corn to get," Hank insisted.

"I'm starving," Al pressed.

The Shadow Cast

Despite Hank's hemming about carrying on gleaning, we ended up breaking for lunch. I imagined Hank's stomach got the best of him.

We wandered over to the woods, really nothing much more than a half-acre cluster of trees. We took seats on a fallen trunk, next to a small brook that eventually babbled into the Otterville Creek. We wasted no time breaking into the basket to start our picnic.

We had not been eating for more than a quarter of an hour when Hank suddenly dropped a leg of fried chicken he had been working on. I caught a glance of Hank just as the chicken hit the ground. Looking at Hank's face, I actually thought I saw the color drain from his skin.

"Hank …" I started to ask him what was wrong when he raised an arm and pointed over towards a mound of tree limbs and long fallen leaves. Looking closely at the clutter, I saw what caught Hank's own attention, causing him to react so deeply.

My eyes locked on to a leg with a shoeless foot, sticking out of the pile of woodlawn litter. In an instant, I felt my gut pitch and roll. As if directed or synchronized, the three of us rose from our seats on the stump and ran, without stopping, all the way back to the farmhouse. Dashing into the kitchen, all out of breath, we caught Hank's mother just as she finished washing up dinner dishes.

"Ma!" Hank groaned, gasping for air. She turned from the kitchen sink and looked from her son's face to Al's to mine and then back to Hank's.

"What happened? Who's hurt?" she asked, instinctively.

62

The Shadow Cast

As quickly and as precisely as we could manage, we explained to Hank's ma what we discovered in the woods. While we spoke, Al actually got weak kneed and took a chair at the table.

Summing up the situation, Hank's mother quickly dispatched directions. Hank was to go round up his father in the barn and take him down to the woods. I was to go with her directly to the tree patch after she telephoned the Sheriff. Al, still seated and blank, was to wait the arrival of the constable at the farm.

The remainder of the afternoon seemed to pass like an early morning dream, a sleepy vision just before the dawn. Although I led Hank's mother back to the spot in the woods where we made our discovery, she prevented me from getting close enough again to see the site.

By supper, the Sheriff had come and gone, along with Doc Spright, the Buchanan County coroner. While at Hank's place, the Sheriff rounded up the shoe we found in the cornfield the day before. The shoe matched a mate still on the dead boy's right foot.

The boy we found in the woods was not a local; he was not recognized by the Sheriff and Doc Spright. The adults all concluded someone had killed the boy somewhere else – perhaps even as far off as Waterloo – and dumped his little body in the woods at night. Once the Sheriff and Doc Spright left, our parents – mine and Al's had come over to Hank's place early on after the discovery – announced that we would all be going to the Ruby Rose Dining Café for supper. The mothers all agreed that they did not feel like cooking – a rare occurrence for women who seemed to prepare

63

even more food when a neighbor or family member passed.

When we reached the Ruby Rose, the adults all sat together at one table while Hank, Al and I took to another by ourselves. The only topic of discussion during the initial part of our visit to the diner was the events of the afternoon.

As the evening wore on, and after supper was served by Ruby Rose herself, I noticed that other topics came up for discussion at the adult's table. By the end of supper, even Hank, Al and I began discussing other topics: fishing, gleaning and winter time matinees at the Regal Bijou Theater in Waterloo.

On that hot autumn night, at the Ruby Rose Dining Café, I realized that despite the tragedy of the afternoon, we three boys could carry on and live hopeful lives in our hometown called Otterville.

Hartford Wayclocks

Seedy.

Passersby of the Longhorn Tavern on Colfax Avenue in Denver, long described the gin joint as 'seedy'. The pub opened up at seven each morning, seven days a week. The Longhorn shut down each night at 2:00am. The place was a haven of regulars.

Colfax Avenue, east from the Colorado statehouse, was the approximation of a red light district, a bawdy strip, in the western capital city in 1968. The Longhorn sat in the midst of the near raunchy blight. Across the street from the bar stood Miss Macie's Triple X Adult Cinema. Next door to the Longhorn, which stood on a corner, was a shanty retail liquor market that fronted a brisk business of working girls.

The Longhorn itself occupied a square building, chipped brick from foundation to midpoint and faded brown-painted wood from there to the roof, which was flat and grisly tar. A solitary door facing Colfax Avenue provided access to the pub, faux steer horns festooned in place right over the entrance. A worn sign to the right of the door, missing a letter, announced "The Longhor_," a misnomer that brought regular smiles to passing folk considering the seedier nature of the area.

Inside, the Longhorn was dark, smoky and reeked of stale keg brew with a misting of other mingled, generally unpleasant odors. A customer could take but several steps through the street door before reaching the bar stand, lined with terribly worn stools. A few scattered tables with rickety chairs sat in other points of the joint, but the bulk of the trade took to the bar stand, sidling up on the grouped stools.

Hartford Wayclocks lived a couple of blocks from the Longhorn in a dingy walkup flat. At sixty-eight, Hartford maintained a thick head of hair, the color of which had turned yellowish like week-old newsprint left in the sun. His cheeks were ruddy, his nose veiny from the drink.

Hartford's clothes were old, worn in spots, but neat and clean. Ram Payton, the bartender normally at post when Hartford Wayclocks came to the Longhorn, long concluded the older man's clothing likely was most stylish thirty years earlier.

All days of the week were essentially identical for Hartford. All weeks of the month, months of the year – all the same. But for cheap decorations hung about the Longhorn – red, white and blue bunting in July; pumpkins in October, garland and tinsel in December – Hartford would have remained oblivious of the holidays.

True to form, on June 9, 1968, Hartford strolled the two blocks from his meager flat to the Longhorn, squinting the entire way to dim the glare from the midafternoon sunlight bearing down on the Mile High City. Hartford's apartment was so dimly lit, and his time on the street so short with his eyelids kept nearly shut, he spent little time adjusting to the dark interior of the Longhorn. He ambled over to the stool he normally took, Ram Payton already tapping a mug of beer the moment after Hartford entered the pub.

"Afternoon Hartford," Ram greeted, setting the frosty mug in front of his customer.

The Shadow Cast

"Hello," Hartford picked up the beer and took a deep drink.

Ram Payton, twenty-three, was a well-scrubbed, well-muscled, blond fellow. He hailed from the gray plains of Eastern Denver, a farming town called Burlington, nearly at the Kansas border. He migrated to Colorado two years earlier to earn enough money to carry on to California and Los Angeles. He hoped for a career in film, perhaps television. He took to calling himself Ram rather than Ron once he hit Denver.

During his nearly two year stint at the Longhorn, Ram learned some about Hartford's past, information that he imagined and hoped would be useful to him when he hit Hollywood himself.

"How are ya doing?" Ram asked, putting his elbows on the bar top, leaning into Hartford.

Hartford shrugged, pursed his lips a bit.

"Been slow here so far," Ram volunteered, tilting his head to two other customers at the opposite end of the bar stand from where Hartford sat.

"Early, I guess," Hartford volunteered. Hartford's voice generally sounded soft, kind, perhaps even plaintive. But, Ram noticed an occasional coarseness to the man's tone, which Ram thought belied a toughness in Hartford that others might not spot.

"Yeah ... it'll pick up, I suppose. I actually just got in a little before you," Ram explained.

"Uh-huh."

Within ten minutes of the arrival, Ram served a second brew to Hartford.

"You know what you were talking about yesterday?

That was real interesting. Really interesting," Ram said.
"What's that?" Hartford replied, absently.

Ram grinned, his smoothly aligned, chalk white teeth
peeking out from behind his lips. "Come on ... you
remember."

Hartford did not.

"Come on," Ram chided in a good-natured way.

"Yesterday?" Hartford asked, more perfunctory and
not as if he was actually searching and screening his
memory.

"Sure."

Hartford mumbled that he did not remember.

Still with a pleasant expression, Ram sighed. "You
were talking to me about Pam Ella Trent, the actress."

Hartford noticeably cringed when he heard the
actress' name spoken. Ram easily noted the
expression.

"I'm sorry," Ram swiftly apologized. Although
Hartford did speak of Pam Ella Trent the prior evening,
he had a half dozen draws before mentioning the
woman.

A half a minute passed before Hartford moved and
when he did he slugged back what remained in his
mug.

"Another?" Ram eagerly asked, hoping he had not
upset his customer.

Hartford nodded. Ram quickly served and noted:
"This one's on me."

"Thanks," Hartford said. His face once more half
slackened to a blasé state.

Ram intended to bring up a different subject,
perhaps the weather or the Presidential primary

election taking place in California. He opted for the election.

"You know, if I'd made it to LA by now, I'd be voting for Kennedy," Ram stated.

"Robert Kennedy …" Hartford mused.

"Yep. He'd be my choice," Ram enthused.

Hartford nodded and then, finally, conceded he did not follow politics much.

"I think it'll be Kennedy," Ram said, somewhat proud to know a bit more about something than did Hartford Wayclocks, who always seemed well-versed about everything to Ram.

"Uh-huh."

Ram was then diverted by his other two customers, needing refills of their cheap whiskey drinks. Despite a loud belch from one of the fellows, neither of them spoke to Ram. He returned to his on the bar position in front of Hartford.

Ram was surprised when Hartford spoke first.

"So, I mentioned Pam Ella Trent?" Hartford asked.

"Yeah, you did." An eager sparkle zipped across Ram's blue eyes.

Hartford solemnly nodded. "Yes, I did know Pam Ella Trent."

"So, Hartford … you've told me you were in show business. But, you said you weren't an actor."

"An actor?" Hartford rhetorically flushed. "No, not an actor. Not me."

Pressing ever so slightly, Ram inquired "So, were you an agent?"

"No." Hartford drank from his mug.

"Producer?"

The Shadow Cast

"No."

"Director?"

Sighing and taking another drink, Hartford responded: "That I was."

Ram stepped back seemingly in sudden awe. "A director," he said, eyes open wide.

Hartford nodded, finishing another mug filled with beer. Ram, not taking his eyes off of Hartford, poured a refill.

"Were you in Hollywood?" Ram asked.

"Hollywood?" Hartford asked in return, glancing down at his drink, intent on avoiding eye contact with Ram. "Yes."

"Gosh," Ram rejoined, sounding positively boyish. "Even New York?"

"Yes, New York, too."

"Movies?" an even more earnest Ram inquired.

"Films," Hartford responded, correcting Ram, as an old hand was wont to do in the business.

"Gosh," Ram replied, looking as if to bust behind the bar. "I want to be in movies."

"Movies ..." Hartford grumbled, finding the word close to foul. "I did films," he muttered, his beer mug almost covering his mouth as he spoke.

"How'd you get into movies?" Ram asked Hartford who suddenly looked tired, worn, pitted out.

"I went to Los Angeles very young," Hartford said, slowly and as if explaining caused him pain. Ram did not notice the stern expression taking hold of his patron's face.

"Yeah?" Ram replied, motioning for Hartford to continue.

70

The Shadow Cast

"Went to work for Regal Limited Studios," Hartford remarked, as if that short statement explained all the rest Ram needed to know. Hartford drained another glass.

"Regal Limited," Ram gasped. "That's Miss Trent's studio, huh?" he asked, referring to the actress. He refilled Hartford's mug as he spoke.

"It was," Hartford confirmed.

"Did you meet her there?" Ram asked. Before he could answer, three younger men entered the bar, a brief flash of outside light bursting through the joint when the entrance door opened. "Sit tight," Ram directed, politely, as he moved away from Hartford to tend to the newcomers, irregulars at the Longhorn that he had not seen before. They looked to be college boys to Ram, perhaps wanderers from the University of Denver in the Southeast quadrant of the city, a piece from the Colfax strip. Although the time was barely past four in the afternoon, the young men appeared well blown by booze even at the relatively early time on a weekday. But, it was the summertime, Ram knew, and variances abounded as much as the weather shifted all about on a Denver day.

The younger men, when served pitchers of beer, took seats at one of the scattered tables in the small pub. They promptly took to a drinking game involving the pitching of a quarter coin.

"So, where were we?" Ram shot out returning to his then favored place in front of Hartford Wayclocks.

Without a beat, Hartford's affected expression appeared to bleat: 'We were nowhere.' Ram missed the dour pout altogether. Hartford knew ignoring or, worse still, brushing past the younger man would detrimentally impact his service at the Longhorn in the future. Hartford lacked the vim to look for a new point to drink, could never muster the vigor necessary to walk any further than the couple of city blocks to the Longhorn.

Feeling forced to answer, Hartford did. "Meeting Miss Trent."

An awestruck flush invaded Ram's face. "Pam Ella Trent ..."

"Right," Hartford grimly replied.

"Now she was a star," Ram remarked, so strongly stating 'star' that he captured the attention of the drunken collegians at the table.

Hartford shifted uncomfortably and finally, awkwardly, bobbed his head in agreement. "She was ..." he whispered. "She was."

Ram and Hartford visited a bit longer, Ram drifting from Pam Ella Trent to Hartford's real relief. Ram was content talking with Hartford, burning to pick the elder gent's brain to his own benefit for his planned journey to Hollywood. The conversation, one-sided as it appeared, shut off when the late afternoon regulars came to root, keeping Ram attending to business with hardly an interruption.

As is the case with taverns, the more crowded the place became, the more solitary Hartford became. He preferred, longed to be, left alone with his drink, etching onward to a blank mind.

Sometime after eight o'clock that night, a frantic looking younger man, who appeared to be a peer of the college boys, but was not, stumbled into the bar from off the avenue. Ram imagined violence on the street but before he could inquire, the young man blathered: "He's been shot! He's been shot!"

Ram concluded violence on the street, right in front of the tavern. Looking down, Hartford muttered: "Kennedy ..."

"Kennedy!"

Pallor descended over the Longhorn almost as if the dark gin joint was swathed in dank black crepe. Hartford left crumpled bills on the bar, silently shuffled halfway down the block not hearing the door to the Longhorn opening or the sound of someone walking quickly up to him. Hartford stumbled, nearly tripping over his own feet, when the follower's firm hand clamped down on his shoulder. Before firm panic set in, a friendly voice sounded from the person clutching Hartford.

"Are you okay?" Hartford instantly recognized Ram's voice.

Hartford turned around, Ram catching the glint of tears in the old man's eyes, little drops reflecting the streetlights lining the avenue.

"Fine, fine," Hartford managed, his voice cracking.

"You left so quick." Although he was now facing Ram, the bartender kept a hand on Hartford's shoulder, squeezing gently.

"Tired ... I'm tired."

"Do you want me to walk you home?" Ram asked. "I'm off in a little while if you want to wait. I'm off at nine.

Hartford thought for a few seconds and then shook his head.

"Are you sure?"

Hartford shook his head once more.

The Shadow Cast

"Heck, Hartford. I'd love to talk to you more about Hollywood, the movies, Miss Trent ..."

When Ram uttered Pam Ella Trent's name, Hartford shook his head more sternly.

"I could even bring along some beer," Ram added.

Hartford slowly declined, but thanked Ram for checking on him.

Smiling, Ram remarked: "Maybe another time, then?"

"Maybe," Hartford replied, turning away from Ram, continuing back on his lonely course to his tiny flat.

Shortly, inside his gray flat, Hartford nibbled on some potato chips that were oily and stale at once. He tuned into his television, an old model that nabbed broadcasts only in black and white despite the colorization of nearly all programming. The screen flickered alive, a reporter of the National Broadcasting Company rehashing the sad news of the savage attack on Bobby Kennedy. The news was the Senator clung to life at one hospital or another in Los Angeles, but a priest had been called.

Hartford drifted into an alcohol-enriched sleep, prone on a natty sofa sloppily angled in front of the television. His slumber was invaded by a dream that haunted his nights countless times since as far back as 1930 when he was but a spry young man of thirty, arrogant and restless, reckless.

In the dream, Hartford revisits a slim dressing room backstage of a performance hall in Topeka, Kansas. He is the director of a traveling revue, making a circuit across the county. The show features the prime subject of Ram Payton's intent interest – Pam Ella Trent.

The Shadow Cast

As the dream unfolds, Hartford presents himself at the dressing room, intent to hurt, not physically but otherwise, Miss Trent. He is joined in his expedition to inflict by two others, men whose faces he no longer recognizes in his nighttime ruminations.

The dreamy caricature of Hartford speaks to Miss Trent, as if his voice engulfed all around, as if disembodied from the person of the night vision.

"We have news," Hartford of the dreams tells the actress.

"Entrez," she responds, grandly making a sweep of her arm to welcome the callers into the snug sanctum behind the sets. In the dream, Miss Trent chirps: "The press will be here soon."

Hearing those words, the specter of Hartford dancing in the real man's slumbering head grins fiendishly.

"This reporter!" Hartford of the night bellows, laughing maniacally.

"A delightful man," Miss Trent mutters, crouching away from the wickedly awesome voice of the conjured Hartford. For the instant, the actress looks more like a cringing kitten than an earthbound star, frightened rather than firm.

"Your reporter friend!" the vision of Hartford shrieks. "He's not a reporter! Not at all! He is an escapee! He's an escapee from a lunatic asylum!" And again, the coarse specter that was Hartford of the dream turns his head back in violent, spiteful laughter.

The sudden blare of a trumpeter playing the nation's anthem on the television, marking the end of the

The Shadow Cast

broadcast day, yanks Hartford from the much-despised dream and back awake.

Hartford returned to the Longhorn the next afternoon about the same time, as was his daily routine. Bobby Kennedy officially was declared dead by doctors in Los Angeles an hour or so before he made pace down the sidewalk to the pub.

Upon arriving, Hartford finds the same two old men to one end of the bar and Ram at post behind.

"Hartford!" the tender happily greeted, wearing a tight fitting t-shirt, equally snug denim jeans, and rattlesnake skin cowboy boots. The sleeves of the tshirt were rolled, a package of Marlboro curled in the fabric on the left arm.

"Hello." Hartford's voice, his tone, drooped.

In a fluid motion, Ram gestured for Hartford to take a seat and poured a brew for the fellow. Hartford looked particularly tired to Ram, burdened.

"Rotten about Kennedy, huh?" Ram asked, guessing Hartford might be upturned by the events of the prior night.

"Yes."

"Hard to imagine."

"Yes."

"They had a glimpse of Jackie on television this morning."

"I see."

"Yeah. And, of course, Ethyl, too."

"Yes."

"And Teddy, the brother."

"Yes."

"And, gosh, other ones who I don't know."

76

The Shadow Cast

Hartford said nothing but rather took in a deep flush of beer. The cold drink rushed his throat and seemed to spread with a pulsing tingle from his head to toes.

"Have you been watching?" Ram asked, meaning the television.

"Yes."

"Me, too. Well, before I came to work."

"I see."

Silence again interrupted by the outside door opening and a local and regular working girl walking inside.

Ram muttered to Hartford: "It's Miss Dee." He sounded unhappy. Ram did not exactly dislike Miss Dee. Rather he resented her because she was the one customer, the one person, who seemed to be able to really snatch and keep Hartford's attention.

Indeed, when Ram mentioned who had entered from behind Hartford, the older man spun on his barstool to face the woman.

"Miss Dee," Hartford said, almost smiling.

"Harty," she purred, sashaying directly to the barstool to the man's right.

Miss Dee bore an affected southern drawl, favored thick and bouffant red wigs, vinyl mini-skirts and fuzzy, scant blouses sans brassieres.

"So what are ya'll drinkin' Harty?" she asked, really seeking a paid-for shot.

"He's having beer," Ram grimly intoned, a possessory thread snaking through his remark.

"What would you like, Miss Dee?" Hartford asked, almost as if he had ignored the terse sounding Ram.

"Oh, my dear, what would I do without the kindness of strangers?" Miss Dee melodramatically responded, a backhand to her perspiring forehead. Ram rolled his eyes, and murmured something about Miss Dee liking pond water. Hartford did not catch the remark, Miss Dee glowered at the bar server.

"A gin fizz," she flatly declared, her cold, calculating eyes tightly focused on Ram.

Ram took his time bringing Miss Dee her desired beverage, intentionally detouring to see if the old gents at the bar's tail end needed anything. He planted the ordered glass so firmly in front of Miss Dee, sprays of liquor and the effervescent flash dashed the bar top.

"A buck," Ram requested of Miss Dee knowing full well Hartford intended to cover the woman and include the beverage on his tab.

"I'll get it," Hartford chimed up. Ram glared at the seasoned woman of the avenue while she proudly posed like a peahen pursued by a brilliantly feathered peacock.

Conscious that Ram kept his eyes peeled in the direction of Hartford although he maneuvered to the bar's opposite end where the two old men sat, Miss Dee slid her barstool closer to Hartford.

"How are you Harty?" she asked.

"Fine."

"Sad news, huh?" she remarked.

"News?" Hartford did not know to what the woman referred.

"That whole Kennedy thing," explained Miss Dee.

"Yes."

"Sad, huh?"

78

"Sad, right," he agreed, sipping from his rapidly depleting mug as he spoke to Miss Dee.

"So, what are you up to today, Harty?"

Hartford shrugged, having no response.

"Me too, don't ya know."

Ram's frown turned scowl grew fiercer all the while he listened to Miss Dee chat with Hartford.

"Ever gone to the Crystal Lounge?" Miss Dee asked, referring to another similarly situated joint a few more blocks down the road.

"No."

"You should go." Speaking louder, Miss Dee remarked: "I go there all the time. The service is great."

Hearing Miss Dee's broadside, Ram would have tossed a drink at the streetwalker had Hartford not been present. Trying to satisfy his burning itch to respond, retort, retaliate, Ram mumbled: "Bitch."

Miss Dee carried on trying to entice Hartford to split from the Longhorn with her to go to the Crystal Lounge.

"No, thanks," he rather meekly rejoined, feeling his face flush because of the woman's spirited, light hearted prodding.

"Come on," Miss Dee delicately pushed, lightly poking a finger at her bar neighbor's shoulder. "We'll have fun."

"Well, I ..." Hartford grew uneasy, but before he tilted and could finish his response, Ram, tightly clutching a bar rag, hollered over: "Need another Hartford?" Ram blared obvious emphasis on the man's name.

Responding to Ram, Hartford managed another: "Well, I ..."

"Let's us have another … at the Crystal Lounge," Miss Dee shot, her stress on 'us.'

Ram moved in the direction of Hartford and Miss Dee, as well as the brew tappers, grabbing a clean mug along the short way. Miss Dee grinned wryly, watching the barkeep's brisk movements.

"Little light there pard'ner … in the little ole' booties," Miss Dee smirked. She laughed at her own jab, a guttural chortle born in dim taverns and on risky avenues.

Hartford thought of moving off to a table away from the bar stand, wanting more than anything else to enjoy, as best as he was able, his beers in peace, the relative peace of a pub.

Ram could not help himself, shot back "bitch" like a lynx plunges to prey, instinctively and swift.

Miss Dee only laughed all the harder as Hartford rocked uneasily on his barstool. The three of them – Miss Dee, Ram, and Hartford – soon fell silent, looking like the graph points of a jumbled triangle.

"Shall we go, Hartford?" Miss Dee finally pierced the quiet.

"He doesn't want to go with you," Ram sneered. Miss Dee followed the barkeep's protestation with a weary word-for-word mimic.

Hartford did not move, did not even budge to touch his mug.

"The Crystal Lounge is a far better place," Miss Dee lightly rolled, moving her face and especially her lips directly next to the older man's right ear. "Real men go there," she added, looking toward Ram for a moment with a glare that suggested she found the person behind the bar less than full fledged.

"He's not going with you," Ram jabbed, his voice gathering a strange sense of urgency. Miss Dee repeated the bartender's words once more in a slippery singsong voice.

Hartford finally spoke up, pretending that he suddenly remembered a task he needed to tend to back at his simple and plain apartment.

"Don't go," Ram rejoined.

"Come to the Crystal Lounge," Miss Dee cooed.

"Really, I can't ..." Hartford answered to both and hurried from the Longhorn, leaving behind a half finished beer. In part, worried that either Miss Dee or Ram might be on his heels, and, to a larger degree because he needed beer, he ducked into the neighboring package store and purchased a six-pack of cheap brew. Brown paper bag in hand, covering the rectangle of the beer package, Hartford hurried to his apartment where he spent the remainder of the night alone watching news broadcasts of the second Kennedy assassination, while drinking a poor man's brew.

At eleven o'clock, Hartford's phone rang. The loud, grating sound of the telephone so surprised the man, he pitched forward in his chair and sloshed beer onto the floor, splattering the beverage so far it even sprayed across the television screen. Hartford could not even remember the last time his telephone rang, but he knew it had to be weeks, perhaps even months. The last caller he recalled was a spinster cousin from Virginia named Priscella, who phoned a few times a year.

The Shadow Cast

He let the phone ring on several unnecessary times finding a pithy pleasure in hearing the sound of a caller. Considering the hour, Hartford was all but convinced the caller had misdialed as he reached for the phone. Tentatively, he said: "Hello?"

"Hartford?" the man on the other end responded. Even though Hartford knew the call was intended, he also readily determined the man on the other end was drunk by the way the fellow slurred and extended Hartford's name.

"Yes?"

"Did I … did I … wake you up?" the caller belched.

"No."

"I'm sorry … I didn't … didn't mean … to wake you up." Another forceful burp followed.

"No. You didn't."

In a playful tone, the caller announced: "Guess who this is?"

Hartford furrowed his brow, perplexed and not inclined for kiddish gaming. "Who is this?" he sounded grim.

"It's me," the man replied, laughing lightly.

Suddenly recognition clicked. "Ram?" Hartford asked, puzzled.

"Well, yeah," Ram replied, still chipper.

"Uh … hello …" Hartford responded, speaking slowly, scratching his head and wishing his beer bottle was within reach.

"Did I wake you up?" asked Ram.

"No."

"What're you doing?"

Hartford stammered, finally, saying only: "Nothing."

"Were you sleeping?" Ram asked still again, sounding aghast.

"No ... no. I've been watching television."

A somber edge in his voice, Ram remarked: "Isn't it sad?"

Hartford assumed the Kennedy death and said: "Yes."

"So what're you doing?" the drunk caller asked, again.

"Nothing."

"I'm off work," Ram volunteered.

"I see."

"I'm still at the bar."

"Oh."

"Wanna come down and have a drink with me?"

"Now?"

"Sure." Ram's tone was eager, enthusiastic, despite his   blurry   enunciation.

"Tonight?"

"Yeah. Come on down," prodded Ram.

"I don't think ..."

Ram cut in: "Have a beer, my treat."

"I'm at home." Hartford stated the obvious.

Ram hesitated for a few seconds and then suggested that he could bring some beer over to Hartford's apartment. "My treat," he said.

Hartford did not know how to respond. He tried to think of when he last had someone over to his flat. Besides occasional visits from old Mrs Phipps who lived in the building, Hartford could not remember anyone calling to visit the apartment.

"So, what do ya think?" Ram asked Hartford.

Almost as if his mouth and vocal cords were working together on their own, "Okay" tumbled from Hartford's mouth.

"I'm on my way, I'll bring the beer. My treat." With that, the phone went dead.

Thirty seconds later, the phone rang again.

"You know," Ram began before Hartford even said "Hello," I got your number from the book, but I'm not sure what apartment." He mumbled something more about having the street address from the directory, but not an apartment number. Hartford provided the needed information and within fifteen minutes, Ram was at Hartford's door.

Before entering the apartment, Ram hoisted the package of beer up in front of his face like a prized trophy of some sort or another. "My treat," he exclaimed from behind the carton filled with six brown bottles.

Rubbing sleep from his bloodshot eyes, the sixtyeight year old and worn man invited Ram inside. Ram gave the flat a quick scan, taking a seat on a threadbare, dull apricot-colored sofa at the opposite end of the small sitting room. A well-scratched coffee table stood in front of the divan, the armchair favored by Hartford off to the side.

Before Hartford drug himself the several steps across the room, Ram pulled on two beer bottles and placed them, one next to the other, on the coffee table. Ram sat to the side of the sofa, suggesting with the brew placement and body movement that Hartford should join him on the couch and not take roost on the nearby chair.

Hartford hesitated but did take a place, awkwardly, next to Ram on the sofa. He nervously picked up a bottle, which Ram quickly opened with the opener Hartford had left on the table during his private drinking time earlier that night.

"Man, I'm sorry about what happened tonight at the bar," Ram said, sounding jocular and referring to the rat-pat with Miss Dee the hooker.

Hartford, not knowing what to say, only shrugged one shoulder.

"She's just out of control," Ram spoke tentatively, as if testing waters with a bare big toe.

Hartford moved his head in such an obscure way he appeared to neither bob nor shake.

"You were telling me about Regal Limited Studios, about you being a director, last night," Ram continued.

Hartford shuddered, thinking about the dream, the nightmare, he had the prior night featuring Pam Ella Trent.

"I'd love to hear more," Ram said, gently pushing.

"I had a nightmare last night." The revelation slipped out in spite of himself, catching even Hartford off guard. Ram moved a little closer to the older gent on the sofa, not wanting to miss out on the opening, the peek into the personal nitch.

"Really?" Ram replied.

Hartford then tried to brush off his remark.

"Tell me about it," Ram swiftly enticed, seeing 'back pedal' written across Hartford's face.

"Oh, I guess it was nothing."

"No, tell me Hartford."

"It was just a strange dream. Nothing important."

The Shadow Cast

"But," Ram responded, "you mentioned it so it must be important." Ram paused for a moment and then added: "I like listening to you."

Hartford found Ram's remark odd and misplaced on a number of levels. Most particularly, Hartford realized he never spoke much to anyone anymore, including the bartender from the Longhorn.

"Oh," Hartford shortly replied.

"Tell me," Ram pushed.

"Well, it was about Pam Ella Trent ..." Hartford's voice trailed off.

"Miss Trent?" Ram perked up, sounding eager.

Hartford nodded.

"Tell me," Ram once again encouraged.

Hartford sat still.

"You can tell me ... anything," Ram gently invited.

Hartford consciously kept from looking directly at his beer-drinking companion.

"I was the director of Pam Ella Trent's last cross country revue," Hartford volunteered, leaving Ram nodding even though he had no idea how the revue of years past related to the nightmare.

Hartford continued. "She was a challenging woman. And I was young. Barely twenty-nine at the time, I think."

"That's young to be working with someone like Miss Trent," Ram interjected.

Hartford shook his head. "Well, not really. You see by that time, Miss Trent's career was in ... well ... I guess you might say a 'dip'." "A dip?" Ram asked.

"You might say," confirmed Hartford.

"I see."

86

"So, my directing the revue ... not such a great thing, no big deal."

"I think it is," Ram responded with all the unbridled eagerness of a happy pup.

"We'd reached Topeka," Hartford went on.

"Kansas?"

"Yes."

"I've never been there," Ram remarked, not knowing what else to say.

"Actually, before we hit Topeka, we were in Kansas City."

"Nope, I've never been there either," Ram noted with a large smile.

"From Kansas City, to Topeka, then to Denver. Here ... Denver." Hartford's voice sounded distant, drifting. He next explained that in Kansas City, Pam Ella Trent met up with a young man.

"He said he was a reporter," Hartford remarked.

"A reporter," Ram repeated the words, his own speech sounding dreamy. He remarked that he hoped when he finally made it out to Hollywood to start his career he would meet some interested reporters.

"You know," Ram said. "To give my career a jump start and all."

Hartford did not respond. Rather, he carried on with his gathering story as if speaking aloud to himself.

"This fellow, this reporter, he really had Miss Trent hooked."

"Hooked?"

"Hooked. Sweet guy, I guess. Just had Miss Trent wrapped around his finger."

"Did he write a bad story?" Ram asked, suddenly sounding worried.

Hartford sadly frowned. "There was no story." "No story?" confused, Ram inquired.

"No story at all. Turns out this fellow who meets up with Miss Trent, who says he's a reporter … turns out he escaped from a mental hospital. Turns out he was posing as a reporter. Duped Miss Trent something awful."

"That is awful."

Hartford pressed on, speaking steadily and altogether tuning out the young man.

"Well, I first found out the guy was a fraud, a maniac of some sort. A nut."

Hartford took a bracing slug of brew. "I went backstage after Miss Trent's show in Topeka, just before the show headed on to Denver."

"Uh-huh." Ram moved slightly closer to Hartford, well sensing the old man's growing vulnerability.

"I couldn't wait to tell her of the fraud. I wanted nothing more than to hurt Pam Ella Trent." Hartford spoke rapidly, his voice belaying a violent intonation. "I went right back to her dressing room and broke the news to her that this reporter … this fellow that she thought sure would put a new gloss on her dulling career … that this reporter was a maniac, a fraud, an escapee from the nuthouse. I wanted to hurt that woman bad, bad, bad."

Ram grabbed ahold of his beer bottle, more by impulse than anything else, a latent response to Hartford's churning voice.

The Shadow Cast

"I traveled with Miss Trent to Denver the next day. And I would not let her live down how she fell for a crazy man pretending to be a reporter. I didn't let up, not the whole way." Hartford inhaled deeply, his body shuddering once more. He nearly shouted, banging a hand on the coffee table.

"I hated Pam Ella Trent."

The two men sat alone in their silence for some minutes, Hartford's face flushed and Ram almost paled. Finally, Ram ventured in a weak voice not befitting his worthy frame: "Well, I guess I didn't like Miss Trent that much anyways."

In response, Hartford moved for the first time since he yelled his vindictive epitaph about the actress. He cocked his head towards Ram and gently stated: "The thing is … the thing was … despite everything I felt about Pam Ella Trent … she was good, one of the best." Hartford sighed and turned away from Ram. "The best actress, really."

Another thick silence invaded the small, dull room. Ram slid a bit closer still to Hartford on the sofa. Setting his beer bottle down on the coffee table, he then slowly extended an arm, which he wrapped around Hartford's shoulders. Hartford did not bridle and did not relax. He displayed no response to the man's gesture, feeling nothing.

More of the silent time passed when Hartford finally declared that the night must end.

"I'm tired, tired," he said.

Keeping his arm around Hartford, Ram eagerly advised that he could stay on for the night. Without reflection, sounding nearly like the voice of resigned death, Hartford simply said "no" in reply.

Discouraged but not knowing how else to prod, Ram stood up from the sofa and took his leave. Just outside the apartment but before he closed the door, Ram asked Hartford if the older man would be at the Longhorn that night, as a new day had started with the passing of midnight. Hartford, not looking at Ram, sadly and simply nodded.

Rather than retire to his bed after the bartender departed, Hartford pulled himself onto the couch fully and drifted into a restless sleep. In the same manner as when he last dozed off on the sofa, Hartford was pestered by the same wrenching night vision portraying him as an unbridled ghoul to the cowering kitten that was Pam Ella Trent in the dream. After the wicked dance played out in his weary head, Hartford awoke, never to find the welcome embrace of a peace filled slumber for the remainder of the night.

At dawn, Hartford found himself engulfed in tremors, shaking with an unexpected ferocity that the sofa rattled on its loose, carved wooden legs. He managed to snatch hold of the bottle left behind by Ram and drank down the lukewarm dregs.

With great effort, he took to his feet, barely able to stay upright as shakes and shudders raked his thin, haggard body. He extended his arm to check the time on his watch. The rattling of his being was so intense he could not well focus on the timepiece.

Shuffling sluggishly across the room, looking every bit the senior chap engulfed in palsy, he made it to a wall clock and squinted at the thin black hands. Finally, by twisting his neck, he was able to make out the hour. Although the Longhorn opened at the impossibly early hour of 7:00am, a full half hour remained before the pub doors opened. Hartford knew the Longhorn was his only easy refuge, as even package stores did not open until later in the day.

Hartford never faced tremors, but he was well aware what sapped at his body that morning. More than a few times, he watched worthless, tired old souls track into the Longhorn, their bodies in uncontrollable spasms calmed only by the drink.

Never paying much attention to his age since rounding out in Denver decades ago, Hartford felt like the withered men he saw with regularity on the brittle Colfax Avenue strip.

With the same puny, shuffled steps, Hartford gingerly made his way to the bathroom. Taking great effort, he managed to squat down to the floor and grasp onto the porcelain of the toilet bowl. Seeking a hopedfor respite, he jabbed a finger into his throat forcing a fleeting retch. Only thick, rank bile dribbled from his instantly aching gut, providing no relief to the rattled man.

On his hands and knees, Hartford crawled the short space to the bathtub and reached up to turn on the water. As best he could, Hartford tweaked the knobs to obtain a warm temperature in the flow.

Lying flat on his back, Hartford wiggled out of his clothes and then hoisted himself up and then into the warm bath water. Although the bath did nothing to calm the man's shakes, the warm embrace of the water cleared his mind a slight bit.

The Shadow Cast

Hartford shut his eyes for a long time, praying the tremors would stop or at least ease. He eventually looked over and up to a small shelf above the tub and off to the left. On the foot long piece rested an old, untouched bottle of aftershave lotion and a glass flask, with an ancient ribbon tied around the middle. Inside the thin glass container were the purple grains of lavender bath salts.

"Pam Ella Trent ..." Hartford muttered, his eyes locked onto the bath salts. The lavender dash belonged to Pam Ella Trent. In Denver, when her revue tour ended so unexpectedly back in 1930, Hartford found himself responsible for taking charge of her traveling wares. In the rush of those mad days, Hartford neglected to pack and ship the container of lavender bath salts. He had the elixir ever since, resting on the same small shelf for years.

Hartford firmly planted his hands on either side of the tub and struggled to pull himself out of the water. Once standing, and trying to balance in the water, he snatched hold of the glass vial of lavender salts. He wasted no time returning to a seated, almost reclining, pose in the bathwater.

He fumbled with the stopper on the bottle for nearly a minute, finally pulling it free. Despite its age, a faint smell of lavender flower lingered in the salts, which were clumped at the bottom and not loose granules of years ago.

Hartford dipped the bottle into the water, filling up the empty space above the hardened salts with water. He then shook the bottle, dissolving some of the salts at the top of the hardened collection. After a bit, he dumped the water back into the tub. He repeated the process enough times to finally clear all the salt from the flask and to turn the water a pleasant shade of pale purple. All the while, a mild scent of lavender filled the bathroom.

Hartford spent the next two hours in the bathtub, regularly adding hot water to the mix to keep the temperature up. Despite his best hopes, the warm bath and the lavender salts did nothing to calm the tremors. He spent another hour laboriously drying off from his bath and dressing. Brushing his teeth proved to be nearly impossible, his shaking hand made keeping a toothbrush in his mouth a virtual impossibility.

When he finally did get dressed, Hartford returned the empty bath salt vial back to its place on the shelf. He walked awkwardly back to his living room, out the door of his apartment and outside to the avenue. The beating heat of the late morning summer sun made Hartford nauseous. He desperately wanted to run down to the Longhorn to escape the broiling sun and to get a bracing drink. He knew the liquor was his only easy remedy. Despite how badly he wanted to make haste, he could barely stand, let alone move more swiftly than a dim plod.

Hartford's legs desperately ached and he was breathless by the time he reached the door to the pub, the entrance under the pair of faux steer horns. He had never been to the Longhorn so early in the day and he never struggled so mightily opening the tavern's door. He was keenly aware that although he had his teeth, he was the tired old soul tracking into the Longhorn, his body in an uncontrollable spasm that only booze would calm.

Being a very different time of day, he did not recognize the faces of the three men seated at the bar. Neither did Hartford recognize the round, flat face of the hefty black-haired woman with broad cat-eye glasses tending bar. He was only relieved that his regular barstool was open, untouched.

He somehow managed to mount the barstool, realizing for the first time that he perspired profusely, cold sweat dripping from his brow and soaking through much of his shirt.

"Hi, hon," the moon faced woman behind the bar greeted, obviously well used to men in Hartford's shape in the morning. In the moment, Hartford realized her nonchalance was quite like that of a nurse tending a patient.

"Wad'ya have, hon?"

"A beer, draw, and a shot," Hartford replied.

"Of what hon?" she asked as she went to the tapper for the brew and referring to the requested shooter.

"What?"

"Wad'ya want for a shot, hon?"

Normally a beer drinker, Hartford was somewhat stumped.

"What do you have?" he asked.

"Oh, hon, we've got it all." She put a filled mug of beer directly in front of her guest.

"Tequila?" Hartford asked, not knowing what to say.

"Now ya're talkin'," she smiled.

"Do you want one?" he asked

"Now ya're really talkin'," she replied, a huge smile ripping across her basketball-sized face.

She filled up two shot glasses with the yellowish liquid.

"Cheers," she said, tipping her shot glass at Hartford. He did the same, although mumbling.

Within less than a minute of taking the tequila shot, the tremors stopped short. A relieved expression washed over Hartford's face.

"Feel better?" the barmaid knowingly asked. Hartford nodded, like a schoolboy coming to an early appreciation of an important fact.

"You just holler if'n you need anything, hon," she chimed, walking over to a waist-high cooler behind the bar that she leaned against. She withdrew a file from her apron pocket and went to work on her red painted nails.

Hartford stayed on his barstool perch until one o'clock, when he paid his tab and returned to his apartment for a nap. A few hours later, feeling rested and calm, Hartford returned to the Longhorn where Ram had taken the bartender's post.

"Hey!" Ram brightly greeted. He quickly advised Hartford that he tried to telephone the older man that morning, but got no answer. "Wanted to see if you were okay."

"I had errands," Hartford replied, for some reason not wanting to tell the younger man he paid a visit to the Longhorn that morning into the afternoon.

"I was worried about you," Ram volunteered. On first blush to Hartford, the bartender did not sound exactly sincere. Ram's words, to Hartford, had a stagy quality, well short of cagey but seemingly off-level sounding in any event.

As in days past, the same two old men sat fixed at the end of the bar stand, focused on their drinking glasses. Through the evening, the tavern ended up doing an unusually brisk business. Ram's service shift ended at nine o'clock, by which time Hartford was well into his cups.

Ram served himself a pitcher of beer and poured a mug for himself and a fresh one for Hartford before abandoning the workstation. He asked Hartford to join him at one of the tiny tables at the edge of the pub. Hartford hesitated for a moment but the full pitcher of beer Ram offered to share, and the prospect of more ale gratis, was a strong draw. Hartford took a seat at the unleveled and unbalanced table with the young man.

"You know I'm going to Hollywood," Ram began.

Hartford vaguely remembered Ram sharing his goal to go further west and nodded.

"I bet you still know people there, have connections," Ram suggested to the drunk old man.

Hartford lied and nodded.

"Knowing Miss Trent and all," Ram continued. "I knew you'd still know people in Hollywood."

Despite his level of intoxication, Hartford concluded that Ram was either ignorant or delusional, or perhaps both.

"You'll fit in well in Hollywood," Hartford managed, his words slurred from a thick, boozed tongue.

"You think?" eagerly Ram questioned.

The Shadow Cast

Hartford thought to himself, 'How would I know, it's been almost forty years since … Pam Ella Trent.' Hartford said, remembering the general battiness of Hollywood, Broadway, and points in between even after four decades: "Sure I do."

"You ever think of going back to Hollywood?" Ram asked Hartford.

Startled, and sounding so, Hartford replied: "Me?"

"Yeah, sure,"

"Me?" he repeated, becoming more puzzled than surprised.

"Yeah, sure."

"No."

"No?" Ram asked, wholly disbelieving that anyone would not want to be in Hollywood, particularly someone who had been in show business.

"It's been forty years, almost," Hartford slowly stated, feeling he made an important and yet obvious statement.

The passage of time, a most significant lapse, failed to appropriately or reasonably register with Ram.

"Maybe you'd think of coming out to Hollywood with me when I go," Ram suggested, with all the force and innocence of youth.

Hartford stared ahead, avoiding Ram's deep, happy blue eyes. In little time they had nearly finished the pitcher of beer.

"Want to go somewhere to talk more?" Ram asked.

By this time of night and certainly after the volume of beer consumed, Hartford normally would have headed home. He did not answer at once.

The Shadow Cast

"We could go back to your place," Ram suggested. "It's much closer than mine. Plus, I don't have a car and we'd have to walk all the way to my place."

Hartford finally nodded and the two men left the Longhorn. They stopped into the liquor store next door to the tavern, Hartford insisting on paying for the package of chilled beer.

Upon reaching Hartford's snug apartment, they both retook the same positions they occupied the night before on the sofa, almost as if no time had elapsed. Retaking the couch, Hartford instantly had two thoughts. First, he thought of the tremors from the morning and almost took to retching on the spot at the prospect of facing the miserable shakes the next morning. He wished he'd purchased more alcohol at the package store.

The second thought dashing into Hartford's mind was the realization he did not finish his tale of Pam Ella Trent and the unplanned ending of her revue in Denver. Maybe it was the fact that he again sat with Ram or perhaps it was using the actress's forty-year-old lavender bath salts that morning, but Hartford felt well compelled to conclude the story. Since the actual events of four decades past, Hartford never spoke of Pam Ella Trent, the final traveling circuit, or the arrival of the revue in Denver.

Hartford meekly remarked that he did not manage to finish his story of Pam Ella Trent.

"You didn't?" Ram asked, sounding as if he forced interest. "I thought you had."

Hartford shook his head as he spoke. "I did not."

The Shadow Cast

Ram slid closer to Hartford, an action repeated from the prior night. "Well do, do finish."

"I told you about the maniac ..."

Ram cut in and said: "Who pretended to be a reporter."

"Who thought he *was* a reporter," Hartford replied.
"Yeah, you told me that."

"I told you I enjoyed ... enjoyed telling Miss Trent she was made the fool?"

"That the fellow wasn't a reporter but was a lunatic?" Hartford nodded.

"Yeah, you told me all that."

"I kept up at it," Hartford remarked.

"What do you mean?" Ram asked, not following.

"I kept at her. Kept at her about being taken in by a crazy man from an asylum." "You did?" Ram asked.

Again, Hartford nodded his head. "Her career wasn't going well then, not at all."

"Uh-huh," Ram said, not because he knew, understood or agreed. He merely muttered to keep the conversation going.

"The revue was going decently, not great, but decently. It could have given her career a boost, I guess. And she thought the crazy man from the asylum was doing a big story on her and the revue. A big story, on the cover of 'Hollywood Chatterbox'." "And it was all a lie?" Ram asked.

"A lie?" Hartford pondered on the words for a moment or two. "Did the crazy man lie? I do not know if he knew the truth. But, there was, of course, no big cover story for Pam Ella Trent."

"Oh."

The Shadow Cast

Hartford thought Ram seemed more intent on his beer than the story of Miss Trent. Hartford continued in any regard, finding a strange feeling of release in sharing the tale despite the halfhearted reception.

"When we reached Denver, everything got worse."

"Worse?" Ram finished off a bottle and started a fresh one.

"Much."

"What happened?" Ram sounded a bit more focused.

"We took the train out of Topeka. There was a terrible storm. The trip was rough. We even stopped at one point altogether when a tornado was spotted in our path. All our nerves were frayed." "A tornado?" Ram asked.

"Yes, yes. But, things got worse in Denver."

"Worse than a tornado?"

"Much."

The two men sat silently, sipping beer. Hartford tried to better collect his thoughts, Ram broke the peace.

"What happened?"

"We finally got to Denver, late. The theater manager here didn't think we'd make it."

Ram broke in: "Because of the tornado?"

"Well, because we were very, very late in making Denver."

"Oh."

"So, the theater manager officially canceled the show."

"But you made it in time for the show?" Ram asked.

"So we did." Hartford sighed.

"What happened then? Did Miss Trent do the show?

100

The Shadow Cast

The show must go on …"

Hartford sadly muttered: "The show must go on …"

When Hartford did not speak again directly, Ram poked him in the side in a good-natured way. "So, what happened? Did she do the show?"

Hartford slowly nodded. "She did the show," he said, hardly above a whisper. He added that hardly anyone was in the audience.

"Because you were late and the theater manager said the show was off, right?"

"That's what happened."

Hartford took a deep pull of beer finishing off his bottle. Ram, as if still behind the bar, hurried to pop open a fresh brew for Hartford.

"But Miss Trent went on anyway?" Ram asked.

"She went on. She did go on."

Ram repeated the singsong ditty about the show going on.

Hartford rubbed his eyes, red from a near complete day of drinking.

"You look tired," remarked Ram.

Either not especially hearing Ram or ignoring him, Hartford spoke on further about Miss Trent's show in Denver.

"The thing is," Hartford explained, "Miss Trent didn't know the theater manager canceled the show." "What do you mean?" Ram asked.

"She didn't know, she never knew that the manager canceled the show, officially, because we were so late making Denver."

Ram asked again: "What do you mean?"

"Miss Trent went on stage, did her bit to a near empty house."

Ram shifted uneasily in his seat, not fully grasping the set up.

"After the show, I went back to her dressing room. Before she could speak, I lied. Flat out lied."

Hartford's voice trailed off as he slumped heavily, his shoulders looking as if tacked down by a great weight.

"What did you say?"

"I told Miss Trent the show flopped. I never mentioned the theater manager canceling the show. Never mentioned it."

"What did she say?" asked Ram.

Hartford continued, well into his own thoughts, and did not directly reply to Ram.

"I told her, lied to her. I told her we canceled the rest of the circuit, the rest of the trip, including her big show planned for Hollywood about a week later. I told her it was all canceled because it was all a flop."

Ram said nothing.

"I thought I'll let her stew in her juices that night and I'd tell her the truth of things in the morning."

Ram smiled. "What did Miss Trent say when you told her the next day?"

Still stuck on a deeply self-plotted course, Hartford kept speaking without particular regard to Ram.

"By mid-morning the next day, it was time for us to leave for the train station, to leave Denver. I was in the lobby and phoned up to Miss Trent's room. She didn't answer."

"So, what happened next?" Ram asked with a budding eagerness akin to a boy at his father's knee hearing of a rollicking adventure.

"Eventually, I went up to Miss Trent's suite. We were at the Brown Palace, such a nice hotel ..."

"What happened then?"

"She didn't answer the door, didn't answer when I knocked."

"Uh-huh."

"Finally, I rounded up a maid and got her to unlock the door, got her to let me in."

"So, what happened?" Ram sounded almost impatient.

"I went into the suite, Miss Trent's suite. Her bed was turned down, but it was obvious she had not slept in it."

Hartford closed his eyes before he continued. "I eventually noticed the bathroom door was open, just a bit."

"'Miss Trent?' I called out. 'Miss Trent?' I called out again. But there was no answer ... no answer. I walked over to the bathroom, pushed open the door slowly. And there she was ..." "Miss

Trent?" asked Ram.

"There was Miss Trent, in the bathtub. The water ... the bath water, it was red ... all red."

Ram sat very still, as if frozen by the spell of Hartford's very words.

"And Miss Trent," Hartford continued, his eyes remaining well closed. "She was gone ... gone in the red water ... dead, dead in the bloody water." And Hartford cried.

The Shadow Cast

Ram wrapped his arms around the broken old man. Before long Hartford slipped away to sleep, a rocky slumber induced mostly by the alcohol. Ram gently removed the old man's shoes and slid him out on the sofa. He found a tattered blanket, which he used to cover Hartford.

Ram took the liberty of using Hartford's untouched bed for his own, too tired to walk home and not certain if Hartford should be left alone.

In the hour just before the dawn, Hartford's eyes fluttered open for a brief, fleeting moment. A smile, thin and gentle, traced his lips. And, at that moment, Hartford Wayclocks was no more.

Snowy Night

The trio kept singing "Auld Lang Syne," over and over and then over again. Harper Faith, the fully perturbed waitress assigned to the men's table, felt on the verge of dousing the loud threesome with a pitcher of brew. She found the man with copper-colored hair particularly irksome; he irritated her even as he sat down at the table upon arriving at the diner two hours earlier when he said: "Sweetie" and then proceeded to pat her ample behind.

As the off-tune trio rounded out the song of remembrance, the copper haired man shouted for "Another pitcher, babe." Harper went to the host station, commiserated with the hostess by cussing and swearing until her face pulsed purple.

Harper Faith was most displeased with having to work the dinner shift on the holiday. But, she drew the short straw. Plus, of all the waiters and waitresses, she was the only one without children. Some of the others were married, some were divorced. Still others were single parents. But, to a person, they all had children at home for the holiday, except for Harper.

Upon drawing the wicked stick that led to her working on that night, Harper reasoned that the diner likely would not be all that busy as people would be engaged in holiday activities at home. Her assumption held true until the copper haired man and his cohorts arrived.

The Shadow Cast

Her only other occupied station contained a solitary gentleman, a man Harper thought to be about seventy. He ordered a Porterhouse with a side of grilled onions and a glass of virgin egg nog.

Indeed, the older gent was so unobtrusive, Harper kept forgetting that he was there at all. Between being irked by the horribly out of tune and out of sync trio and generally miffed about drawing the short straw, Harper found herself losing track fairly frequently that evening.

Harper started to sneak off to the restaurant's rear delivery door, behind the kitchen, for a smoke break. Halfway to her desired destination, she stopped short realizing she had not popped by the kindly gent's table in some time. She hurried around back into the dining room. Reaching the man's post, she apologized for not being back to him sooner and asked if he needed anything.

"You know," he said in a voice that made Harper think what a wonderful grandfather he would be, kind and loving, "I'll take another slug of this."

"Sure," Harper smiled, sincerely finding herself grinning. She took the man's glass and went back to the kitchen and poured him a fresh egg nog.

Returning to the man's table, she took a closer look at the chap. He did not look familiar to her, the restaurant having a goodly share of regulars. The man also looked tired, very tired and worn, to Harper.

"Are you from around here?" Harper asked.

The man looked as if he was on the brink of bursting into a gut-busting laugh.

"My, no," he said. "I'm actually from quite far off."

Harper imagined Peoria.

The Shadow Cast

"Born and raised here," Harper volunteered about herself.

"I'm Nicholas." The old man struggled to stand as he introduced himself.

"Sit, sit. Don't get up for me," Harper extended her hand, shook his and gave him her name.

"Pleased to meet you," the old man graciously said.

"Same to you," she replied, thinking about a smoke once again. "You just let me know if you need anything else," she added, leaving the old man's table.

Harper retraced her steps back through the kitchen, on this occasion reaching the delivery door. She ducked outside, into the freezing Illinois winter night. She wasted no time in lighting up, finishing her smoke off in little time, not wanting to be out in the cold for too long.

Returning to the dining room, the loud trio was crashing through "Auld Lang Syne" for the umpteenth time. She rolled her eyes as the liquored up males once more butchered the lyrics.

"Go home," she muttered to herself. "Go away."

She glanced over at the old man, to see if the tragic rendition of "Auld Lang Syne" bothered him. He seemed well content, enjoying his egg nog and looking as if he were staring out the window and across the parking lot at the occasional car motoring down the roadway in front of the diner.

Harper thought about returning to the man's table to chat with him a bit further, but then thought better of it. He looked pleased enough to just be left alone and Harper did not want to bother him.

The Shadow Cast

Just as she was about to turn away and walk back into the kitchen, the old man cocked his head and looked in the general direction of where Harper stood.

The old man's kindly glance compelled Harper to move in his direction.

"Are you doing okay?" she asked, finding herself smiling again.

"Oh, yes, I am," he responded emphatically.

Harper noticed he finished off his meal plate and that his egg nog was nearly gone.

"Would you like some dessert? We have great pie."

He rubbed his hand on his chin, thinking.

"You know," he said, "I just had my beard shaved off this afternoon, so I'm not too used to actually feeling my chin."

He chuckled, a happy laugh.

Harper smiled, waited a moment, and then lightly prodded him further about dessert.

"You know," Harper said, putting her hands to her full hips, "the pie is on the house, this being a holiday and all."

Smiling all the while, he deliberately squeezed shut both his eyes as if to say 'How nice of you.'

"What kinds do you have?"

Harper rattled off the diner's fresh made, homestyle pie menu.

"Hmm," he replied, once more rubbing his fingers on his newly shorn chin. "How about a nice slice of blueberry?"

"My favorite," she honestly said. "Whipping cream?"

"Oh, please," he heartily replied as if Harper suggested something or another tremendously grand.

"Just like I like it," she added, leaving his table to fill his request.

She realized, on walking back to the kitchen, that the entire time she visited with the old man, she totally tuned out the noise rumbling from the three top table. She thought that she just might take a break and have a slice of blueberry pie herself; with the visitor if he did not mind the company of a waitress.

She found the diner's owner idling away in the kitchen and asked him if he objected to her taking a short break to have some dessert with one of her customers.

"It's a holiday after all," she remarked.

The owner agreed, noting: "Yeah, it's slow, too."

Harper put two slices of blueberry pie, warmed, with whipping cream on the side onto a serving tray. She filled up a couple of glasses of egg nog and then made her way back out to the dining room.

As expected, the drunken trio was well into "Auld Lang Syne," although Harper thought the song sounded more and more like "Camptown Races" as the night wore on and the men's singing ability degenerated further.

She walked up to the old visitor's table, placing one of the pie slices in front of him before she asked if he minded some company over dessert.

"That would be grand," he said, starting to stand in order to more gallantly extend Harper a seat.

"Sit, sit," she said, smiling at the comely gent.

Both the old man and Harper took pleasing first bites of the berry pie and whipping cream.

"Very good," he complimented.

"The pie here, it's always good," replied Harper.

"Very tasty," he reaffirmed.

"So," Harper continued. "You mentioned that you are from pretty far off ..." She allowed her voice to trail off, hoping to elicit some more information from him in order to move into smooth conversation.

"Yes, I am."

"I'm from here," Harper said with a shrug. "My whole life."

"Seems to be a nice town."

"I suppose." Harper spoke in the manner of all people who resided in the smaller towns of their birth into adulthood, a tone rife with resignation.

"Did you have a nice Christmas?" inquired the old visitor.

With another slump of her shoulders, Harper again said: "I suppose."

"You had to work," he stated the obvious.

Harper echoed: "I had to work." She added: "We drew straws to see who'd work."

He smiled and nodded as if he truly understood how Harper felt at that moment.

"I worked today myself," he remarked. Hearing that, Harper almost responded that he looked to be beyond his working years, but she caught herself.

"You and me," she ended up saying, identifying their commonality.

"You and me," he repeated, cutting off another bite of pie with his fork.

"Do you have children?' he asked. Something in his inflection, the rise and fall of his voice, made Harper

110

wonder for a moment if he knew the answer to his question.

"No." Her face looked downcast when she spoke about not having a child.

"You're young," the old man said, desiring to buck up his suddenly sagging table partner.

Harper nodded. She knew she was young, but she also understood the pratfalls and limitations of living in a small town. She also knew that she had not had a date with a fellow in a few years.

"You never know what the new year will bring."

The old visitor's tone was so encouraging she believed him, almost.

"So, will you be heading back home?" Harper asked, not having paid attention to the fact that Nicholas did not tell her where his home even was located.

"Oh, yes. Once I finish up here, I head back home."

"That'll be nice for you."

Harper looked more directly into the gentleman's eyes. She realized that old man's eyes were a color that she could only describe as being Christmas green.

"You have such pretty eyes," she remarked, speaking before she considered her words.

He flushed, his cheeks turning a bit rosy.

"Thank you, Miss Harper," he replied.

Fully engrossed in visiting with the old visitor, Harper did not at first hear the copper-haired, inebriated man at the three top table clamoring for another pitcher of beer. When she did finally catch the boisterous call for service, she politely and reluctantly excused herself from Nicholas.

The Shadow Cast

Harper hurried and tapped a fresh pitcher, dropping it off with the loud threesome without even directly acknowledging them.

In barely a few minutes, she was reseated with the old man.

"Do you like the pie?"

"It's delicious," he replied.

"We have the best."

"You seem to," he agreed.

They did not speak for a couple of minutes while they each finished the pie slices.

"I end up traveling a good deal around Christmastime," the old man volunteered between sips of egg nog.

"Really?" asked Harper. "Why's that?"

He patted his lips with his napkin, then smiled. "My work," he softly explained.

"So, you're away from your family a lot at Christmas?" Harper asked.

"From my wife, I am."

"No children?"

"No children. Just my wife and me."

"What do you do?' Harper asked him.

"Shipping, I guess you'd say."

"I see," Harper said although she really did not.

He nodded, taking another swallow of egg nog. He eased back in his chair.

"You know, even though I find myself traveling at Christmastime, I always meet good people along the way, folks I never forget." "That would be nice."

He nodded in agreement.

The Shadow Cast

"I remember a poor, young lad in Iowa, many years back. Back during the Depression ..." His voice trailed off, a smile still on his face.

Harper thought to herself: 'Boy, you are old if you were working way back in the 30s.'

"Uh – huh," she said, waiting to hear more of the old man's tale.

"Well, Miss Harper, I came to know this young fellow, probably about twelve or thirteen, 1 suppose." Harper nodded, taking some egg nog.

"He lived at his grandparents' house in a little Iowa town. He lived there with his father, who had been a farmer. But, because of the Depression, because of financial troubles, the farm was lost. They had to move into town to live with the grandparents."

"Oh, how sad," Harper remarked.

"Yes, of course, losing the farm was rough. You see, Miss Harper, life was even tougher for those folks. The boy's mother had died not all that long before they lost the farm. Consumption is what they called it at the time, I think. Tuberculosis."

"Oh, dear," Harper sadly responded.

He carried on with his tale of the boy in Iowa.

"You see, Miss Harper, I would see this boy quite often sitting on a fence watching some ponies that were kept in a pasture not far from where he lived."

The old man took a generous slug of egg nog to refresh his throat. The break in his story, though minimal, was enough to allow for the sound of the raucous men at the other table to pierce Harper's concentration. They wanted another round.

Harper apologized to him, told him she would return "in a jiffy," and excused herself.

Snaring another fresh pitcher of brew, Harper reluctantly returned to the trio's table. Right after she set the new pitcher in front of the group, but before she could escape the table side, the man with the coppercolored hair reached out and wrapped his own arm around Harper's midsection.

"Hey babe," he blathered, "when 'ya gonna' sit with us, babe?"

Saying nothing, she yanked herself free of the groper and returned to the safety and comfort of the old man's table.

"I'm sorry," the old man said when she retook a seat at his table.

"For what?"

"For them," he explained.

"Oh, please," she chided. "They're not your fault." Pausing, she added: "Or my concern, for that matter."

Harper encouraged him to finish his story of the teenage boy in Iowa.

"Like I said," he went forth, "I saw this young lad regularly, watching these ponies in a pasture. Shetland ponies, as I recall. When I saw the boy, each time I saw the boy, he looked to be carrying the weight of the world on his shoulders."

Hearing that, Harper sighed.

"Turns out," he said, after acknowledging Harper's sympathetic sigh with a nod of his head and a blink of his Christmas green eyes, "turns out the sad looking lad had a younger brother and a younger sister. Twins." Harper's eyes echoed the sentiment of her sigh.

114

The Shadow Cast

"The boy finally confided in me," the old man stated to Harper. "He finally told me there was no money to buy his little brother and sister Christmas gifts. Not a spare penny, Miss Harper."

Feeling for the boy, as the old man obviously still did as well, Harper shook her head.

"Miss Harper, you see I just could not let that be."

He went on to explain that he himself arranged for a pony to be delivered to the boy's home on that Christmas Day so long ago.

"And the best part, Miss Harper," he added with a brilliant twinkle in his eyes, "the very best part was that the pony was pregnant and had twin colts that very spring."

"A pony for each of them," Harper said.

"A pony for the boy and for his brother and sister."

Placing both of her hands on the tabletop palms down, Harper declared: "What a nice man you are."

The old man flushed red, as he had earlier, his cheeks each casting off a soft rosy glow.

"You would have done the very same," he told Harper.

They chatted on a while longer when he turned the discussion tables around to Harper's life.

"So, Miss Harper, tell me more about your life," he suggested. She realized she sounded trite, but nonetheless asked: "What's there to tell?"

Nonplussed, the old man said he imagined she could tell a good deal. "Well ... like I said ... I'm from here ... originally."

"Yes."

The Shadow Cast

"And I work here," she said, gesturing around the dining room with her right hand.

"Do you want some coffee?" she asked, intentionally trying to divert the conversation away from her and her life.

"No, thank you," he graciously declined. "But if you do ..."

She shook her head. "Keeps me awake."

"Me, too." He chuckled. "You know, I have a long trip home to make yet tonight. So, on second thought, maybe I should have some."

"You do want some?" she asked.

"Let me wait and see. Tell me more about yourself, your life here."

"Well, let's see." Harper paused, trying to decide what to tell the man next. "I'm an only child. Both my folks have passed, going on four years for Ma, five for Pa."

She stopped speaking, in a manner that led the old man to conclude that the woman at his table finished with what she was willing to share.

Assuming she was single, Nicholas asked if she ever married.

Her expression slipped and he immediately regretted the question and wished he could stuff the words back into his mouth. Nevertheless, Harper answered after a moment and explained she had once, some twenty years back when she was just over eighteen.

"He left, for good, when I was pregnant ..."

Her voice trailed off.

The Shadow Cast

"And the baby?" the old man asked with transparent hesitation.

"Adopted. I put him up. Thought it was best."

He wasted not a beat telling Harper that he was sure the child, her child, thought about her and wished her the best.

"Maybe so," she said, in an obviously doubtful tone.

"I'm certain," he said with a firmness that startled Harper.

Before she could say anything further, the restaurant's door opened and a young man walked in, wearing a stocking cap, hunter's plaid coat and carrying a knapsack on his back.

"A customer," she muttered, sounding disappointed because the arrival of the new patron would take her away from the old visitor.

"Will you be here for a bit longer?" she asked him.

He smiled and said: "A bit longer, yes."

Harper stood, went over to the young fellow and asked if he wanted to be seated in the smoking or nonsmoking section of the diner.

"Nonsmoking, please," he replied and looked as if he wanted to say something else. Harper waited for him to speak further and when he did not say anything more, she led him off to a table between the three top and Nicholas. She noticed that the threesome had stopped singing, for which she was relieved, grateful. But the men showed no sign of getting ready to depart, which made Harper moan, softly so as not to be overheard by her new customer.

Harper spent about ten minutes getting the young man settled in and his order taken and turned in to the solitary cook behind the grill. She also dropped a new,

117

full pitcher off at the table of three men, wanting to get back to the old man and avoid having to deal with the dreaded copper-haired man for at least a while longer.

When she returned to the old man's table, he was finishing off the last of his egg nog.

"Would you like more?" she asked before retaking a chair.

"Oh, no, Miss Harper. But, you know, I will take that cup of coffee."

"Surely."

She retrieved fairly fresh cups of coffee for the both of them.

When she returned to the table, the old man mentioned to her that he frequently told the young lad in Iowa something that always seemed to cheer the boy up.

"What's that?"

"I used to tell the boy: 'Think the best thoughts and the best will come to you.'"

Harper smiled and told him that he spoke a nice sentiment and she would do her best to keep it in mind. Nicholas, saying nothing, nodded deeply while keeping his eyes closed. For a moment, Harper wondered if the old chap was checking into her own mind to see if she was thinking the best of thoughts.

Before either of them could speak any further, the man with the copper-colored hair called out for Harper, hollering for his group's tab. She felt relieved that they appeared to be ready to depart. Even if she had to endure another smack to her behind, which she surely hoped to avoid, she knew that they would be out the door in due course.

The Shadow Cast

She wasted not a moment in getting the three top's bill settled. And she managed to dodge an incoming palm swipe aimed towards her rear end.

Right as she dispatched the obnoxious trio out the door and into the night, the solitary young man's order was up. Retrieving the meal, she went directly to his table.

"Here you go," she said, sounding more genuinely happy than she had all night. The conversation with the old visitor had brightened her spirits and lightened her mind. The three men departing helped even more.

"Can I ask you something?" the young man asked Harper. She assumed he wanted ketchup or some other condiment.

"Sure."

"Is your name Harper Faith?"

She thought nothing unusual about the query. Being in a small community, such a question was common. Harper thought she probably knew the young fellow's mother.

"Yes," she said, with a smile.

"My name's Mitch," he quickly responded. "Mitch Conley."

Harper engaged her memory, trying to place the Conley surname. She drew a blank. Before she asked if she was a friend of his folks, the young man said:
"This is hard."

Pausing, he inhaled deeply and continued.

"About nineteen years back, you had a baby. You had a baby boy."

The young man, Mitch, took in a second generous breath of air.

The Shadow Cast

"Well, ma'am, that's me. I'm that baby, I'm that boy."

Neither Harper nor Mitch said another word for over a full minute. Indeed, Harper held her breath. Eventually, Harper turned around to see if Nicholas heard the conversation.

Much to her surprise, the old man was no longer seated at the table. Instead, she saw some cash piled next to his empty pie plate. Somehow the old visitor managed to depart the diner without her seeing him leave.

Not knowing what to say in response to Mitch, Harper nervously dashed over to the old man's table and fumbled around with the money he'd left behind. On top of the cash for payment, he left a note that said: *"Harper,*

Think the very best thoughts and the very best will come to you.

Merry Christmas,

Nicholas."

Harper picked up the note, tears welling up in her eyes. She returned to Mitch's table, sitting down across from the young man. She spent the remainder of Christmas with Mitch, her child. She listened to his stories, tales of his life so far. When it came her turn to share with Mitch her own life's tale, she spoke first of an old man named Nicholas.

The Bouillon Cube

"It's what?" Hester DeWayne asked of her gentleman caller, Richard Therese.

Richard, who fancied himself an inventor, regularly paid a call upon Hester DeWayne and had done so for over a year, since the springtime of 1924. On most occasions of his visits, Richard carried along his latest invention, the fruit of his heartfelt tinkerings.

In April of '24, on his first trip to Hester's parlor, Richard Therese brought a Victrola he had somehow rigged up to a gasoline powered engine.

"Just think," he explained after presenting his creation with a flutter of hands and an enthusiastic "tada." "Just think, Miss Hester. With a bucket of gasoline, a Victrola can play on and on without winding once."

"Oh, my," Hester said at the time, clutching a lace hanky to her ample bosom. Hester, then twenty-six, was a full-figured woman with raven hair and chocolate brown eyes. Her father, Clyde, was the local physician in the tiny hamlet of Rossville, Kansas, just ten miles from the state capital city of Topeka.

Unlike Hester DeWayne at barely five feet in height, Richard Therese was tall, lanky, and almost spindly. He was thirty when he presented Hester with the petroldriven Victrola.

"Should I crank it up, Miss Hester?"

"I thought that with gasoline you didn't need to turn the crank," she rejoined, puzzled.

"Ha, ha," he guffawed. "Figure of speech, really. I mean, shall I turn on the Victrola?"

Hester hesitated for a moment, trying to imagine how the contraption might work.

"Come on," he prodded. "It wasn't easy getting it here in the first place."

"Well, all right then," Hester relented.

Within a minute, Richard fired up the engine and had the record-playing machine twirling at top speed, too fast in fact. For a couple of seconds, the tune emitted from the Victrola appropriately, but as the machine picked up speed, the sound pouring out from the solitary scope was akin to that of furious felines of alley cat stock.

In little time, the parlor filled with foul smelling ash gray smoke fuming from the pumping engine.

"Good heavens," Hester yelped, unsure whether she should use her hands to fend off smoke reaching her nose or to cover her ears to block the racket from the music player.

Despite his best efforts, Richard could not shut down the Victrola. Dense smoke ended up billowing from the DeWayne residence on Spruce Park Avenue, bringing round a wagon and crew from the volunteer fire department.

Surprisingly, three weeks later, Hester agreed to another visit from Richard Therese. She cautiously opened the door to her family home, making certain that Richard had no machine, motor or engine in tow.

The Shadow Cast

The family's maid had not yet succeeded in cleaning the smoke stains from the parlor walls.

"Come in," she cautiously invited.

In the parlor, they stiffly chatted for half an hour.

"How are you?" Richard asked.

"Fine."

"Good."

"Yes," she concurred.

"I'm well," he remarked.

"Good."

"Yes," agreed Richard. "Your father?"

"Fine."

"Good. And your mother?"

Hester advised: "Well."

"Good."

"Yes." Hester asked about Richard's parents.

"Good."

"Both?"

"Yes."

"Good."

"Yes," he nodded.

After more than thirty minutes of stilted conversation, Richard reached into his suit coat pocket after telling Hester he wanted to "show her something." She thought, on the spot, of dashing off to the kitchen to fetch a pitcher of water. She felt certain Richard was poised to fetch something from his clothing that most likely would spark, smoke or catch fire.

She furrowed her brow, confused, when she caught sight of the two-inch long stick that appeared to be covered with gaily colored paper. He held up the stick, fiddled around with it for a moment. In an instant, the stick transformed into a tiny umbrella, purple, pink and pale blue.

"What's that?" she blurted.

Proudly, Richard explained: "An umbrella."

"Umbrella?"

"Yes, an umbrella."

Hester touched the tiny device.

"Paper," she muttered

"What?" asked Richard.

"Paper," she replied. "It's made of paper."

He nodded, beaming brightly. "And colorful."

"But, it's paper," she protested. "And too small."

"Too small?" he asked.

"Too small. And paper."

"Why … yes," he finally agreed.

"What good, Richard, is a tiny umbrella made of paper?"

Glum all of a sudden, Richard shrugged and muttered something Hester did not understand.

Despite being flattened by Hester's critique of his diminutive paper and stick umbrella, the visit ended quite well. In Hester's mind, any time with Richard Therese that concluded without the need for fire fighters was well spent.

Richard continued to call on and visit Hester with regularity. By the springtime of 1925, he saw Hester weekly. Hester eventually became used to, or at least not surprised by, the queer and unusual items Richard created. As a result, when he came bearing a half-inch wide flaky, brown cube, Hester was puzzled but nonplussed.

The Shadow Cast

When Hester asked: "It's what?" Richard promptly piped back: "Bouillon." "Bouillon?" she asked.

"Bouillon," he confirmed.

Slowly Hester reached across the coffee table in the parlor where Richard placed the little cube. She lightly touched it with her right forefinger.

"It's what?" she questioned Richard again.

"It's bouillon."

"Like … the soup?" she asked.

He nodded.

"But …" she said, hesitating.

"Yes?" Richard replied, sounding encouraging.

"Well, Richard, it's just a square."

He nodded.

"A square, Richard."

"Of bouillon," he remarked.

"A square of bouillon?" she squinted her eyes as she spoke and looked again at the solitary cube on the table.

"Yes, Hester. A bouillon square."

Hester sucked in her upper lip, sitting still and quiet for a couple of minutes.

"What do you do with it?" she asked.

"The bouillon square," Richard replied.

She nodded.

Previously, the maid had brought in a tray loaded with hot water in a pot, tea, cups, saucers and wafer thin cookies.

"Let me show you," Richard replied.

He picked up the cube and dropped it into an empty teacup. He handed the china piece to Hester.

"What do I do with this?" she asked.

The Shadow Cast

Richard gestured towards the teapot. "Pour water on it," he advised.

"Do what?" she asked.

"Pour water on it," repeated Richard.

"In the cup?"

"Right, Hester. In the cup."

Hesitating a bit, Hester picked up the teapot and poured the hot water into the cup and over the bouillon cube.

Instantly, the square dissolved and the hot water turned an opaque brown.

Hester gazed into the cup and then looked up at Richard smiling.

"Soup?" she asked.

He said: "Yes." He then asked Hester if she noticed anything else in the cup. Hester took a second glance into the teacup and did see something lying at the bottom.

"What's this?" she asked Richard, keeping her eyes in the cup, trying to better make out what rested at the bottom.

"It was hidden in the square," he explained.

"Hidden?"

"Yes … I made the square of bouillon with … that … inside."

"But what is it?" Hester pressed.

Richard picked up the teacup and drank the bouillon. When he finished, he set the cup back down on the coffee table. He motioned for Hester to look again.

Seeing clearly for the first time what lay at the teacup's bottom, Hester let out a surprised gasp.

"For me?" she cried.

126

The Shadow Cast

"For you," Richard tenderly replied. He picked up the teacup again and tipped it sideways. An engagement ring slipped from the china cup into his hand.

Quickly he wiped the ring dry with a neat linen napkin from the serving tray. Speaking no further, Richard slipped the ring onto Hester's finger.

Vardaman Said: My Mother is a Fish

"I'*fe* torn it up twi*the*," Hank White, a sixteen-year old sophomore with mangled speech explained as he sat across the desk in my snug, smoldering office that May afternoon. Spring came early that year (1963) to the Shenandoah Valley, eventually dragging summertime weather in its wake even into May. Looking back on that spring, I can't recall if April came in or out like a lion or a lamb. I do recall that May flamed forth like dragon's breath.

I knew Hank White from his position in the front row of my American Literature class that school term. Every term during the ten years I taught English courses at the Massanutten Military Academy in Woodstock, Virginia, I seemed to have a student like Hank White of 1963. (I came to the Academy fresh from my graduation from the University of Virginia in Charlottesville.)

Hank White (like the other similar boys in years past) stood out from his peers precisely because he was so plain. Hank was just enough overweight to be soft looking without appearing fat. His color was pale but not paper white enough to look sickly. He rarely spoke out in class, a fact which I attributed to some sort of speech problem he carried.

Hank White's course work was capably undertaken (competent to be sure). He never came with anything outstanding (brilliant), but he most certainly never turned over lacking (poor) work.

The Shadow Cast

In short, I'm certain Hank White never (ever) crossed my mind outside of class until that afternoon in the spring when he presented himself at my office.

Even though I engaged a rickety steel fan to try and circulate air in my cramped quarters, the office was so hot as to be barely tolerable at all. The tight compartment was essentially windowless save for a small two-paned portal I managed to prop open a bit (exactly one inch, I measured). Because of the heat, my eye glasses slid to the end of my nose, leaving me to look across my desk at Hank White over the tops of the frames. Clearly, I saw, the boy was frustrated.

"You've what?" I asked in response to his initial proclamation.

"I'*fe* torn it up twi*the* … my paper."

I assumed (rightly so) that Hank White spoke of shredding his assigned term paper for my class. The project was due two days hence and was worth fifty percent of his grade. His selected topic was a critical review of William Faulkner's novel "As I Lay Dying." He was the only one of my students to select a true Southern writer for his American Literature opus (and I was pleased).

Why the boy was tearing up his paper (twice, indeed) I could not fathom – so I inquired.

"I keep getting *th*tuck."

"What?" I did not understand (literally).

"*Th*tuck. You know. *Th*tuck!"

I did not know (at least immediately). I thought: "*Th*tuck? What in God's pastures is 'thtuck?'" Fortunately, before I sought a definition from the boy, something clicked in my heat-sizzled head.

The Shadow Cast

"Stuck?" I asked.

Hank White nodded.

At the moment I began to try to divine the heart of my student's troubles, I caught a glimpse of (zeroed in on, really) an especially ugly pimple just above Hank White's lip and directly under the tip of his nose.

Hank started talking about his term paper plight using words I could (for the most part) understand. I, on the other hand, took up staring at the red (really rosy) pimple, not especially hearing what Hank said except for an occasional "thtuck" which registered (somehow).

I finally caught focus when Hank, in a pleading (almost frantic, really) tone implored: "What am I going to do?"

My instant response was (almost): 'Good Lord, man, pop the blister!'

Catching myself (barely, really), I pushed my glasses up my nose and muttered something about "Faulkner not being easy."

"*Th*ath why I picked him. *Th*ath why I picked the story anyhow," Hank rejoined.

Not knowing quite what to say, but recognizing Hank said "stuck" ("thtuck" really) a number of times, I finally inquired;

"So why are you … where are you … how are you … stuck, then?"

Hank wasted no time opening up Faulkner's book to a chapter commencing with the line: "Vardaman said my mother is a fish."

I gulped (twice, in fact).

Hank pointed (jabbed at, really) the offending sentence.

"See that?" he demanded. "Do you see thi*th*?"

I did. I nodded.

"Thi*th* i*th* why I'm *th*tuck," he explained.

I nodded (again). But (alas) my attention somehow was back on Hank White's pimple. My focus was on the cruel blemish a second time when Hank (still pleading, almost frantic) asked me: "What do*th* thi*th* even mean, 'my mother i*th* a fi*th*'?"

"Mean?" I asked.

He nodded.

"That?" I pointed at the sentence in the Faulkner book.

Hank nodded (again), asking (a second time): "What do*th* that mean, 'My mother i*th* a fi*th*?'"

I picked up the book. I poked my specs back up on my nose again. The sentence seemed to float off the page right before my eyes (probably the heat, I imagined). But, there it was, that sentence:

"Vardaman said my mother is a fish."

Faulkner's "As I Lay Dying" was not on the general reading list in my American Literature class. Hank White selected the piece himself. At that moment, I wished the boy would have picked Fitzgerald's "Gatsby," Steinbeck's "Pearl," or Hemingway's bit about tolling bells.

I read "As I Lay Dying" ten (twelve, perhaps) years earlier when I was a collegian. The book itself (Faulkner's, that is) was broken up into numerous short chapters telling of and recounting the death of a family's matriarch. One chapter presented the tale from the vantage point of one character, the next chapter featuring another character, and so on (and back around again).

The Shadow Cast

The sentence in question ("Vardaman said my mother is a fish") was in a chapter written from the point of view of the deceased woman's youngest son (a child). Vardaman was another character, a brother to the boy, I thought.

"I mean," Hank carried on, "I thought, at fir*th*t, that thi*th* wa*th* the crazy *th*on imagining hi*th* dead mother wa*th* a fi*th*."

I nodded, vaguely recollecting one of the characters being off the center.

"Well, then ..." I began to respond (before my eyes went back to the pimple). Suddenly, I found myself wanting to ask: 'Good Lord, man, doesn't that hurt (like hell)?'

Instead, as if out of nowhere, I suggested we take a walk.

"What?" he asked, shifting (nervously, perhaps) in his seat.

"A walk, then. Let's do that. Go for a walk."

"Walk?"

"Indeed, yes. A walk. Out of this office. It's so stuffy and all. Take some fresh air. Think this through, then." He hesitated, but agreed.

Side by side, we walked out of the Humanities and Arts building, into the midafternoon sun. Although it was very hot outdoors as well, the breeze and the open space combined to make for a more pleasant state.

We walked for some distance across the Academy campus grounds to a neat stand of maple trees (speaking little, really). Coming to rest in the shade of an old, expansive tree, we sat on a bench placed near the stout trunk.

The Shadow Cast

Sitting next to the grand maple, I realized (for the first time, unbelievably) that Hank White's garbled speech was not only different in technique but in tone from my other students. Hank White did not have a local southern flavor like my other charges (or old Mr Faulkner, for that matter).

"Say, Hank, I don't rightly know where you're from …"

"Otterville," he shrugged.

"Otterville," I repeated, imagining a tiny, tiny hamlet somewhere in Old Dixie (but where and why no drawl in boy's speech).

"Virginia, then?" I asked.

He shook his head and said, "Iowa."

Startled, I repeated "Iowa" (twice).

Hank nodded.

"How did you get here?" I asked, mildly gesturing towards the Old Main building.

"A conte*th*t," he flatly stated.

"A what?" I asked, not getting what he intended to say.

"A conte*th*t. I won a conte*th*t. Fir*th*t Pri*th*e."

"Oh, I see then. A contest." He

nodded (most matter of factly).

"What sort of contest?" I asked.

"E*th*ay," he replied, smiling for the first time (shyly yet with pride).

I sat still (for a moment or so), trying to figure out "e*th*ay."

"Essay contest!" I shot out, more in a triumph at my deciphering ability than in furtherance of our conversation. I had the sensation we were playing a party game, almost like charades.

"Ye*th*. Fir*th*t Pri*the*."

I must have looked puzzled because Hank quickly explained first prize was a scholarship to the Academy. There was a girl prize winner, too, but Hank could not recollect where she got to go to school.

"The paper had the conte*th*t," he added. "*The Des Moin*the Th*unday Regi*th*ter*."

Hank volunteered that he was raised on a farm, dairy cattle and corn as a crop.

"Otterville i*th* very th*mall," he remarked.

"Well, so is Woodstock," I noted, the locale of the Academy.

With my remark, Hank White laughed (a truly hearty chuckle, in fact). Otterville, he explained, was much, much smaller.

"A general *th*tore, a *th*ervi*th* th*tath*ion and the Ruby Ro*the* Dining Café," he remarked, leaving me with no idea what a "*th*ervi*th* thathion" or a "Ro*the*" was at the time. (I later figured he'd said "service station" and "rose" as in the "Ruby Rose Dining Café.")

"Do you know why I picked Mr Faulkner'*th* book?" he eventually asked me while we sat on the bench under the maple tree. (I, of course did not.)

"I don't."

"The title, it caught my eye," he said.

"Really?" I asked, believing it all suddenly and somehow rather maudlin.

"Becau*th* of th*omething that happened when I wa*th* a kid," Hank said, all the while he looked across the campus, which sat on top of a gentle slope, the highest

134

point in Woodstock. I followed his line of sight; he was looking off into the distance, off to the Massanutten Range of the Blue Ridge Mountains. He seemed to train his scope on the Medieval looking structure, nestled between two rises of the Massanutten, which was the Wayclocks Institute (some sort of asylum).

Sitting together, I realized the boy's mother (maybe his father) must have died.

"Oh, I'm sorry," I replied (instinctively, really).

He shrugged.

"Your mother? Or your father? Or one of them passed, then?" I asked.

Instantly he stiffened (rigid as if made of concrete like our bench).

"Oh, no," he replied, wide-eyed. "My folk*th*, they're fine. It'*th* not becau*the* of *th*omeone I knew," he continued. I did not yet understand what he meant and asked him to explain.

"We were gleaning," he said.

"Cleaning?" I asked, believing he garbled his speech again, but in a new way.

"No … *gleaning*."

"Gleaning?" He

nodded.

"What's that? Gleaning?"

"My*th*elf and two buddie*th* … every fall, we'd go out to the corn field*th* after the combine*th* and what not…"

"After the what?"

"The combine*th*."

"What?"

"The combine." By making the word singular he helped me understand. "The ma*th*ine that pic*th* the

135

corn. We'd go to the corn field*th* and pick up ear*th* of corn that the combine didn't get."

"You'd pick up ears of corn … that the combine did not get?" I asked.

"Right."

"And that's gleaning?" I surmised.

"You got it," he replied (happily).

"Okay," I said to encourage Hank along. He went forward to explain how one fall, at harvest when he was about twelve, he and his buddies came across a body, the body of a boy hidden in a pile of brush in a wooded area at the edge of the cornfield at his own family's farm. He told me no one ever discovered who the boy was or where he was from. Hank said the sheriff confirmed the boy had been shot (and killed) and that his body was dumped (and hidden) in the woods.

"Then I *th*ee thi*th* book by Mr Faulkner and I think I'd read it, that it'd make *th*ome *th*en*th*," Hank summed up this thoughts. He concluded, on his own, that the book, "As I Lay Dying," would help him make some sense about the boy he'd found dead in the woods. But Hank said (sadly) now the book he picked made no sense to him.

I looked at Hank (differently than I had before). I recognized that this was no plain boy, not a nondescript youngster at the front edge of my classroom. I no longer noticed the pimple.

"You know, Hank," I said, "I think you've got something here. Maybe something you don't see just yet. And, perhaps just something Mr Faulkner did not exactly intend himself."

As I expected, Hank looked baffled.

136

The Shadow Cast

"What do you mean?" he shyly inquired.

"I think this sentence, that doesn't make any sense …" I replied. "I think it does have something to do with the boy … with the boy whose body you found. A dead child, Hank, that really makes no sense … not at all. Never has, never will."

He agreed, looking relieved to appreciate that some things in life really never will make a lick of good sense. He seemed relieved to know he wasn't the only one who felt that way and it wasn't childish to feel that way.

"Maybe Vardaman, too, sees that some deaths, maybe all deaths, make no sense and is trying to express that absurdity."

With my student under the old maple tree that May day, we discussed the mysteries of life and those of death the rest of the afternoon. We worked on various theories.

We considered the possibility that Vardaman believed in reincarnation and thought his mother had come back as a fish.

We even considered that perhaps in death we are all like a fish: unbridled, carefree, at peace. Or, perhaps, in life we need to endeavor to be more like a simple fish, enjoying the brook, tackling the currents as they come, 'going with the flow.'

Down at Sunset

Two hours past midnight and traffic thinned on Sunset Boulevard running through the heart of West Hollywood. Sunset Boulevard connected Beverly Hills to Hollywood to Santa Monica Beach and the brisk waters of the Pacific Ocean. Sunset Boulevard – the Street of Dreams.

Besides headlights from passing motorcars, the Boulevard was kept illuminated at the odd hour by the glow from red, blue and yellow neon lighting along the strip of street making its way through West Hollywood. Most of the curled and boxed letters and shapes of twisted glass filled with neon gas promoted tawdry joints – peep show cinemas, adults-only book stores and narrow, dank gin holes.

The autos stripping up and down the Boulevard in the dark time past midnight either were driven well above the posted speed limit or well below the course allowed. Drivers behind the wheels either were both eager and anxious to make haste out of West Hollywood or were intentionally trolling at low speed like fishermen casting and reeling slowly, purposefully.

Ram Payton, clad in a tight pair of fading blue jeans and a sleeveless muscle shirt, covered by a black leather jacket, slowly paced west on the sidewalk on the south side of the street, his cowboy boots making a clacking sound on the concrete which echoed in the night. A smoke, Marlboro Red, dangled from his lips.

The Shadow Cast

Ram arrived in Los Angeles almost twelve months earlier, leaving Denver, Colorado, and a pleasing job as a bartender at the Longhorn Saloon. He headed west, after several years of scraping together cash and countless hours plotting and planning. Ram came to California, in cliché fashion, to act.

In January, in the late 1960s, Ram arrived by Greyhound bus in Los Angeles. With a worn suitcase in hand, one latch completely sprung, Ram departed the bus station and spent a couple hours wandering the streets of LA. Eventually, he alighted in a custard shop in a ratty neighborhood. Outside the tiny establishment, a nearly empty Los Angeles Times stand stood bearing a couple of that day's edition. Ram bought one before entering the shop and ordering a vanilla custard and cherry cola with a maraschino floating on top.

Occasionally taking a spoonful of custard and sips of cola, Ram perused the classified advertisements looking for a furnished apartment. With the money Ram squirreled away from his days tending bar in Denver, he believed he could find suitable digs in the City of Angels.

Paying little attention to the other goings on in the custard shop, Ram did not see the bald, fortysomething year old man sitting a couple tiny tables away staring at him. After Ram studied the newspaper for a full quarter hour, the man across the way from Ram cleared his throat, twice, to garner Ram's attention. Failing, the man spoke out. "You there ... Excuse me ... You there, with the paper."

Ram, paying only half attention, looked up and over,

139

not particularly thinking the speaking voice beckoned for him. Glancing in the direction of the speaking fellow, Ram realized the man was staring directly at him with a sly smile. "Me?" Ram said, his voice sounding craggy from lack of real use since leaving Denver.

The middle-aged man nodded and asked Ram if he were new in town. "I've never seen you around," he said, keeping the thin smile in place.

"Uh-huh," Ram acknowledged, cautiously.

"I can always tell a newbie," the stranger stated, promptly.

"A what?" asked Ram, uncertainly.

"A newbie," the man repeated, speaking a bit louder.

"A newbie?"

The man nodded.

"What's that?"

The stranger chuckled. "A newbie?"

Ram bobbed his head.

"Well, my friend," the man replied, "a newbie is someone who is new to our fair city." The stranger gestured expansively as if presenting Los Angeles at the tips of his fingers, his smile remaining.

"Ahh," understanding, Ram replied.

"You must have come to our fair city for Hollywood," the stranger stated, a firmer and more definite expression crossing his face. "You've come to be in pictures."

"Pictures?" Ram asked, momentarily thinking of drawings.

"Motion pictures," the stranger replied with strong emphasis on the word 'motion.' "You're here to make movies, no?"

"Yes," Ram quickly shot back.

"Then, my friend," the man rejoined, "I'm glad to meet'cha."

Ram soon found an apartment and a job, a flat off Santa Monica Boulevard and a bartending position three nights a week at a tavern in West Hollywood called 'The Happy.'

Ram's apartment was more of a room and a small one at that. The place lacked a proper kitchen leaving Ram to rely on take away food orders and soup he could warm on a hot plate with loose wiring. Two intersecting drapes cut off a corner of the room where a toilet and claw leg bath tub were plumbed.

Not letting even a week pass following his arrival, Ram began trooping to cattle calls, casting sessions for movies and television at which scores, even hundreds of eager, anxious men and women hoped for a break and a part in a film or in a program. After two months, Ram put in at least twenty cattle calls, no parts offered.

Ram's only respite from the frustration of mounting an acting career was found in the few hours a night a few nights each week he worked at The Happy. Quite like his tenure at The Longhorn in Denver, Ram developed a close rapport with a troupe of regular patrons: LaVerna, a whiskey voiced and retired makeup artist from Calamouth Studios; Stephen, a struggling screenwriter slightly older than he; and Calvin, an elderly gent who alternately billed himself as a cattle baron from North California, a Bourbon count or a compadre of Oppenheimer who he assisted in creating "The Bomb." Many a shift, all three patrons were bar-side during Ram's time on the clock.

"Shit, I miss the old days," LaVerna rasped, her yellow hair haphazardly bobby pinned in a lopsided pile on top of her head.

"As do I," Calvin chimed in, with regal airs, an ascot badly knotted about his throat.

"Any luck yet?" Stephen asked Ram, the two men regularly comparing notes on their lack of progress in the business of Hollywood.

"I have an audition tomorrow," Ram replied, speaking as if the next day's cattle call was an event of personal invite.

"Great!" Stephen supportively enthused.

"You should go made up," LaVerna advised. "I can make you up, you know. I did all the greats. Gable, Leigh, even Crawford on two pictures. Two pictures I did Crawford."

"I'd like to meet Joan Crawford," Ram said.

"I courted her once," Calvin interjected, himself even believing to be true his claim of wooing the screen queen. Ram and Stephen knowingly and benignly grinned at each other.

"What a bitch, huh, Calvin?" LaVerna asked, downing the dregs of her glass of rye.

"She was most challenging, indeed," Calvin retorted. "A most challenging woman, indeed."

"A major bitch," LaVerna growled, lighting up a cigarette.

"Indeed, challenging." Calvin repeated himself, intentionally staring off away from the bar as if recalling a misty memory long past.

The Shadow Cast

And so the conversation meandered most nights, the only variance being in how Calvin presented: Cattleman, count or rocket scientist.

Fletcher Hecht, the bald man who snared Ram's attention at the custard shop during his first day in LA, kept tabs on the young want-to-be thespian. In time, Fletcher Hecht joined the regulars at The Happy.

Fletcher made a practice of extolling Ram on his movie star looks. Ram did fit the bill of a stereotypical Hollywood dashing man. He was twenty-three, wellmuscled, blond, well-scrubbed and wholesome looking. One would readily believe he hailed from the small farming town of Burlington in Eastern Colorado as he did.

"Keep your chin up," Fletcher stated at the start of Ram's duty shift at The Happy following a particularly disappointing audition.

"I'm trying," Ram replied, sounding rejected, a despondent chord in the young man's voice.

"Hell," LaVerna cut in, "you'll be big. And when you make it I'll do your face. I did all the greats, including Crawford – the bitch."

Calvin, wearing an ill-fitting Bolo tie, sighed. "Aah, good old Joany. We were to get hitched right up some years back," Calvin as the cattle baron stated.

Not long after Ram arrived in LA, Fletcher Hecht invited him to lunch at a decent though inexpensive Hollywood bistro. Not knowing the difference between an expensive hot spot and otherwise, Ram thought he was dining fine, an illusion Fletcher encouraged. At the lunch, Fletcher explained that he promoted models, male models, from time to time and that he was interested in arranging some gigs for Ram. Initially, Ram declined, not wanting to veer in the slightest from his quest towards film.

Fletcher remained relentless in his pursuit of Ram, however, and by summertime had worn Ram down. Ram's pre-California savings nearly dried up by June and the tips from The Happy, although decent from his regulars, did not provide him enough cash to survive. He continually nipped into his cash reserve.

"I can arrange some private modeling," Fletcher explained to Ram one early evening at The Happy.

"Hell," LaVerna tossed in, interrupting the conversation between Fletcher and Ram, "I'll do your makeup."

Ram smiled politely at LaVerna, thanked her, and went back to his discussion with Fletcher Hecht. For a second time, Fletcher invited Ram to a dinner, at the very same restaurant Ram thought fashionable.

The remainder of Ram's duty shift sailed quickly by the night he agreed to Fletcher's advance and proposal. At The Happy that night Ram believed he was on his way.

Two nights later Ram ate with Fletcher Hecht. Fletcher explained that he had an unusual assignment for the young man hoping for a break, if he desired to take the task on.

"Unusual?" Ram asked, the smile not leaving his face.

"Well, yes, you might say so," Fletcher Hecht replied, lighting up a long, thin cigarette, a kind normally favored by uppity ladies sneaking a smoke. "But, Ram, the ... assignment, you see ... the assignment will bring you into contact with very exciting, very important people ... men in the business, men in film."

"Really?" Ram enthusiastically replied.

"Oh, yes, yes," Fletcher assured.

"So, what do I do ... exactly? Where do I go? When do I go?" Ram rattled off questions at lightning speed with the earnestness of a Boy Scout told of an upcoming jamboree.

Fletcher Hecht explained more of what he had in mind: what in fact he had planned for Ram. Plying the bartender who wanted to morph into a star of film with generous servings of cheap booze, he relaxed Ram well enough to gain his trust fully and his acceptance of the deal.

Ram returned to his apartment, the room, drunk but excited that he broke through, broke in. He felt filled with the confidence that tended his spirit during his days at The Longhorn in Denver, the burst of energy that one day he could – and would – take on Hollywood. Finally, curling up under his sheets, Ram felt certain that triumphant day had arrived.

The next morning, Ram rose early, his head throbbing from the booze. He shivered in his makeshift lavatory and dressed in his best set of clothes. As a treat, he walked to a nearby International House of Pancakes and splurged on breakfast; hot cakes, Ozark sausages, home fries and fresh orange juice.

Following his celebratory meal, Ram took his wellworn car and drove west on Sunset Boulevard to Beverly Hills. He parked on a side street just out of the posh berg's corporate limits and walked the several blocks to Rodeo Drive. In his best clothes, he did not want to be seen presenting himself in the upscale district in a rusting, smoking auto, certainly not in his time of triumph.

He spent the mid-morning hours window shopping, casting content rather than longing glances at the beautiful merchandise perfectly displayed behind immaculately kept glass. Ram, for the first time in his life, felt like he really belonged. On that morning, strolling Rodeo Drive, he felt as good, as deserving – and the same as – the other smartly attired men and women making their ways around and about.

Watching the reflections of passersby in store windows, Ram imagined taking lunch with one, sharing martinis with another, enjoying a swell gala with yet another. On occasion during his morning walk-about, another person on the Drive nodded "hello" or "good day." The sporadic tip of the head left Ram fully convinced that he had arrived on the Street of Dreams.

Night fell over Los Angeles, more like a torn blanket than a whole one providing sure and steady warmth. Night in LA was a festive time, the unpredictable part of the day when an unwary person might just as easily tear loose from the worn linen as stay neatly and safely cocooned until the dawn.

Following the specific directions of Fletcher Hecht, Ram arrived at the appointed hour in the lobby of a smaller hotel in Glendale, far from an exclusive inn although Ram could not discern the difference. Pulling a slip of paper from his pocket, Ram checked and rechecked the room number Fletcher gave him earlier in the day, where Ram was to report for the setup assignment.

The Shadow Cast

In addition to the hotel address and room number, Fletcher Hecht gave Ram a few pills, pink ones, small, that Fletcher encouraged Ram to use before the appointed call.

"They'll relax you, Ram," Fletcher promised. "Make the work a bit ... easier. You'll see."

Before leaving for the hotel, Ram dry swallowed a couple of the tiny pink tablets and did feel lighter, calm, relaxed as Fletcher guaranteed. In fact, Ram felt oddly giddy, despite the task ahead.

Once in the hotel, he wasted little time in taking the elevator to the fourth floor. A young couple took the same lift up with Ram. He avoided eye contact by staring at the dirty, threadbare carpet, which he imagined had been a shade of green, with some sort of pattern that was obscured by ground-in soil. On the ride up, Ram caught himself making a clicking sound with his tongue against his teeth. Had he looked up from the floor, he would have seen the odd glare he received from his two fellow passengers in response to the rapid fire click-click-click emitting from his mouth. He stopped the tongue clacking momentarily, but restarted unconsciously in the swim flowing from the pink tablets.

Once off the lift, Ram walked the dimly lit corridor to the number 416. Running his hands over the front of his shirt, he then rapped on the door. After a few seconds, the door opened, a pale, pudgy man with a wispy comb-over taking the knock. The man standing opposite Ram wore a vibrant blue silk blouse, the top four buttons opened revealing coarse graying chest hairs.

147

The Shadow Cast

In greeting Ram, the man answering the door spoke in so overtly an effeminate manner that Ram broke into a broad smile in spite of himself. Ram felt lucky that his expansive grin was read merely as being an unspoken and jocular "Hello."

"I'm Ram," he said to the portly fellow.

"I bet you are, I bet you are," the holder of the door shot back, rapid fire.

"Fletcher Hecht, he set this up," Ram continued.

"Entrez-vous," the bald one rejoined with his best attempt at a French accent, more Marie Antoinette than Charles DeGaulle.

Hesitating slightly, but mentally awash in a hazy blur as a consequence of the pink tablets, Ram entered.

During the scorching months of summer in Los Angeles, Fletcher Hecht continued to send Ram to snatches of men, mostly gathered in seedier hotels, men who paid money to Fletcher to have the muscled Ram appear, disrobe and, usually, dance around in the cramped quarters. Some nights Ram was spared sweating gropings by the middle- to senior-aged men gathered about. Most times, however, Ram ended up subjected to advances more severe than a brush with sweaty palms.

Through the days of summer, Fletcher paid Ram a fistful of cash following each appearance. Fletcher continued to assure the starry-eyed Ram that important contacts were made with Hollywood honchos each time he stripped.

At the beginning of August, what Ram believed to be a fairly well set boundary tumbled. From his first night on the tawdrier hustlings at the bidding of Fletcher Hecht, Ram was approached by red faced patrons who

148

offered him even more cash than that tendered by Fletcher for a private, personal show. By the late summer, Ram's taste for illicit highs outstripped the pink tablets Fletcher provided freely to him before a call. Consequently, despite the cash he earned from Fletcher, and the tips from The Happy, Ram continually found himself short on green backs.

On a night in early August, Ram agreed to a personal encounter with a paunchy fifty year old man for fifty bucks, a fortune to Ram. As the month wore on, Ram received more regular offers from men in attendance at his hotel performances for quiet, lonely encounters. Enjoying the cash, and not much minding what this or that man did to him behind closed doors, Ram found himself eagerly accepting the bits.

By the fall, Fletcher Hecht learned of Ram's side hustle. Fletcher was not upset with the idea of Ram privately servicing men from the parties. Fletcher Hecht was furious, however, that Ram failed to include him with a cash cut. Like slashing a blade, Fletcher Hecht severed Ram's services.

Into the autumn, Ram continued to stand duty a few nights a week at The Happy and made an occasional cattle call during the day. He immediately felt the impact of the loss of flesh traded for cash, and Fletcher Hecht's little pink tablets. A couple of older men he privately engaged kept paying for quick-spent contact with Ram, but for the most part the cash pipe dribbled dry.

Directly after Thanksgiving, Ram went to his last cattle call. The disappointment, the rejections mounted beyond a point that even pink tablets and other shady remedies could relieve. On the last night in November,

The Shadow Cast

Ram drove east on Sunset Boulevard, thinking of the morning he took the same course, then headed to Rodeo Drive, in the wake of the news that Fletcher Hecht had modeling work for him. The end of November trip ended far short of Rodeo Drive, in West Hollywood, where Ram pulled his aged auto off of a side street and posted himself on a corner of Sunset.

From that point onward, Ram ended up walking Sunset a few nights each week to hustle what money he could in anonymous encounters in the rear seats of automobiles driven by cruising men, mostly older, with loose cash.

In his tight, faded, blue jeans and sleeveless muscle shirt, cigarette burning, dangling from his lips, Ram stood alone, for a moment, on the Street of Dreams.

In a Back Row

Hester Therese topped the scales at three hundred pounds and lumbered with difficulty up the sidewalk to the Jayhawk Theater in downtown Topeka, Kansas. The evening air was heavy, laden with summer thick humidity. Sweat poured down Hester's face and neck, and rolled down her back, staining her simple and cheap, plain and thin pale blue cotton smock.

She wore thick soled black shoes, deeply scuffed from near constant wear. Her nude-colored panty hose, a runner slicing through the right leg, bagged miserably as if sadly melting in the oppressive summer heat.

Hester turned thirty-two a couple of months earlier. By the time she reached her thirtieth year, Hester thought she was a widow and believed her three-yearold daughter had been stolen away, kidnapped most likely by vagabond hobos that regularly traipsed through the railway town of Topeka. In the two years after her third decade of life, Hester's once shiny, raven-colored hair had fastly faded to a flat gray. Her formerly deep chocolate-hued eyes also seemed to dull, their coloration slipping to a cardboard box brown. Her always rosy lips and flushed cheeks paled, turning a sad pallor akin to the grim tone of one who had passed away.

After her wedding day, six years before, Hester and her betrothed, Richard Therese, moved into a lovely Victorian home in the Potwin Place district of the Kansas capital city. Potwin was a three-block-wide

151

stretch of exceptional residences boasting burgeoning families and well set retired folk living easily as knit neighbors.

Just before the celebration of the marriage's fourth year, Hester and Richard's three-year-old daughter, Victoria Kay, vanished from a playpen set on the comfortable front porch of their rambling home. The toddling girl was gone, with no trace.

Authorities were summoned, police resplendent in their crisp navy uniforms. Pastor Price from the First Congregational Church provided comfort to the distraught, desperate parents.

"We are not rich people," Hester protested, pleaded, at the time. "Why would someone take our baby? Why would someone take our Victoria Kay?" In fact, Hester's father, a doctor, was rather well to do, but she never understood money.

Through the first day of the kidnapping, and the second and then the third, Richard barely spoke, said almost nothing. And then, during the night of the fourth day, all the while Hester slept, Richard disappeared. While Hester was upstairs, deeply sedated with the remedy of Dr Hildegard, some disturbance occurred, or seemed to, in the front parlor. In the morning, when Hester roused, she found the parlor a wreck and her husband nowhere to be found. Blood thought to be Richard's was splattered all about.

Again, authorities were summoned, the same police officers in their same spotless garb. Pastor Price was on the porch directly after the arrival of the detectives. And Hester Therese unraveled.

The Shadow Cast

In the hours, then days that followed, no ransom demand came to secure the return of little Victoria Kay. No word came from anyone who might have undone Hester's husband. Although no body was found, the constabulary determined Richard Therese was killed, by rambling, ranging hobos, Hester thought. Dirty scavengers had taken her child and butchered her husband, leaving her behind and all alone.

Hester stayed in the roomy Victorian manse for a year after the mysterious tragedies. But her personal funds drained low and Hester abandoned the tree-lined neighborhood with block ending grassy roundabouts for a dingy, two-room flat downtown, across the street from the steam plant. Her father tried, indeed insisted, she take his money. He loved her and wanted Hester safe. But, she would have none of it and, in her overwhelming, irrational grief, severed all ties with the good, old doctor.

In another year, the youthful colorings of her hair, face and eyes shrunk away while her once healthy body sickly plumped. Hester eked out the most meager existence, at first by mending dresses for the women of the Potwin Place neighborhood. Eventually, Hester no longer ventured from her grim, slim flat and took in no more sewing. She came to rely on the state dole, mostly paid to the grocer's delivery boy, who kept her stocked in meager rations.

Hester's only luxury, indeed her only nexus with the world beyond passing on government bestowed cash to the grocer's boy on Wednesday mornings and the landlord on the first of the month, was a subscription to 'Hollywood Chatterbox', the infamous yellow sheet

The Shadow Cast

hyping the affairs of actors and actresses, film players, stage performers, merry vaudevillians.

One month, she read in her precious copy of 'Hollywood Chatterbox' that her favorite actress of stage and film, Pam Ella Trent, had taken to tour. Most wonderful of all for ill Hester Therese was the fact that the traveling circuit of Miss Trent's revue would bring the beloved performer right to Topeka, directly to the gracious Jayhawk Theater.

Scrimping and pinching, Hester managed the monies necessary to buy a solitary ticket to the show, a seat in the back row.

She made purchase of the golden colored ticket, with stylized print like Hester had not seen in years, two weeks before the day of the great performance. By day, she kept the ticket wrapped in a worn handkerchief, tucked next to her bosom. By night, the ticket went safely beneath the pillow on her bed. She so feared of the return of the vagabond hobos who she imagined snatched her daughter and sliced short the life of her husband that she could hardly sleep at night. She was so very certain the hobos would come and make off with her ticket to the Pam Ella Trent Revue, the only precious possession she had since losing Victoria Kay and Richard.

Clutched in her damp hands, as she slowly plodded down the sidewalk to the Theater, was the edition of 'Hollywood Chatterbox' extolling Miss Trent's traveling show. Hester hoped against hope that she might actually see the good lady and get her to write her name across her picture in the magazine story.

The Shadow Cast

Hester reached the Theater only a couple of minutes after the doors were opened to take in patrons for the night's show. She stopped directly outside the highly shined bronze doors leading into the lobby. A life-sized poster was mounted to the left of the doors, a colorized head to shoe portrait of Pam Ella Trent in a beaded golden gown.

Hester gasped at the sight of the fashionable picture. She slowly raised her hand and lightly touched the glass covering the image, reverently like a humble penitent revering an icon.

The doorman, watching the sweating, plump woman finger the placard piece of Pam Ella Trent, swiftly moved to Hester's side. Judging by her attire, he prepared to shoo her down the sidewalk and away from the Theater.

"Please ..." he began.

Hester quickly turned to face the entry attendant. She fumbled into a pocket on the side of her shapeless dress, pulling out her precious pass to the revue. She held the ticket in front of her worried face looking like a frightened woman holding a holy object to ward off evil.

"A ticket," she stammered. "I have a ticket."

The doorman grunted, gave Hester a visual once over, rolled his eyes, and mumbled "Really" with disgust, disdain and walked back into the lobby. Hester kept the ticket in front of her face for a full minute fearing the doorman would return.

She eventually peeked through an opened bronze door into the resplendent lobby itself. Returning the ticket to her pocket, fearing someone would take it from her, Hester slowly plodded into the ground floor lobby.

The Shadow Cast

A pleasant looking usherette greeted Hester after she made her way across the entrance to one of the doors leading into the performance hall's main house. "Good evening," said the usherette dressed in a smart navy uniform with red piping. "Can I have your ticket, please?"

Hester hesitated but finally turned over the tab to the usherette. The young Theater guide looked closely at Hester, then smiled.

"You know," the usherette said, her voice pitched at a whisper, "I'm supposed to keep all tickets. But, you know, I think you might like to keep yours?"

Hester's eyes opened wide, a smile spreading across her lips. In a hushed tone, as if speaking in a cathedral, Hester asked: "Really?"

"Sure, why not?"

The usherette showed Hester to her seat in the very rear row of the Theater. "Enjoy the show," she said handing Hester a program.

Hester gushed, "Oh, I will. I will."

Even though Hester sat in a back row, she suddenly looked more than happy, indeed nearly regal. The Queen of England could not look more content in a royal box. She clutched the program tightly at her bosom, not wanting to even open the petit book for fear breaking the cover might somehow dissipate the magic of the night.

In little time, the house of the Jayhawk began to fill with theater goers. Ladies in fine gowns and gentlemen in rich evening attire filtered through the doors and were seated, all taking places in more choice positions in the Theater. Hester remained all alone in her rear row, except for an elderly chap who was ushered in about twenty minutes after she arrived.

At almost curtain time, the same usherette who initially seated Hester returned to the back row and stood next to where Hester sat.

"Excuse me," the usherette said, causing Hester's heart to fall. Hester was sure the usherette reappeared to escort her from the Theater, probably because her dress was old and worn looking and not fresh and pretty like those of all the other women in the house. She felt tears well up in her eyes.

Not looking up at the usherette, Hester muttered, like a whipped pup: "I have a ticket." She started to reach into her pocket to retrieve the Theater pass the usherette returned to her earlier.

The usherette, after Hester's remark, smiled, a soft smile like a patient parent. "Oh, yes, ma'am ... I know." The usherette leaned in closer, as if she were a friend of Hester's. "You know, there are a few open seats ... down closer to the stage. I thought you might like to move down to one of them."

Hester could not believe her ears, the invitation seemed to her truly unreal. "But, I don't have any extra money," she said.

The same benevolent smile crossed the usherette's face a second time. "No, Ma'am ... no need for more money. Your ticket is good enough, just fine. There is no extra charge for moving to a better seat."

"Really?" Hester put a finger to one ear and pressed, thinking she really did not correctly hear the young usherette. Confirming what she told Hester the usherette nodded her head.

The Shadow Cast

"Now?" Hester asked, excitement easily edging into her voice.

The usherette nodded again and Hester awkwardly worked her way to her feet. With some effort, Hester made her way down the back row and out into an aisle. The usherette guided Hester to a prime seat in the fifth row.

Flustered upon taking her new spot, Hester nonetheless managed a breathless "Thank you."

In the minutes before the curtain rose, Hester worked hard to calm her breath. The excitement of being in a row at the front even caused her pulse to race. Once again, Hester clutched the evening's program to her chest, hoping to ease her happy heart which she felt certain could be seen pounding through her thin cotton smock.

Directly before the start of Pam Ella Trent's revue, a proper looking man close to Hester's age worked his way down the row of seats in Hester's direction. She shuttered, squeezed her eyes tightly shut, well certain that the approaching fellow was the Theater manager. Still fearing she was destined to be thrown out into the street, a lonely tear dribbled from Hester's tightly closed eyes and across her chin, landing at the tip top of the Theater program held tightly near her heart.

Sensing the man at her side, Hester waited for his likely angry words to flow forth. She imagined he would promptly proclaim: "You there! The woman in the old, worn dress! You there! Get out! Get out at once! Here you do not belong!"

Instead, the neighboring chap took the open seat right next to Hester. "Excuse me," he whispered.

158

The Shadow Cast

Hester, her eyelids remaining held down like solid gates beyond a deep moat, whimpered a "Yes?" "Are you alone?" he asked.

Hester slightly raised one lid, catching a glimpse of the man with a most earnest face seated at her right.

"Uh-huh," she replied.

"Me, too," he rejoined, a merry chirp in his voice like a carefree garden lark. "I'm so excited."

Slowly opening both eyes full, Hester said: "So am I."

"I'm Handy Weather," the fellow introduced.

"I'm Hester Therese," she replied.

Introductions made, the house faded to black and the marvelous Miss Trent took to the stage. At intermission, Handy and Hester – both nearly in a swoon from watching their favorite player – walked to the lobby together.

"Can I get you anything?" Handy asked Hester as they both stood at the crowd's edge.

"Huh?" Hester asked.

"Anything?" Handy explained. "Do you want anything to drink?"

"You mean like refreshments?" she asked.

"Sure," Handy replied. He gestured towards the lobby and bar where patrons lined up to retrieve beverages and finger-sized snacks. "What do you want?"

Hester hesitated, did not respond.

"I'm treating ... It's my treat," Handy prodded.

Barely above a whisper, Hester spoke. "I might like a cream soda, please." Hester and Handy made for the lobby.

The Shadow Cast

"One cream soda it is," Handy replied, joining the queue near the bar, leaving Hester near the entryway into the house.

A few minutes later, Handy rejoined Hester, two foamy cream sodas in hand. They quickly finished the carbonated concoctions because the lobby lights shortly began to flash, signaling the intermission's imminent end.

Returning to their seats for the second act, the twosome occasionally exchanged whispers back and forth during Miss Trent's performance. Both Hester and Handy looked sad when Pam Ella Trent took her final bow.

Together Hester and Handy slowly made their way from the theater house amidst the jocular crowd of fellow theater-goers. Reaching the lobby, Handy spoke to Hester, the eager smile again dashing to his face. "Say, Hester," he said, "would you like to go for a coffee, maybe some pie?"

"Coffee," Hester replied, almost reverently. "Pie?"

"Sure," Handy replied. "I'm treating."

Hester nodded, with reborn enthusiasm. Together, Hester and Handy exited the theater. Walking side by side into the night, a gentle rain began to fall.

The Nickel Brit

I graduated one year early from Buchanan County High School in Winthrop, Iowa, a tiny town about an hour north of Cedar Rapids. At seventeen, desiring to study music performance, I traveled 1,500 miles from home to Winchester, Virginia and the Shenandoah Conservatory of Music. I arrived in Winchester in the fall of 1964. I arrived with my violin in hand.

My travels to college marked my first airplane trip, a rough and rocky trip from Cedar Rapids to Washington DC and National Airport, where I caught a diesel smelling bus to Front Royal, Virginia. At Front Royal, I was picked up in a ramshackle truck that looked to be about twenty years old or perhaps more, driven by a strange fellow, maybe ten years older than I was that year. The odd bird waited for me at the Greyhound Bus Depot in Front Royal holding a ratty cardboard sign that he'd obviously used at least two other times. Towards the top of the two foot long and one foot wide brown placard was the name 'Madeline O'Day' crossed out. Under the drawn out name was a second one, 'Tim Sommers' also dashed through.

Under that name the stranger wrote my name, 'Wayne Price.'

"Excuse me," I said upon approaching the man. "Are you from the Conservatory? Shenandoah Conservatory of Music? Are you here for me?"

The man was wearing what looked to me to be second hand clothes, the kind of garments I saw on men when driving through seedier spots in downtown Cedar Rapids to my Aunt Karen's house in the suburbs. He wore a threadbare tweed jacket, both elbows patched. His shirt, a thin fabric perhaps once white, but now a sickly gray quite like I imagined prison sheets, was buttoned to the top with the collar taking a stranglehold about the fellow's neck.

He wore a red bow tie and faded brown woolen slacks. His shoes were seriously scuffed, the soles obviously barely held in place and, I imagined, riddled with holes.

When I asked the man if he was from the Conservatory, he bowed to me deeply, like an actor I saw in a movie about World War II, an actor portraying a Japanese admiral surrendering aboard the USS Missouri. He then spoke, with an unusual accent that I assumed to be British, although his speech did not sound quite right, not like the English men and women I saw and heard in movies and on television. I never met anyone from England growing up in Winthrop, Iowa. The more exotic visitors to Winthrop came from Des Moines, Omaha and the Teglers welcomed occasional visitors from Denver.

After the fellow finished his bow, he asked: "Are you Master Wayne Price?"

"Yes, sir."

"Then, Master Price," he replied, "your chariot awaits." He broke into a seemingly violent coughing fit after he spoke.

Once he recovered, we collected my luggage and walked from the depot. He led me to the rickety truck that would serve as my chariot to my first day at college, the kind of ride I often saw on Iowa dirt roads.

The Shadow Cast

As we maneuvered away from the crowded bus station, I asked the fellow his name.

"Henry William Hamilton, at your service," he replied.

"Do you work for the Conservatory?" I asked.

"My yes, I do," he replied.

"So, are you from London or something? I mean, with your accent and all?"

"Oh, yes, quite right," he replied, adding his family lived on an estate directly outside the limits of Greater London.

"I'm from Iowa," I offered.

"Ah, Iowa …" he replied, nodding his head knowingly. "Verdant green pastures, thriving livestock, crisp blue skies that wander on for scores of miles … Iowa."

"You've been there?" I asked, as we motored out of Front Royal and north towards Winchester.

"Goodness, how I wish. There is so much of the Americas I wish to see, including the middle west of the United States. Alas, for now, I find myself too busy to travel much beyond Virginia."

"Are you a professor?" I asked.

"Of a special sort," he quickly responded, a ready answer.

"I'm going to be a music major … performance," I advised, sounding more certain of my decision after my arrival in Virginia than I was in Iowa.

"Ah, music … Our school is known for music. And the theater, as well."

"Patsy Cline, she was from Winchester, right?" I asked.

The Shadow Cast

"Indeed ... born and raised. But, of course, on the road with her career before she ever could set foot on the Conservatory campus. And then, of course, the plane crash ..." His voice trailed off.

We reached Winchester in about forty-five minutes. Henry William Hamilton dropped me off in front of the red brick dormitory that would be my home for the next two terms, my freshman year.

Hoisting my luggage from the back of the truck, I thanked Mr Hamilton for the ride.

"Please, call me Henry," the young professor said with a poignant look in his eyes.

I would have liked to shake his hand, but my own were fully occupied with my luggage.

"Let me give you something, for luck," Henry said. "For luck as you begin your college career."

He reached into his pant's pocket and removed a coin that I did not get a close look at. My hands loaded, he slipped the coin into my shirt pocket.

"An English sovereign ... pure gold ... Victorian ... for luck."

"Thanks ... Henry."

I made off to the dorm to get settled in my room. I forgot all about the coin in my pocket until I began to change out of my clothes for bed that night. Reaching into my pocket, I fingered the piece, pulling it out. Holding it up, I immediately recognized it, a currency bit I saw nearly every day. Henry William Hamilton gave me a nickel, a United States five cent coin, for luck.

A month passed before I laid eyes on Henry William Hamilton, the Brit who gave me the nickel. In fact, from the night I discovered that he gave me the American

164

five cent token rather than an English gold sovereign, I thought nothing of Henry William Hamilton or his coin until that morning after first period when I saw the fellow amble out the door of the theater arts building.

In spite of myself, and in spite of his cheap gift, I found myself smiling as I watched Henry Hamilton walk from the building in my direction. On that morning in mid-September he was dressed quite like on the day I made his acquaintance. However, his bow tie was green rather than red.

When he reached speaking distance, I greeted him with a polite "Good morning, Mr Hamilton … Henry, I mean."

He stopped walking, looked me up and down, his expression puzzled, the epitome of the befuddled, eccentric, young professor. Before he could say, "Do I know you, lad?" or something of the sort, I reintroduced myself. "I'm Wayne Price … You came for me at the bus depot in Front Royal. You gave me the … coin."

"Ah, indeed," he replied, his voice sounding British, but different somehow from a month earlier. Perhaps he had an autumn cold, I thought. "Master Price of the Iowa Prices. Yes, I recall you well. Has the sovereign brought you luck?"

I did not know quite how to respond. Perhaps he mistakenly believed he gave me a British coin rather than the American pittance. Unsure what to do, I smiled and said: "Yes."

"Very well, then. And your studies, Master Price, they go well?"

"Pretty good. Getting into the routine."

The Shadow Cast

"Ah, yes, so it goes." Right as the words left his mouth,
he coughed harshly, deeply.
"And you, Henry, are you … well?"
"Oh, indeed. Well fed, well rested … very well."
We visited a bit longer, about the pleasant weather
and the marvelously colored trees, fall bursting forth up
and down the Shenandoah Valley.
We parted ways and I continued on to my dorm. My
roommate, Cliff Simon, was struggling, prepping, really
cramming, for an examination when I returned. I tried to
keep quiet and went to my own desk, opening up the
seldom used center drawer. Inside the space were
some receipts, a couple of scraps of paper and cocktail
napkins scribbled with different co-ed's names and
phone numbers, and the nickel the Brit gave to me on
my first day in Virginia.
I fingered the coin for a minute or so and then
decided to interrupt my roommate, who was also a
music major.
"Do you know a Prof named Hamilton?" I asked
Cliff.
"Hamilton?"
"Yep," I confirmed.
"There's a Hamilton who's a Prof in the theater
department," Cliff advised. I figured that must be Henry
William Hamilton, the Brit with the nickel.
"I guess that's him. From England?"
"England?" Cliff asked. "What do you mean?"
"I mean, this Professor Hamilton that I'm asking
about, he's from England …"
Cliff shrugged. He did not know. He knew the name
and that was all. I held up the coin and explained how

The Shadow Cast

Henry William Hamilton picked me up at the bus depot in Front Royal, giving me the nickel for luck.

"He slipped it in my shirt pocket; my hands were full with my luggage. He said he was giving me a gold sovereign from England."

"And it's just a nickel?" my roommate asked.

"Yep," I said and nodded.

"Weird," he remarked and I agreed.

A couple more months passed and I found myself in the theater arts building as part of the orchestra for the annual Conservatory Christmas concert. While replacing a broken string on my violin, I caught sight of Henry William Hamilton sitting towards the rear of the auditorium where we rehearsed. Getting my string in place, I walked back towards Henry.

"Henry?"

Catching his attention, he looked at me, that time with recognition.

"Master Price," he smiled.

"Checking out the rehearsal?" I asked.

"Indeed I am. It's been so enjoyable thus far."

Henry's accent, British sounding to be sure, once again sounded different than on the day of my arrival and even slightly unlike my second encounter with the man outside the theater arts building. I chalked up the slight differences I perceived to the fact I had seen the fellow on only three occasions and never met a Brit in my life before encountering him.

"I play the violin," I said, slightly raising my instrument.

The Shadow Cast

"So I see, Master Price. A lovely instrument, to be sure," Henry remarked, reaching out to lightly touch the violin with a couple of bony fingers.

"I guess I should get back," I remarked, meaning to the orchestra pit and practice.

"Play well, Master Price."

I told Henry I would try my best. Before I reentered the pit, Charlene Lamont stopped me by lightly taking hold of my arm. Charlene was a senior and first violin of our special Christmas orchestra.

"How do you know him?" she asked, with a touch of disdain, I thought, and a slight nod in the direction of Henry William Hamilton. "Him?"

She nodded.

"You mean Professor Hamilton?"

Charlene gave me a puzzled expression followed by a wry grin. "No," she said. "I mean his son there." "Who?" I asked, confused.

"Professor Hamilton's son," she replied.

"His son?" I returned. "I don't know his son. I know Professor Hamilton, but not his son."

Charlene's expression remained unchanged.

"Wayne," she continued. "You were just talking to him … Professor Hamilton's son, I mean."

"What?"

"Over there," Charlene said, tilting her head in the direction of Henry William Hamilton. "You were just talking to him, that man over there. He's Professor Hamilton's son."

"His son?"

"Uh-huh."

"But," I stammered, "I thought that was Professor

The Shadow Cast

Hamilton ..."

"You wiener," she riddled. "That's his son. The coocoo one."

Before I was able to question Charlene any further, we were called back to carry on with the rehearsal in the orchestra pit. I did not have the chance to speak with Charlene further until after the rehearsal. I managed to catch up with her right outside the theater arts building, both of us well bundled up to ward off the surprisingly blustery winter night. By that time Hamilton, whoever he was, had left and was no where to be seen.

"So, what do you mean ... he's coo-coo?" I asked.

"Just what I've heard," Charlene said with a shrug. "Something that happened and made him drop out of school here, I think."

"Maybe people think he's an oddball because he's English," I suggested.

"English?" Charlene shot back, clearly surprised.

"Yeah, maybe because he's a foreigner, people think he's odd."

Charlene laughed. "What makes you think the Hamiltons are from England?"

I hesitated, but finally explained Henry William Hamilton, the professor's son, told me he was from England, outside London somewhere. "Plus, he has an accent."

"I bet he does," Charlene replied snidely. "What else did he tell you?"

"I guess he told me he was a professor ..." I let my voice trail off, awaiting the next zap from Charlene. She laughed again.

"No, he's not. His father is a Prof in the theater arts department. They're from Richmond, the Hamilton family. Henry ... Hank Hamilton ... his family calls him Hank ... is the youngest child. He has a loose noodle in his noggin. He went to school here, almost graduated in fact. Years ago. Studied theater arts, but something went wrong when he spent a semester abroad and got really ill. Wayne, he's coo-coo, as I've said. After he quit school, his father got him a job here at the Conservatory, kind of a jack of all trades deal. Something must have happened to Hank that no one talks about ... Something changed him when he was away."

I cut in and remarked: "That's why he picked me up at the bus depot in Front Royal."

"Yep," Charlene replied. "He does stuff like that ... pick up people who need rides, file things in the Administration Building, stuff like that. He's perfectly harmless, just coo-coo."

Charlene smiled at me and I returned the look and added a brisk shake of my head.

I mumbled something like "Live and learn" and said "Good night" to my fellow violinist. I walked back to my dorm, flurries of light snow swirling about my ankles.

The Christmas concert was a success, my examinations were survivable. When the time came for me to retrace my steps back to Iowa for the Christmas holiday break, I signed up to ride along on a Conservatory van to Front Royal where I could catch a bus to Washington National Airport and a plane on home to Iowa.

The Shadow Cast

On the morning of my departure, I waited in front of the Administration Building with a half dozen fellow students, awaiting the ride. At ten that morning, a blue Ford van pulled to a stop in front of the Admin Building. The driver, as I pretty well expected, was Henry William Hamilton.

Shifting the vehicle into park, but keeping the engine running to keep the van warm inside on that December morning, Henry then hopped out and began helping us with luggage.

Eying me, he greeted, "Master Price," once more in an English accent that I then knew was fake.

"Hello, H-Henry," I sputtered, thinking for a moment about calling him Hank. I looked at him a little differently, but with it being the Christmas season, I thought twice about spoiling Henry William Hamilton's illusion. He was, indeed, every bit the harmless man Charlene Lamont described. And, regardless of his ruse, Henry William Hamilton was likable if nothing else. And he had tried to make me feel welcome.

Christmas was a happy time in Iowa. My little hometown of Winthrop was unchanged and I took tremendous comfort in that fact. After a couple of weeks, the time came for me to return to Virginia and to my studies.

Finally reaching Front Royal and the bus depot, I expected to be picked up by the faux-Brit, Henry William Hamilton. Instead, a fellow student on a workstudy program was paid to haul me to Winchester.

"I thought Professor Hamilton's son did this job," I remarked as we pulled out of the bus depot parking lot. The driver, a sophomore I did not recognize, said he

171

heard the professor's son took ill over the holidays. "Got real sick and then died," the driver said far too matter-of-factly for my tastes and temperament.

"What?" I shot back in alarm.

"He died," the driver replied with a 'so what' shrug.

I pressed the driver for more information, but he obviously knew nothing. After a few minutes of questioning the fellow, I fell silent for the remainder of the trip to Winchester.

Reaching the dorm, I hurried to my room to find that Cliff, my roommate, had not yet returned from the holiday break. I spent the remainder of the afternoon and the early evening alone in my room, simply feeling sad about the apparent demise of Henry William Hamilton.

At some point in the early evening, I thought about the coin given to me by Henry William Hamilton, the nickel I kept in the center drawer of my desk. I opened up the desk drawer and fumbled around, finally feeling the cool metallic disk stuck in the very back. I pulled the coin out, noticing at once and before I laid eyes on the piece that it did not feel quite the same.

Raising my hand, I took a look at what I held. Between my fingers I did not clasp a US nickel. Rather, in my hand I held a golden Victorian sovereign emblazoned with the profile of the plump old queen. In that instant, while holding onto the shiny coin, I felt the gentle spirit of the peculiar man I would forever remember as the Nickel Brit.

Letters To Saint Nick

My wife and I retired to Miami Beach in the fall of 1960. We cast ballots for John F Kennedy from a voting booth set up in the lobby of the Eden Roc Hotel, a couple blocks from our snug bungalow just off Collins Avenue.

Our only son, his wife and our two granddaughters traveled from Kansas City to Miami Beach by train to spend Christmas and a winter vacation with us. Our older granddaughter was six and our younger just two.

On one afternoon early in the New Year, I sat on a bench at the beach with my older granddaughter. While looking out over the crystal Atlantic Ocean and enjoying a warm breeze, the little girl, done up in pigtails, asked me what I remembered about my favorite Christmas.

"That's easy," I thought to myself, and proceeded to tell her about Christmas 1932.

I turned thirty-two years old in '32 and was the Executive Vice President of August J Crosby Dry Goods Co., the department store founded by my own grandfather and ran by my father in a huge granite building at 12th and Main in downtown Kansas City, Missouri.

Since well before I was born, the Crosby store had a Christmas tradition of answering letters from children to Saint Nick. I explained to my granddaughter that Santa was such a busy person he needed help answering all the mail he received.

Right after Thanksgiving 1932, my father called me into his office to tell me he had decided I would be one

The Shadow Cast

of the people at the store assigned to answer Santa mail. I would spend every afternoon until Christmas writing back to children who had written to Santa Claus care of the store.

I can still remember how fiercely I protested.

"Oh, come now!" I exclaimed. "You can't be serious!"

My father said nothing in reply. He let me rant, rave and protest the assignment until I ran out of steam. He then said: "You start this afternoon."

I stalked back to my office, still fairly fuming with anger. I was the Executive Vice President of the Crosby Co department store. I did not want to be stuck writing letters to children.

At noon, a stack of a couple dozen letters from children was delivered to my office.

"Take these away, take these back!" I yelled at the hapless and helpless mailroom boy. I can still picture his horrified expression as he sprinted out of my office, leaving the letters on the edge of my desk.

I left the letters alone, intending to carry them down to the mailroom myself, unanswered, at the end of the day. I spent the remainder of the afternoon inspecting various departments in the store to make sure all was running smoothly in preparation for the holiday shopping season. I found myself still at the store, a couple of hours after closing, sitting alone in my office.

I idly picked a letter off the top of the stack just as I was preparing to leave. I read the child's missive to Saint Nick.

Dear Santa Claus,

My name is Rowan. I am nine. My Mama works. She works for some people at the Country Club Plaza.

174

The Shadow Cast

They are rich. We are not. They are white. We are not. For Christmas I would like a truck. The truck does not have to be new. Just a truck. That would be swell.

Your friend,
Rowan Washington
PS. Can you tell the people my Mama works for to let her stay home with me for Christmas?

I sat back down in the big, leather chair behind my desk. I wondered, even if I was going to answer these letters, what would I say to a boy like Rowan?

"Sure, Santa will bring you a truck. Maybe even a new one. And, if your Mama worked for me she could have a day off on Christmas to be with you," I thought. But I knew that neither of Rowan's two requests of good, old Saint Nick would come true.

Leaving the office that night, I left Rowan's letter on my secretary's desk, along with the envelope and the boy's return address. I wrote a note to my secretary:

Please see if you can find this child's mother and a phone number.

The next morning, I returned to work and my office. As always, my secretary, Margaret, was waiting for me with a cup of coffee. She also handed me a sheet of paper with a woman's name and phone number.

"What's this?" I asked. I didn't recognize the telephone exchange and had forgotten about little Rowan Washington.

"The name and phone number you asked me to find."

"Oh, right, right," I muttered, taking the piece of paper and my coffee into my office. A short time later I

175

rang Rowan's mother's phone number, getting no answer. I imagined she must be at work, likely a maid or cook for one of the wealthy families who lived at the Country Club Plaza, based on what Rowan wrote in his letter to Santa. I tucked the slip of paper into the breast pocket of my suit jacket, intending to call the woman later in the day.

I paid no attention to the other Santa letters on my desk until the same mailroom clerk dashed in and out of my office just after noon making a deposit that doubled the size of my stack. Margaret poked her head into my office, grinning mischievously like a carnival barker.

"Keep yourself quiet," I said after which she withdrew, chuckling lightly.

Within the hour, I picked a letter off the top of the stack. The child wrote:

> Hi, Santa!
> It's me! I'm fine! I hope you are fine! Mommy is fine!
> Daddy is fine! Billy is fine! My cat is fine!
> XXX
> Betsy Lou Spaine

"Now this letter I can handle," I thought. I yelled for Margaret to come into my office to take a letter. She appeared, still wearing the same wry grin.

"I don't take Santa letters," she advised. "You have to write them by hand." As she spoke, Margaret handed to me a stack of stationery emblazoned with:
Santa Claus
North Pole

The Shadow Cast

I moaned as Margaret made her exit. Nevertheless, I took a piece of Saint Nick stationery and scribbled out a reply to Betsy Lou Spaine. I wrote:

Dear Miss Spaine:
I am pleased to hear of your family's good health.
Cordially,
Santa Clause

I did not realize that in my haste, I misspelled "Claus." I proudly trooped out of my office and dropped my response on Margaret's desk directly in front of her as if to say: "Take that."

Margaret looked at the letter and said: "Boss, this is a rotten letter. And you misspelled Santa's name."

She pulled a red pen out of a desk drawer and marked up my letter like a frustrated fifth grade teacher.

Shortly, I redid the letter to Betsy Lou, spelling corrected and to my secretary's satisfaction. Passing over the revised version to Margaret, I received a passing mark.

Curiosity got the best of me and I picked another letter off the growing stack on my desk.

Dear Mr Claus,

I am writing to you for both my sister, June, and I. I am ten. She is three. She cannot write by herself and Mom and Dad said I have to write for both of us.

I have been good this year, even though I am ten. My sister has been good because she is three.

Would you please bring me a baseball, a mitt and a bat? I want to play baseball and need these things to play.

The Shadow Cast

Would you please bring my sister, June, a dollhouse? I guess some dolls, too. Okay?

Thank you, Billy
Jones
670 31ˢᵗ St
Kansas City, Missouri

"Margaret!" I shouted, my office door being left open a crack for when I needed to call for my secretary. Entering into my office, she mocked me dryly. She had worked for my father and known me since I was a child.

"You bellowed?" she said.

"Go down to Sporting Goods. Bring me a couple of baseballs, a bat and a mitt that will fit a boy who is ten. Then go to Toys and bring me a dollhouse and couple of dolls."

Margaret saw that I had a Santa letter in front of me on the desk. But that did not stop her from saying something about "Playtime, Mr Crosby?"

When Margaret returned with the items I needed, we packaged them up and I had Margaret take them to the mailroom to be sent off to Billy Jones and his little sister June. I told Margaret to try to find a phone number for the Jones family on 31ˢᵗ Street to let the parents know the desired gifts from Saint Nick were coming.

I read and responded to a dozen more of the Santa letters on my desk, just like I did with Billy and June Jones. Wrapped up as I was in my doling out toys and gifts, I lost track of time. Margaret had left for the day and the sun had set.

I picked up the telephone and rang up little Rowan Washington's home, this time reaching his mother.

178

The Shadow Cast

After explaining who I was and mentioning Rowan's Santa letter, Mrs Washington provided me with the information I desired. Clicking off the line from the woman, I set about the task of creating a Christmas I hoped Mrs Washington and her boy would always remember.

The following day, I took lunch with Hubert Van Gibb. Hubert and I were students together at Maur Hill Prep during our teenage years. We met at 1:00pm at the Cattlemen's Club overlooking the freight district and stock yards.

Hubert reached the Club ahead of me and graciously stood at the table to greet me when I arrived. "What a nice surprise to hear from you last night," Hubert said as we sat down, referring to my phone call inviting him to lunch.

"It has been a while," I replied. "How's Estelle?" I asked.

"Very well. You know, bustling about for the holidays."

I nodded politely and he asked me how the store was doing. I asked about his wife, he asked me about the store. Never before had I felt more single, like the consummate bachelor, which I really had become.

We both ordered London Broils and gin martinis, two drinks apiece.

"Listen, Hubert," I said, halfway through our luncheon, "I understand you and Estelle have a cook named Mrs Washington."

Hubert eyed me suspiciously, probably thinking that I intended to hire his house help away from him.

179

The Shadow Cast

"It's not what you think," I said, responding to my companion's droll expression. He took a sip from his thin martini glass and nodded for me to carry on.

From that moment, I rambled for over ten minutes, telling Hubert about the Santa letters coming to the store, how I really did not want to do the project – at first – and, I told him about the letter from Mrs Washington's son, Rowan. By the time I finished my tale, poor Hubert Van Gibb had no idea what I wanted of him, my remarks were so jumbled.

"What I want ..." I finally, flatly stated, "what I want is for you to give Mrs Washington Christmas Day off so she can be with her boy."

Before Hubert could object, or laugh in my face, I quickly told him I would arrange for full catering of Christmas dinner, whatever Hubert and Estelle wanted, the best of everything, from the Hotel Savoy. All free of charge.

Hubert thought for only a moment, and then shot his right hand across the table to shake mine. "It's a deal!" Hubert happily agreed.

Feeling pretty pleased with myself, I headed back to my office at the store. Whistling as I walked past Margaret's desk, she merely grinned, slightly shaking her head.

In my absence, another delivery of a couple dozen Santa letters had arrived and was sitting on my desktop. I wasted no time in diving into the new letters and the leftovers I had not finished previously. As with the day before, I lost track of time and ended up writing letters and gathering gifts until late into the night.

180

The Shadow Cast

I decided to and did in fact arrive at my office very early the next morning, just after dawn, to go back to work on the Santa Claus mail.

The second letter I read that morning was from a little boy aged six.

Dear Santa Claus,

My name is Ricky and I just turned six. I live with my Momma. I don't have a Daddy.

My Momma and I live in a house just off the Farmers' Market. Our house isn't big and I'm afraid you don't know where it is. Momma explained to me last year that our house is hard to find, sometimes, and you not coming to visit wasn't because of me.

So, Santa, this year I drew up a map with this letter so that you will find my Momma and me.

My Momma works when she can up at the Hearty Perk coffee plant on Central Avenue in downtown. I just started the first grade.

For Christmas, I really don't want much at all. Just a football. That would be swell. But mostly, I'd like something for Momma. She is very pretty, you know, and she works very hard. If I could, Santa, I'd buy her a nice dress. The kind of thing the women wear when they go shopping downtown. She is just as pretty as they are.

My Momma, her name is Dahlia, just like the flower. So, Santa, if you can't bring the football, it is okay, but please follow the map and bring a dress for my Momma. Thank you.

Love. Your pal,
Ricky Nicks

181

Paper-clipped to the letter was a crude map evidently drawn by the boy himself, using red and green crayons.

I read Ricky's letter over once more and then yet again.

With the little Christmas colored map in hand, I dashed out of my office, passing my puzzled looking secretary in the hallway as she arrived at the store for the day's work. I did not give her the chance to ask where I was going.

Pulling my car out of the store's parking plaza, I sped through the downtown streets filled with the rush of people trooping to work. Even in the heavy traffic, I still managed to make the Farmers' Market in less than fifteen minutes. Following Ricky's hand-drawn map, I was on his street, a narrow dead-ender, and a few minutes later, I reached the house Ricky Nicks and his mother called home. A tiny patch of winter brown grass fronted the yard behind a fence of bent, rusting chain link. A small mongrel dog was chained to the remains of a tree, really a glorified stump, in the yard. The dog didn't bark or even stand up.

The house itself was tiny, having only a door and a solitary window on the front face. It looked empty at the moment and for a time, parked in front of the property, I found myself fighting a rigorous impulse to walk across the yard and sneak a peak in the little window.

Something about the boy's letter to Santa Claus led me to reckon that even though he and his mother were in dire financial straits their home would be warm and pleasantly comfortable inside, no matter how plain and simple.

The Shadow Cast

I lost track of time, sitting in front of Ricky Nicks' house. An old, brittle woman deliberately walking near my parked car, scowling, caught my attention and prompted me to motor off back to the store.

I spent the remainder of the day picking out toys for Ricky Nicks. I then went to the Women's Boutique in the store to select some dresses and accessories for Ricky's mother, Dahlia.

"So, what size, Mr Crosby?" the boutique clerk asked me when I told her I desired a selection of nice dresses for a woman, for Christmas gifts.

I shrugged, having never seen Dahlia Nicks.

The clerk, an older woman, smiled. She was used to waiting on an occasional male customer shopping for a wife or a girlfriend. I did not immediately pick up on the fact that the sales clerk assumed I was shopping for a particular personal lady friend.

"So you don't know her size, then?" she asked.

"No, I guess I don't," I replied.

Trying to be helpful, the clerk asked how 'my lady friend' looked, size-wise, in comparison to her.

"You know," I honestly replied, not thinking the situation through fully, "I don't know what she looks like."

The sales lady frowned, indeed nearly grimaced.

I fumbled a confused semi-explanation after which I eventually retreated from the boutique, telling the puzzled clerk I would be back when I had some idea what size dress was needed.

Returning upstairs to my office, I found Margaret waiting, wearing an earlobe to earlobe grin and looking

183

like a person who succeeded in a particularly mischievous prank.

"Maralee just called," Margaret said to me as I entered into my office suite.

"Who?" I asked, slowing my pace slightly although still progressing towards my private office.

"Maralee," she repeated in a manner making it clear that Margaret believed I most certainly knew a woman named Maralee.

"I don't know a Maralee." I brushed off Margaret as I side-stepped past her desk.

"You just talked to her," Margaret retorted as I prepared to shut my office door on her.

"I didn't just talk to her," I replied. "I just got back from the dress boutique." I shut my office door on Margaret, but not before I heard her begin to chuckle.

I reopened my door, only a crack, with an inquisitive look.

Margaret rolled her eyes. "Maralee is the clerk in the boutique."

In turn, I crossed my own eyes, exited my office and said: "Say ..." I explained Ricky Nicks' letter to my secretary and my dress size dilemma.

"So, boss, you want me to guess for you?" Margaret teased, obviously pleased with my somewhat lighter mood in recent days.

"No," I replied, but I did ask if she would accompany me to the Nicks' house directly after work. I told her I would deliver some Santa gifts for Ricky and Margaret could estimate Dahlia Nicks' dress size.

Margaret protested a little, but then thought the better of her first instinct to refuse to accompany me.

184

The Shadow Cast

She realized the jaunt I proposed might be amusing. Certainly, she found the whole developing escapade to be out of what she perceived to be my common character. She agreed to tarry along with me that evening.

A few minutes after five, Margaret and I left the store and, once more using the red and green crayon map, headed off to the Nicks' house by the Farmers' Market. With us, we had the gifts for Ricky intended to be packages from Saint Nick on Christmas Day. And, Margaret had orders to look Dahlia Nicks over and see what size dress the woman likely wore.

Arriving at the Nicks' house, I saw a light glowing in the one front window.

"Here?" Margaret asked.

"Here," I replied, finding myself scanning up and down the block to see if the scowling old woman from earlier that day might be out and about. No one seemed to be stirring that chilly, November evening.

We both got out of my car, each with armfuls of gaily wrapped gifts. I looked at Margaret and saw that she was smiling. She, in turn, looked at me and said: "Boss, you're smiling."

Reaching the small concrete stoop, we juggled our loads to free up a hand between us to knock on the door. Giving up on that idea, I rapped on the door with one of my wing-tipped feet.

Promptly, the door opened and there stood a woman, a few years younger than me and a smiling boy with big, blue eyes.

"Hello," the woman greeted, at once matching the smile of the child at her side.

The Shadow Cast

I quickly identified Margaret and myself, explained we were from the Crosby store and that Santa Claus asked us to lend a hand and help get some gifts delivered before Christmas.

"My letter!" the boy, Ricky, gleefully exclaimed.

Margaret, quick on her feet and knowing about the dresses yet to be delivered, wasted not a beat in explaining that there would be another delivery in a day or so.

Dahlia hesitated, pausing for a few seconds, then did in time invite us into the house.

Ricky wasted no time in relieving Margaret and then me of our burdens. He placed the gifts around the small Christmas tree in the corner of the living room. As I imagined while parked outside that afternoon, the house was simply decorated, yet warm, comfortable ... lovely.

Dahlia Nicks had coal black hair, pulled back from her face with an ivory-colored clip. She wore no makeup, but rather had a rosy glow about her face. Dahlia's eyes seemed as dark as her thick hair. And her smile ... her smile made her all the more beautiful. Within the minute, I realized – as did Margaret – that I was staring at Dahlia Nicks.

Margaret cleared her throat intending to cut short my intense gaze at Dahlia Nicks. I managed to look away at Margaret's prompting, but in no time my eyes were glued on the woman once again.

Dahlia offered us tea, which Margaret declined for both of us. Dahlia thanked us profusely for the gifts, making it very apparent that we had fulfilled her child's dreams for a merry holiday.

Feeling as if we overstayed our welcome, Margaret tugged on the sleeve of my suit coat. "We have to be going," she said.

As Margaret and I moved toward the door, I blurted out that I would be back the next day with more gifts.

"Gee, this is so swell!" Ricky happily exclaimed.

"Ricky!" Dahlia gently scolded. "Really, Mr Crosby ..."

"Wayne," I cut in.

"What?" Dahlia asked.

"My name," I clarified. "It's Wayne."

Dahlia blushed. "Well ... Wayne ... You really have done more than enough."

I waved her off and assured her I would return the next day, at about the same time if that was acceptable to her. Rather than saying something along the lines of "That's fine," she seemed to carefully pick her words and said: "We'll be home."

Once back in my car, heading back to the store, Margaret said: "She's a four."

"What?"

"A four," Margaret said in a tone which indicated she was stating the patently apparent.

Not comprehending, I asked "For what?" and half expected Margaret to reply "For you." "A size four," she dryly stated.

"Oh, yeah. Right. Great. Maybe tomorrow you could help me pick out some dresses."

She nodded in agreement. Feeling as if I needed to make my actions all the more proper, I reminded Margaret that Ricky asked Santa for a dress for his mother.

The Shadow Cast

"Of course," Margaret replied, a grin creeping across her lips.

When I arrived at work the next morning, I intended to take care of some more Santa letters. I found that I could not concentrate on that task or anything else. Dahlia Nicks, Ricky's mother, stayed on the tip of my brain since the night before.

The minute I heard Margaret enter our office suite, I left my office to meet her. Not letting her take a seat, I grabbed her by the arm.

"Dresses, Margaret, dresses."

I led her out of our office and down to the women's dress boutique. Margaret chuckled mischievously the entire way to the department.

She held her tongue while she helped me select half a dozen dresses that she thought would look nice on Dahlia Nicks. Although she made no remarks in jest, I could readily tell from her expression that she was biting at the bit to rib me about what she perceived as my interest in Dahlia Nicks.

Repeating our ritual from the day before, Margaret and I wrapped more packages destined for the Nicks' household. With the gifts prepared, I spent the rest of the morning reviewing departmental inventory reports. At noon, Margaret poked her head into my office.

"Need anything, boss?" she asked.

"Lunch," I replied.

"What would you like?"

"Let's say we go get lunch," I suggested. Margaret and I almost never ate together.

"Well," she said, piping up her voice.

"Well, let's go," I said, getting up from my desk.

188

The Shadow Cast

I took Margaret to the Hotel Savoy for our luncheon. Over lobster bisque, Margaret brought up Dahlia Nicks.

"So, boss, tell me ... What do you think of Dahlia Nicks?"

I verbally stumbled, like a high school freshman called to the blackboard. "What do you mean?" I finally managed.

She smiled, but in a kindly fashion, gentle.

"Well, boss, it seemed to me that our Dahlia Nicks strikes your fancy."

"Oh, gosh," I muttered, relieved that at least I did not say 'Aw, shucks.'

"She's a lovely girl," Margaret said.

"Well ... I ..." I could not escape the minor at the blackboard feeling.

Margaret rolled onward, pleasantly yet persistently.

"You should take her to dinner," Margaret finally pronounced with granite certainty.

"How is your bisque?"

"Take her to dinner." Margaret's course was well plotted and she was not to be detoured.

We finished lunch, returned to the store and went about our business for the remainder of the afternoon. At five, like the day before, I left for the Nicks' home over-loaded with parcels. On this trip, I went alone.

Dahlia, or perhaps Ricky, must have seen me walking up the cracked sidewalk to their house. They opened the front door just as I reached the stoop.

Dahlia, slightly smiling, nodded her head. "You really shouldn't have ..."

Before I could speak, Ricky spoke up. "He didn't. This stuff's from Santa."

189

The Shadow Cast

Dahlia patted her boy's head and acknowledged that he was right.

Standing in the living room, Dahlia offered me some hot tea. "It's cold out there," she added.

"You know," I replied. "Tea, hot tea. That sounds great."

"Please," Dahlia said. "Sit." She pointed at an old sofa she covered with an afghan.

While Dahlia left the room for the kitchen to fetch the tea, Ricky sat down, Indian style, next to me on the sofa.

"Ain't Santa swell?" Ricky asked me, looking at the pile of wrapped presents under the tree. "And now I don't have to worry that he can't find our house."

I nodded, smiling at the little boy. I had an urge to give the young fellow a hearty hug.

"You know, I wrote Santa a letter and gave him a map I made myself so he wouldn't get lost. And best of all, he sends you early so I don't have to worry any more about Santa getting lost and not finding us, you know."

I had seen children in and out of our store every day. But, looking at Ricky, I could not recall ever seeing a happier child.

"That's right. I'm sure Santa just wanted to make sure you and your mom got your presents and that you did not lose sleep over him coming," I said.

"Here you go," Dahlia announced, returning to the living room with a pot of tea and a couple of cups and a frothy glass of milk for Ricky.

Over tea, Dahlia and I talked about Ricky and his schooling, Dahlia and her work at the coffee plant and now as a receptionist at a doctor's office. Dahlia was a proud woman and remained ill at ease about accepting the gifts I brought from the store, but she balanced her rightful pride against her son's obvious happiness.

I found myself losing track of time, a common occurrence for me those days. I finally apologized for staying so long after I had been at the Nick's home for over an hour. Standing to leave, I racked my brain trying to come up with another reason to make contact with Dahlia and her son.

"You know," I finally said, just before I opened the front door to depart.

"Yes?" Dahlia replied.

"The store ..." I stammered. "The store also has arranged for Christmas dinner for you, Ricky and anyone else."

Dahlia pursed her lips, readying an objection.

"You've done more than enough."

"No, no," I responded, firming up my voice. "It's just part of what we do. We have dinner delivered to your house Christmas Day."

I made a mental note to call the Hotel Savoy to arrange for a second catered meal for the holiday.

With a little friendly arm twisting, Dahlia gave in and told me she was having her parents over to her home for Christmas dinner.

I bid Dahlia and Ricky a final goodbye and headed home, very light hearted. Although I resided alone in an apartment on the Country Club Plaza, I did not feel as if I lived in an empty dwelling.

After taking dinner, I bundled up and went back outside. The Spanish style buildings of the Country

The Shadow Cast

Club Plaza, an elegant shopping district south of downtown Kansas City, were all decorated for the Christmas holidays. Despite being in the midst of the Depression, twinkling lights decorated the buildings, a bright reminder that despite the hard times, good times could still be had.

I wandered around the Plaza for a couple of hours. Each time I passed by a couple walking arm in arm or hand in hand, I could not help but practically stare at them. Often we exchanged pleasantries as we walked on in our separate directions.

By the time I returned to my apartment, rather late at that point, I wanted to ring up Dahlia Nicks. I held myself, controlling my urge to telephone this woman I had just met lest she come to conclude I was knocked off my rocker.

The next morning at the office, Margaret wasted no time in asking me how my return trip to the Nicks' home had gone. I almost broke down and told Margaret what was on my mind, perhaps even in my heart. I suspected that Margaret was well aware of my feelings. Nevertheless, I ended up telling her that all went "Fine, just fine."

I did end up telephoning Dahlia Nicks that evening on the pretense of finding out what menu she had in mind for Christmas dinner. I phoned her again the following day, a Saturday, contending I had accidentally misplaced the original menu. And on Sunday, I called Dahlia again saying that we had not discussed dessert for the meal, even though I knew we had chosen pecan pie and whipped cream topping.

The Shadow Cast

When Monday evening rolled around, I summoned enough courage to make a truthful telephone call to Dahlia Nicks. I spoke so rapidly, I was convinced that Dahlia did not understand what I had said when she replied, "Yes."

"You will?" I asked, surprised.

"Ricky and I would love to join you for dinner tomorrow night," Dahlia said, making it clear that she did understand what I had proposed, my invitation to her and her son.

The three of us dined together the following night and a full five more times before Christmas. Finally, Dahlia and Ricky invited me to join them and her parents for catered Christmas dinner at their little home. "And that," I told my little granddaughter sitting next to me on the beach some thirty years later, "that was my most favorite Christmas, I do believe."

She played with the new toy in her hands and I looked out at the ocean again thinking of all the other wonderful Christmases in the intervening years. She looked up at me with eyes as blue and almost as wide as the ocean and said, very seriously: "You know, Grandpa ..."

"What's that, dear?" I asked.

"My daddy's name is Rick," she said, adding, "And Grandma's name is Dahlia."

"I know," I said.

Sparkle's Gone

My seventh birthday ended up a big stinker. The day started out pretty fine, though. At eight in the morning my mom, dad and grandma Nanna came upstairs into my room, singing 'Happy Birthday,' waking me into what seemed to be a nice summertime day in my little hometown of Strasburg, Virginia.

My mom's mother, grandma Nanna, lived with my folks and me in our three story, tin-roofed house, painted a neat white, just across from the Parker-Fine Funeral Parlor on Oak Street in our little town of a thousand folks.

I never thought much about living across from the funeral parlor until 1967 when I turned seven, the year of my stinky birthday. But after birthday number seven, I would never look across the street from my front lawn the same again.

Mom and Nanna could carry tunes well. They both sang in the Shenandoah Baptist Church choir. All of the Archers in Strasburg, my family and my kin, went to worship every Sunday morning at Shenandoah Baptist. My dad did not sing with the Shenandoah Baptist Church choir because he was a musical fright. Despite his rotten-sounding singing, he was always the loudest even at Sunday services when the pretty-sounding choir sang, and certainly when my folks and Nanna woke me to the 'birthday song.' Dad also got the words to songs mixed all up most times. On my sixth birthday, Mom and Nanna smoothly sang:

194

The Shadow Cast

"Happy birthday to you!
Happy birthday to you!
Happy birthday Dear Clay!
Happy birthday to you!"

Dad, on the other hand, loudly managed:

"Happy day Clay!
Birthday to you!
Happy! Birthday!
Dear Clay!
To you"

Very loudly.

My dad's scratchings actually roused me from sleep, alarmed and terrified, until I saw the happy expressions of my family and realized the racket was only Dad trying out a song.

I scrambled out of bed after the bedroom concert, scrubbed my face and teeth, pulled on short pants and a clean T-shirt. Within the hour, three of my buddies would be over at our house; Kenny Walker, Patrick Jonas and Shoe Landeau. Shoe's name was really Mark. When we were in kindergarten the year before, Mark religiously put his shoes on the wrong feet after naptime, gaining the nickname 'Shoe,' thought up by Patrick Jonas himself. All the adults called Patrick Jonas 'clever,' Kenny Walker 'trouble,' and me 'nice.' Adults did not say much about Shoe, other than "he really tries, huh?"

Shoe's papa actually went to the Parker-Fine Funeral Home when we four boys were in kindergarten.

195

The Shadow Cast

Shoe's papa went boozing at the Harvest Pub in town and ended up getting smashed by a train after passing out on the railroad tracks while trying to walk home.

After I dressed, I wasted no time getting downstairs for breakfast and to wait for the arrival of my buddies. Because it was a weekday, the very first part of July, Dad had to go to work even though I was out of school for the summertime. Dad sold auto insurance from an office on Main Street in Strasburg. Nearly everyone in town who drove got their auto insurance from Dad, except for a spinster lady named Priscella Wayclocks whose house we all avoided on Halloween and when selling greeting cards for the school PTA. Even though our parents tagged along, except for Shoe's papa who was run down by the 525 to Baltimore, we never went to Priscella Wayclocks' front door.

Some of the older boys, from Mamie Dowd Eisenhower Junior High, did toss toilet paper into Miss Wayclocks' trees at the start of summer. I was surprised when the toilet paper did not burst into flames considering the witch us younger kids thought lived inside that house at the end of Maple Road, Miss Wayclocks.

Dashing into the kitchen on my birthday for breakfast, Nanna blurted out: "Our big boy!"

She said that, even though I was about the shortest boy in my school class, except for Freddy Tender. Folks around Strasburg said Mr Tender, Freddy's pop, still made moonshine even though it really wasn't necessary with package stores and all. Pastor Crimshaw's wife from Shenandoah Baptist Church said about old man Tender: "You can take some people out

196

of the hills, but you can't take the hills out of some people."

I didn't know what Mrs Crimshaw meant by that, but I guessed it had something to do with the Tenders coming from West Virginia and their having a still in their back yard and a 1948 Ford pickup truck in front, propped up on cement blocks. Anyway, Freddy Tender wasn't coming over for my birthday.

After Nanna proclaimed me a 'big boy' in the kitchen, my Dad piped up: "He sure as cotton is a big fellow." Dad's speaking voice was just fine, not rottensounding like the way he sang.

My mom, not to be left out, piped in: "My little man."

After she said her bit, she held up a plate heaped high with pancakes.

"Look, little man," she said, looking like a magazine model advertising a griddle. "Hotcakes!"

She put the platter of golden brown cakes on the table, where she'd already set out bacon, sausage, chopped up grapefruit and buttered grits.

We were all eating when Shoe and his mother, a woman my Mom called mousey, showed up on our front porch, lightly knocking on the door.

"I bet that's Mrs Landeau and Shoe," Mom said.

"Why doesn't she use the bell?" Dad asked.

Whispering, leaning forward and acting like Mrs Landeau could hear through brick walls, Mom replied: "She's mousey ... very mousey."

"I'll get it," I declared, jumping from the table and making for the door in a split second. I lead Shoe and his mousey mother into our kitchen. When Mrs Landeau saw Mom, Dad and Nanna sitting around the table crammed with food, I thought the woman was going to faint. I really saw the color just wash right out of her face. She gasped: "Oh, Lordy … we're early!" She looked directly down at Shoe. I thought, at first, she was checking to see if he had everything on the right foot. "Mark, I thought you said we should be here at nine o'clock?"

Before Shoe spoke, Mom got to her feet saying: "It's fine, fine!" She told them both to join us. Shoe looked to be about ready to take a chair when Mrs Landeau spoke.

"No, no. We've eaten."

She spoke in such a way that I imagined she thought Mom believed the Landeaus to be charity cases in need of food with Shoe's pop being squished by a train and all.

"Nonsense," Mom quickly replied. "Sit. Have some coffee, juice at least."

Mom shuffled off to the cabinet to retrieve fresh plates for Shoe and Mrs Landeau. I kept my eyes on Mrs Landeau who kept her own on Mom. Mrs Landeau looked like she didn't know whether to sit, run off or puke her guts out from nerves. She finally sat and I took to eating my pancakes again.

Mom dished up healthy servings for Mrs Landeau and for Shoe. They both looked at their plates like Mom handed over Martian food for them to eat. I figured Mrs Landeau felt she was being impolite interrupting our breakfast and felt impolite if she did not eat and had no idea what to do. I figured Shoe plain, flat out had no idea what to do.

Mrs Landeau finally poked at her eggs and, on seeing her move, Shoe dove in, finishing off a couple of hot cakes in nothing flat.

"When will you be back?" Mrs Landeau asked Mom after a few minutes.

"Oh, probably about nine or ten tonight. You know, the boys are just sleeping here."

Mrs Landeau nodded. I looked over at Shoe who was slurping on eggs.

"Can you believe it?" I asked my pal.

"Huh?" he asked, a glob of egg falling out of his mouth.

"Gross," I smacked. Shoe blushed. Mrs Landeau, taking it in – flopping yellow eggs and all – looked like she was about to faint.

Shoe mumbled an apology and I asked him again if he could believe our imminent good fortune.

When my other two buddies arrived, Mom was driving us off to Washington, DC an hour and a half away. Once there, we were off to the WWBC television studios to be on the 'Sparkle the Clown Show.' After that, pizza pies at 'Little Roma Pizza Palace' in Georgetown. Kids having birthdays and their pals got to sit in the audience and get introduced on the 'Sparkle the Clown Show.'

Shoe nodded and smiled, a shy boy's agreement that we had a grand adventure ahead.

Our breakfast group had nearly finished the meal when the front doorbell sounded. I darted out of the kitchen to greet the callers who turned out to be Patrick Jonas and his mother. Kenny Walker and his Mom were pulling up to the curb in front of our house at that very moment.

Within an half an hour, the visiting mothers were going their own ways and Mom was hauling Patrick, Kenny, Shoe and me down Interstate 66 to Washington, DC. We spent the first forty miles of our journey debating pizza toppings for that night's suppertime treat. Each of us boys favored a different topper and finally decided we would each choose one item when time came for supper.

Before noon we were motoring across the Roosevelt Bridge into downtown DC. We needed to be at the WWBC studio by two o'clock and Mom decided she needed to feed us boys. Mothers and food. Mothers and sleep. Mothers and baths. At least us guys enjoyed eating, especially getting meals out, which was a rare treat.

Mom was one of a handful of women in Strasburg in 1968 with a college degree. She spent four years at Georgetown University in DC and knew Washington well. She drove us to a sandwich shop on Capitol Hill, eventually finding a parking space not too far from the diner.

"Maybe we'll see the President," Shoe stupidly said as we walked down the sidewalk toward the sandwich place.

"Yeah, right," Patrick snorted, with all the boyish indignity he could muster.

"We might," Shoe plodded.

"Yeah, right," Patrick retorted, his tone remaining the same.

The Shadow Cast

"If I saw him, I'd kick him right in the nuts," Kenny blurted out, earning a swift, "Kenny, your language, please," from my Mom.

Kenny's brother Billy was off in Viet Nam. I figured he could kick LBJ wherever he saw fit because of all that war stuff and his brother having to fight and all.

When we reached the deli, Mom made us take seats at a table covered by a blue and white checkerboard patterned cloth, while she went to the counter. Knowing Mom, I understood that she did not want to endure four boys at the order stand trying to make up their minds on what to eat. Plus, we likely would each pick malteds and pie slices and nothing more.

Before too long, she joined us with a tray of sandwiches. A high school-aged girl who worked at the deli followed behind, wobbling a tray of sodas.

As we ate, our talk turned to the 'Sparkle the Clown Show.'

"Can you believe it?" I asked my pals again.

"Sparkle the Clown has been on TV since 1952," Patrick smartly advised.

"Maybe I'll kick him in the nuts then," Kenny pounded out for no obvious reason other than to nicely rile up Mom.

She did not disappoint and admonished my buddy with a seemingly stern: "Kenny ... your mouth ... please."

Shoe asked: "Does a clown even have nuts?"

The other three of us, plus even Mom, laughed.

Before long, we all piled back into the car and headed off to WWBC. We were at the television studios in no time at all.

The Shadow Cast

Not one of us four boys really knew what to expect of a television studio. We imagined quite a grand place, considering the importance of the work that went on there.

When Mom pulled the car off the road into the parking lot next to a building that looked like nothing more than a nearly windowless concrete rectangle, we assumed she was lost. I asked: "Are we lost?"

A bit of an edge existed in my voice, fearing we might end up being late for the show.

"We're here," she replied.

"Here?" I asked, puzzled.

Patrick followed my tone and wondered aloud: "You mean this is a TV studio?"

Kenny was looking around, possibly for nuts to kick. Shoe, having no concept of anything, was unfazed by our arrival at the gray concrete rectangle.

"Come on, boys," Mom directed, ushering us out of the car and down a concrete sidewalk that was the same dull color as the entire building itself.

Much to my surprise, and that of my three pals, when we walked into the studio building, we found ourselves in a warm looking reception area. I guess we all expected more concrete, probably even concrete furniture. Instead, the reception room had comfylooking sofas, chairs and tan shag carpeting that looked brand new.

In an instant, the receptionist directed us down a hallway which led us to a door outside studio number four where a line of other kids and parents was forming, waiting to enter into the happy domain of Sparkle the Clown.

The Shadow Cast

After we stood in the line not moving for several minutes, I complained to Mom that if we didn't get inside soon, we'd miss the whole show. An old man in an ill-fitting guard's uniform sat in a chair next to the door. While Mom assured me we would be inside the studio in plenty of time for the start of the show, Kenny looked at the guard idling doorside.

Kenny then leaned over and whispered to me: "I can kick him in the nuts."

He pointed towards the old fellow at the entrance. I giggled in response. Patrick tugged on my shirt wanting to know what Kenny said. Shoe was rocking back and forth in a manner that I knew meant he needed to pee. Looking at Shoe shifting around, I panicked.

"Good God," I blurted, repeating a phrase I heard Nanna use with some frequency.

"Clay!" Mom scolded, not pleased yet also puzzled. "What's wrong?" I
pointed at Shoe.

"What?" Mom asked, following the course of my directing finger.

"What?" she asked again.

Sounding rather like a parent himself, Patrick explained that Shoe needed to use the toilet.

"And we're gonna miss the whole show!" I moaned.

Quite like a ballet dancer I once saw, Mom grabbed a hold of Shoe by the hand and seemed to float down the hall back towards the reception area. She turned back to Kenny, Patrick and me as she walked on and told us to save a couple of seats if she did not make it back with Shoe by the time the doors opened.

The Shadow Cast

"They're never gonna make it," I groused to my remaining pals. "They're gonna miss Sparkle and the whole show."

"I should've kicked him in the nuts," Kenny said, being the one who made good sense at the moment.

Calmly, Patrick with his still father-like tone told us that he was sure Mom and Shoe would be back with us in plenty of time. He proved correct. And as if on cue, the old, rumpled guard opened up the door and began ushering the folks in line inside Sparkle the Clown's television studio.

Edging down the hallway closer to the door, I actually could feel my heart pounding in my skinny chest. I wanted to tell Mom and my pals how excited I felt; wanted to tell them about my hard-thumping heart. But, I just couldn't speak, not a single word.

Entering the studio, I gasped, my eyes darting from the stage and set that I had seen so often on my television at home to the three big broadcast cameras to the cluster of lights hanging from the ceiling. Most of all, I was immediately hit by how the studio felt. A blast of cold air greeted my Mom, my pals and me when we walked into the cavernous room. I shivered, my Mom catching the reflex.

She leaned over and explained to my buddies and me: "With all the lights and equipment and whatnot, they have to keep the studio very cool."

Learning these television secrets, which my very own Mom knew well was a moment of pride for me in the eyes of my mates. We took our seats in the studio and good ones we had, right up front, almost in the center.

The Shadow Cast

"This is so great!" I exclaimed.

Patrick, Kenny and Shoe all agreed. I'm sure Mom did too even though she got busy talking to another mother seated next to her.

For nearly ten minutes, the four of us boys kept our eyes peeled on the stage waiting for Sparkle the Clown to bound on out. We expected to hear Sparkle's happy: "Hey, ho, boys and girls … A hippy dippy to ya!"

And then we would say: "A hippy, dippy to ya, Sparkle!"

And we'd be saying it right in front of Sparkle, right on television, for the whole world to see. Even if it wasn't the whole world, it would at least be greater Washington, DC and parts of Maryland and Virginia, Mom explained in the car on the trip to the studio. She assured me everyone in Strasburg could get – *would* get – the broadcast.

Ten minutes passed, which seemed like ten years to me. I said: "Mom, if this show doesn't start rolling, I'll be an old man … I'll be seventeen before long."

Mom laughed, finding something or another humorous despite my most serious tone.

"It'll be fine," she assured.

"But Mom, the time," I pointed at my trusty Timex, a Christmas gift from the year before from Grandma Nanna that I wore to all major events like trips to be on television.

Before Mom could say 'It'll be fine' again, she looked at my watch, then her own. At about the same time, I became aware of similar rustlings around the studio.

The Shadow Cast

"You know," Mom said, realizing as I did that it was show time, in fact two or three minutes past show time. And the 'Sparkle the Clown Show' broadcast live.

The murmuring all around us increased, and one particularly boisterous mother blurted out for all to hear: "What's going on around here?"

I was most happy that my Mom did not grouch out loud like that woman. Before any one of the other mothers piped up too much, a pudgy, bald man with tiny round glasses, who was obviously sweating despite the polar temperatures, squirmed uncomfortably onto the stage. The entire audience piped down as if the little man on the stage had asked us to be quiet.

From where I sat in the good seats down front, I could see the man's eyes dart back and forth, right and left, like a white mouse in a cage in Mrs Grimm's classroom back at school. He finally spoke: "Boys and girls ..." he began, and then cleared his throat. I figured if he had a frog in his voice he should have cleared it out before he walked onto Sparkle's stage in front of all of us kids and our moms.

"Boys and girls ..." he said again, wiping sweat off his forehead with the back of his hand.

Kenny mumbled: "Gross." And I agreed by nodding.

"Boys and girls ..." he sputtered for a third time. "I have
news ..." He shook his head. Mom mumbled to the woman next to her:

"I bet it's the President, just like with Kennedy."

"Bad news," the fellow went on. "Sparkle's ... Sparkle's ..."

The bald man on the stage gave out a mighty sigh.

The Shadow Cast

"Sparkle's gone," he blurted.

"Where to?" I asked Mom in a heartbeat. She furrowed her brow and put a forefinger to her lips, seeming sure the little bald fellow would say more.

"Sparkle's gone," he said again. Tightly shutting his eyes, he spoke further. "Sparkle's passed on."

Horrified gasps and dismayed moans filled the auditorium. At that moment, my seventh birthday ended up a big stinker. But, I remained calm and still.

The pudgy, bald man repeated "Sparkle's passed on" a second time as if us kids hadn't heard the rotten fish news the first time. Mom looked like she was ready to clamp her hands over my ears like she did when bad speaking adults said something nasty in my presence.

All of a sudden Shoe Landeau burst into tears. He was the first kid in the whole place to cry and he turned out to be the only boy who really cut loose. I figured Kenny Walker would do some nut kicking if Shoe didn't shape up.

I leaned over to my Mom and whispered in her ear: "What do we do now?" I then added, as if my mom was somehow oblivious to the racked and sobbing Shoe: "Shoe's crying Mom."

"I know, I know," she said, speaking to me using a different tone than I had ever heard her use with me prior to that day. Stunned, nearly, by her inflection, her manner of speech, I asked: "What?"

Mom naturally thought I had not heard her and said: "I said, I'm not sure." The tone remained the same. "I think we need to get Shoe out of here."

"We?" I asked as I came to understand the reason for my Mom's vocal shift, her change in style. She had

The Shadow Cast

taken me into her confidence that day. On my seventh birthday, on the set of the Sparkle the Clown Show, I grew up a little in my own mother's eyes, and in my own.

"We need to calm Shoe down," Mom somberly said. "Let's get out of here."

With some effort, Mom and I were able to cajole Shoe out of his seat. Kenny and Patrick were at the door in no time. I overheard Kenny suggest to Patrick that they sneak backstage to see if they might happen upon Sparkle, or what was left of the dead clown.

With my newfound status in Mom's eyes, I was not pleased to hear the boys' conniving. I scowled my disapproval, which I was certain registered with Patrick and Kenny.

By the time we reached my mom's car, Shoe had pulled himself together, more or less.

I retook my seat in the front passenger spot, where I had ridden into the city earlier that day. But on this occasion, I felt different. I felt older, almost more like a person of my Mom's age than a squirrely boy like Shoe.

Although my seventh birthday ended up a stinker with Sparkle croaking off and all, I took my first, tentative step on a long walk that eventually led me out of boyhood.

There were still plenty of rafting trips left down the Shenandoah River with my pals. There was camping and other happy adventures in the woods of the Massahutten Mountains near home. There were other birthday parties. And, alas, there were even more than

The Shadow Cast

a few times when I cried, sometimes kind of like Shoe Landeau at the Sparkle the Clown show.
  But, I was on my way.

Sitting with Jackie

Soft candlelight from the votives flickered off the worn, silver rosary beads in her hands. She slowly made her way around the prayer chain, quietly invoking the Lord, the Virgin and the Holy Spirit.

She traveled by train the day before, from Winchester, Virginia. The train came to Winchester, the one that ran to Union Station in Washington near the Capitol building. The rail trip took over four hours, because of stops along the way, beginning in Front Royal and lastly in Arlington, before heading into the District of Columbia.

Her final destination was where she then sat in prayer: St Matthew's Cathedral off Dupont Circle, the young President's church.

The past few days had been long for her. At seventy-five years, and in fragile health, she tried to avoid events and situations, places and people that might cause her undue and unnecessary agitation. But there was no way she could avoid the horror and, finally, the sadness of recent events.

On the day it happened, she was in Robert E Lee Park back home in Winchester. She had a small bag of peanuts with her as she sat on the green painted iron park bench. She nibbled on a peanut or two and then tossed out several to the pigeons that collected about her perch.

The weather was brisk although she did not feel particularly cold. The prancing pigeons kept her mind occupied. Not far from where she sat, a younger woman, bundled up as if it were the depths of winter, sat on a bench knitting and listening to a tiny transistor radio. From where she sat, she could not make out a word. She could tell it was playing but the sound seemed so unclear to her.

She was scattering peanuts to the birds, but suddenly she was startled when the woman with the little radio all at once jumped to her feet, moaning as if in great agony.

"Bug bite" she imagined at first but soon realized that it was too late in the season for such insects. Before she could focus more fully on the plaintive sounds from the neighboring woman, that woman with the radio dashed over to her own bench. The neighboring woman held her little radio, clutched it madly.

"Listen! Listen!" the youthful lady implored, shoving the transistor unit in front of her. "Listen!"

Befuddled though she was, she nonetheless cocked her head to take in the broadcast. She at once became aware of a grim sounding voice, a man with a tone that suggested the weight of the entire world was on his shoulders.

And then she heard the news. The President, her President, had been shot in Dallas, Texas, a short time prior. The neighboring lady joined her on the bench and the two women listened intently to the broadcast.

Mike Broemmel

Neither woman said anything. Neither woman moved much at all.

The Shadow Cast

After what seemed like an eternity, the news broadcaster announced: "The President ... is dead."

As quickly as she could, she collected her wits. Arrangements needed to be made, she knew, and right away.

She purchased a train ticket from Winchester to Washington the next morning. The planned trip would be her first since moving to Winchester from the small town of Woodstock forty miles south in the Shenandoah Valley.

She moved from Woodstock some five years earlier after her husband died. Lung cancer took the man she spent forty-five years of her life with. They had no children and that always saddened her, but her husband worked for the Massanutten Military Academy and that brought them into regular contact with bright and, most often, polite high school aged boys.

The following morning, the day after she purchased the ticket, she was on board the train bound for the nation's capital. The day was sunny, the sun piercing through the train car's window making for comforting warmth, snug and tight. Had she not been heading to the District for such a sad occasion, to mourn the fallen President, she should have found the day pleasant, indeed lovely.

She dozed off for forty-five minutes towards the end of the rail jaunt, awakening as the train clacked and rattled to a halt at the Arlington Station.

Finally arriving at Union Station, she walked the several blocks to the massive national Capitol Building. A queue of mourners, a line of human folk longer than anything she had ever seen, stretched around the

The Shadow Cast

Capitol Building. Americans and other nationalities were waiting their turn to file by the bronze-looking casket.

She wished to join the queue but she knew her old, brittle knees could never manage the extended wait. The next day, however, she knew she would go to the Cathedral to properly mourn and pay her humble respects.

At around mid-afternoon, she trudged down Pennsylvania Avenue, away from the Capitol and towards the White House. Making her way down the expansive, grand avenue, with the fine museums of the Smithsonian off to her left and countless unidentifiable edifices housing offices of the government to her right, she struggled to fight back tears.

The familiar red, white and blue flags of the grieving nation, fluttered all around her, pulled only to half mast. People, young and old, joined her on the sidewalk and in the street connecting the presidential manse with the congressional edifice.

By the time she reached the White House, she was so out of breath that she had to grasp a firm hold onto the tall, iron fence enclosing the executive residence. Gasping for air, struggling to regain her breath, she looked across the neatly manicured lawn to the North Entrance, festooned in grim crepe of black, an honor guard resolutely on duty.

Keeping her eyes on the White House, outfitted for death, she found herself thinking of her own husband. For almost a full three years before he finally passed, he struggled, greatly and diligently, in an ultimately futile and fatal battle. Her husband was a proud man Mike Broemmel and showed her how to be a proud woman. All through the years of their marriage, he had worked custodial duty at the Massanutten Military Academy. Although his detail required the cleaning of latrines and chores of the like, he held his head high when he strode over and across the gracious campus. She knew her husband's tasks in life may have been simple but the man she loved simply did them well.

Her husband's harsh and long illness sapped their savings, leaving her penniless and alone. What little money she had been able to save and tuck away through all of 1963 and most of the year before had gone to purchase the train ticket from Winchester to DC and, after the funeral, back home again.

After standing in front of the White House for over an hour, she delicately crossed the street into Lafayette Park. She found a bench, much like the one she favored back home in Winchester at Robert E Lee Park. Just like at home she nibbled on peanuts, feeding a goodly share to the pigeons strutting near her feet.

When night fell, she curled up on the park bench and fell into a restless, anxious sleep.

The next day, she was transfixed, watching the procession down Pennsylvania Avenue. She cried, desperately, when the casson carrying the President rolled by.

After the sun set on her second day in Washington, some time after the President was laid to rest in Arlington National Cemetery across the Potomac River, she reached St Matthew's Cathedral. The Requiem Mass for the President had long ago ended.

The Shadow Cast

Even at the late hour, people sat and knelt scattered throughout the cavernous church, deep in prayer.

She slowly made her way up the main aisle of the Cathedral. She took a seat at the end of a pew in the front row to better see the altar and to be closer to her God.

She pulled her Rosary out of her worn woolen coat pocket and began her prayers. After finishing the first two decades on the blessed beads, she noticed a man's handkerchief, neatly folded on the pew next to where she sat.

Earlier that day, a black-clad woman seated in the same pew and attending the funeral Mass had used the pressed handkerchief to dab tears from her eyes, a linen piece she borrowed from her husband's closet that morning. Monogrammed on the white square cloth, in silken black thread, were the initials 'JFK.'

Victoria Regina

Barely sixteen, I tended the stables, along with my father. His wife, my mother, was on the kitchen service under the Royal Baker.

Mine was a lonely watch amongst the Queen's horses. I lived the life of a bat during those years of my youth; sleeping by day and attending my duties through the night.

At dusk, I reported to the stables where I would remain until the dawn. My actual regime was simple. Throughout the dark hours, I strolled by the pens, cleaning up promptly after any horse who defecated. I carted the manure far off from the stables, well out of sight and breath of the Royal household.

Since the death of the consort, Prince Albert, the Queen had taken to spending nearly all her time away from London. The Queen also enjoyed time at Osborne House. Most recently, she sought refuge far off in the Scottish Highlands at Balmoral with all her children save the Prince of Wales, who remained behind at the behest of Benjamin Disraeli, Her Majesty's Prime Minister.

I knew all of the scuttlebutt by listening to the older men tending the Queen's stables. I also well knew that not long ago the Prince of Wales himself took to be very ill. I knew not what afflicted the heir to the throne. No one spoke with specifics regarding what ailed his Royal Highness.

I did know that because of the Prince of Wales' poor health, Her Majesty and the rest of the Royal Family

216

had returned from Scotland that very afternoon, the first time the Queen had been at the castle and in London for a goodly time. I learned of her return hours after her arrival.

Regardless of the excitement amongst the servants accompanying the Queen's return, my life and my duties were unchanged. Reporting to the stables at dusk, I began my trooping of the stalls to remove and clean after the Royal beasts.

Sometime around the midnight hour, while I rested from hauling dung out of the stables, I heard the sound of someone walking down the main corridor of the stables, stalls lining each side of the walkway. Oddly, the steps taken were not the heavy plodding associated with the booted men who tended the Queen's steeds. Obviously to me it was a woman with light feet.

Still holding onto the fouled shovel I used to clear off the horses' waste, I walked in the direction of the slowly moving walker. Reaching the main corridor, I squinted in the darkness and did then make out a figure strolling slowly in my direction.

"Who would invade the Queen's stables in the cover of night?" I wondered to myself. "What woman walked before me?"

I do not know if the walking woman noticed me, although I stood directly in the middle of the long corridor. Even in the gloom, I could see that she looked into each stall she passed, as if checking on the horses.

The Shadow Cast

As the woman drew closer to where I stood, watching, I could see that she was well dressed in rich, heavy garments, a veil falling from the crown of her head and covering her face. As best as I could tell, the woman seemed to be dressed in black from head to toe.

I took a few cautious steps in the direction of the midnight trespasser, not certain as to what I should do or what I should say. No one came to the stables this hour of the night, let alone a woman who seemed to be on a casual, carefree stroll.

I thought the sound of my own boots on the floorboards would divert the woman's attention. Even though she was certainly aware of my presence, she continued her idle stroll, looking from stall to stall and horse to horse.

I walked a bit further, taking several more steps. In a few moments, the woman was but several yards away. And, at that moment, I made out the visitor: Victoria, our queen.

My mouth slacked open, dropping as I feared I would at any moment.

In my frantic head, I tried to recall all the rules of royal etiquette, which I really did not know, never imagining an occasion when I would so directly face the Queen.

"Perhaps," I thought, "I should just turn and walk away. Or, perhaps, I should drop to my knees."

Before I could consider all of my options, reasonable and right or unreasonable and wrong, she spoke.

"Good evening." Her voice was softer than I imagined a Queen to speak. She sounded no different than many of the handsome women I encountered in my regular wanderings about London proper.

I stood, silent. The Queen lifted the veil covering her face and let if fall behind her head.

"The horses seem well," she said, not so much addressing me but summing up her inspection of the stalls.

I managed a garbled: "Yes, Ma'am."

"And you are?" she asked of me, holding her hands together in front of her as my own mother did rather frequently.

Once more, I stood silent. I could not easily make out the expression on her face in the darkness. But, I thought I detected a smile.

"Young man," she spoke, more firmly yet not harshly. "What is your name?" "Randall," I muttered.

She did not hear me as I was not speaking clearly or loud enough.

"Speak up," she scolded.

Doing my best, I blubbered: "Randall."

With my name now between us, Queen Victoria extended a lace gloved hand in my direction.

"Well then, Randall, I am pleased."

I gawked at her hand as if I were looking upon an object I had never seen in my life. I did not know what to do. Was I to shake her hand? Was I to bow? Was I to say something to Her Majesty?

Nothing that ran through my mind seemed appropriate. I ended up making an awkward step in her direction, extending my arm slightly, and finally tangled up my own feet and fell to the boards. The shovel I had

The Shadow Cast

been holding went flying, a tiny spot of horse dung flying off the spade, landing on Her Majesty's chin.

Looking up from my less than advantageous place on the ground, I imagined that my Queen would promptly dash off to retrieve the Court executioner to have me summarily beheaded. Instead, she bent over a bit, gazing down at me with the same kind expression on her face.

She reached into a pocket somewhere on the side of her expansive dress and pulled out a delicate handkerchief. In one fluid movement she wiped her chin and returned the lacey cloth back to her hidden pocket.

"Randall. Are you all right, boy?" she asked.

My lips began moving, rapidly, but I failed to succeed in forming a single audible sound.

"Can you rise?" she asked, although I took her query to be directive and I scrambled to my feet.

Standing, I managed a muttered "I'm sorry, Ma'am."

I doubt she really could make out what I said to her, but the Queen gently nodded and advised me not to worry.

"I am," she remarked, "as you can see, in the stables. So I expect a dirty mark or so, Randall."

Despite her seemingly understanding words, there I stood in front of Her Majesty, Queen Victoria, of the United Kingdom of Great Britain and all her Domains, Empress of India, and so on and so forth. And, I had just struck Her Majesty in the face with horse dung, squarely on her chin. I nearly wet my trousers at the consideration of my harrowing circumstances.

"Walk with me," she directed. I took a post some steps behind Victoria, as I had seen one person or

220

another do at the Trooping of the Colours and other royal processions.

"Randall," she sternly stated after we had taken a few steps.

"Ma'am?" I asked, softly.

"I said walk with me, boy."

I scrambled up to the Queen's side.

"I thought ..." I started to explain that I believed I was to walk behind her.

"Yes, yes," she said. "At times, that is what we do. But, Randall, in the stables at night we can walk side by side."

She continued to make her way through the stables, walking down side halls and taking a look in each stall. By the expression on her face on each occasion, the Queen seemed to recognize each horse specifically.

We finally reached a stall where a horse had relieved himself and which I had not yet cleared off because of my walk with the Queen.

I gasped at the sight of the raw waste.

"What is it, boy?" she asked.

I pointed at the pile of wet and steaming manure.

"As I said, Randall, I expect a dirty mark or so in the stables."

"It's my job, Ma'am," I explained.

"I see. Well, do not let me hold you back from tending to your affairs. I shall continue to walk about and you meet me in the tack room once you finish with this horse."

I scrambled off to retrieve my shovel, leaving the Queen on her slow stroll about the horse stalls.

While I was cleaning up the stall, I heard the Queen calling for me from perhaps fifty yards off.

"Yes, Ma'am?" I shouted back, taking care to set my shovel aside to avoid any more mishaps.

"Come, boy," she directed.

Beating a rush, I was at her side in a matter of seconds. Sometime after I left to clean the fouled stall, she had lit a lantern and was intently looking into the stall directly in front of her.

"Look here," she said, nodding her head into the stall.

I looked inside the pen to discover a mare and her newborn colt, the little beast just then trying to get on his feet.

I gasped, this time with delight.

"Beautiful, is it not Randall?" she asked.

"Yes, Ma'am," I replied, keeping my eyes glued on the little colt.

Once the newborn colt managed to gain his legs, the Queen said: "Come along."

We walked to the tack room next to the stables where we milled about for a couple of minutes. I was certain that someone would come for her at any moment. Certainly queens, kings, princes and princesses were not to wander around in the middle of the night.

She started to head out of the tack room and I assumed I would dash back to my post clearing manure. Once more, she said: "Come along."

I felt I needed to tell her I needed to return to work.

"But ..." I muttered, again feeling like I could wet my breeches.

"You have somewhere to be?" she asked, her voice truly regal.

"Well, Ma'am." I cast my eyes to my boots, looking like a waif-like character by Dickens. "I need to keep the stalls clear."

With that explanation, Her Majesty tumbled into a deep laugh.

"My boy," she said, once stifling her hearty chuckle. "You would prefer clearing manure to walking with me?"

Instinctively, I replied "Yes Ma'am," believing I demonstrated devotion if not enthusiasm for my position at the stables.

She smiled broadly and made a remark I did not understand. "I would imagine my ministers feel the same but they lack the compunction to tell me so."

"Yes, Ma'am," I replied, not knowing what else to say.

"In any event, Randall, we shall walk." I wondered if 'we' meant 'her' or did she want me along? She solved my dilemma by stating once more: "Come along."

We walked slowly towards the castle itself, ending up in a well-tended rose garden.

"I enjoy the roses, Randall," she said.

"Yes, Ma'am," I replied, nearly mechanically, regimented.

"Do you?" she asked.

"What Ma'am?"

"Like the roses?"

"Yes, Ma'am, I do. Very much, Ma'am." "Good then," she crisply replied.

The Shadow Cast

I nodded, wondering if I had yet been missed in the stables. Surely no one would believe I had been walking with the Queen.

"My husband enjoyed these beds," she remarked, referring to the rose garden with an obvious note of sadness in her voice.

"Yes, Ma'am."

"He and I would walk here often, Randall."

"Yes, Ma'am. The Prince was a good man," I volunteered. "I often heard my father say 'The Prince was a good man.'"

"Yes, Randall. He was a good man."

"Do you miss him much, Ma'am?" I wanted to slap myself as the words tumbled from my mouth. I doubted a boy of my station was to ask a question of his Queen.

Her Majesty stopped walking before she spoke. I was certain I was in for a royal scolding.

"Randall, I miss him as if my own heart were stolen from my very body ..." Her voice trailed off into the night.

"I'm sorry, Ma'am."

The tiny lady stood on the tips of her toes and gazed up to meet my eyes. "Thank you, Randall. You are a most kind young gentleman. You make your parents proud."

I stood there mute, not knowing what to say in response to the Queen.

She stood, looked around at the fragrant blooms, and then bid me farewell. She walked off towards the castle, I on back to the stables. Every few steps, I turned around, looking over to the Queen until she vanished into the black of the night.

The Ladies of Eden Roc

"He did what?" Teda Fineberg asked her nearly constant cohort, Lilly Rosenthal.

"Umbrellas," Lilly replied. Both women had solid, stout, New York accents.

"What?" Teda rejoined.

"Umbrellas," repeated Lilly.

Teda and Lilly sat under a pale blue and white striped patio umbrella on the deck around the pool at Eden Roc Hotel on Miami Beach.

"Umbrellas," Teda repeated the word of her friend, pointing directly upward at the canvas contraption covering them both from the sun's late morning rays.

"Not umbrella-umbrellas," Lilly explained, raising her hand in front of Teda's face while holding her thumb and forefinger about an inch apart. In a slightly lower voice Lilly added: "Umbrella-umbrellas."

Teda mimicked Lilly's hand gesture and said herself: "Not umbrella-umbrellas but," and in a lower voice, "umbrella-umbrellas."

"Right," Lilly chirped, smoothing a hand over her shellacked bouffant hairdo. She kept her hair dyed fall apple red. A widow for five years, and in her sixties for seven, Lilly spent a month each winter at Eden Roc with Teda.

Teda, like Lilly, had a puffed and well teased hairdo, hers dyed jet black. At sixty-six, Teda was a year younger than Lilly, although she had been a widow for a year longer.

225

The Shadow Cast

Teda asked: "Do you mean umbrella-umbrellas?"
Lilly nodded.
"Like the tiny paper things in drinks?" Teda asked.
"Uh-huh," replied Lilly. "That's right."
"And he invented them? This fellow you met invented them?" Teda, part impressed, part skeptical, enquired.
"Uh-huh, that's right."
"Those little umbrella-umbrellas in drinks?"
"That's right," replied Lilly. "Uh-huh."
Solemnly, Teda noted: "I like those umbrellas."
Equally somber, Lilly herself remarked: "Oh my, so do I."
"They're swell," Teda said.
"Swell," Lilly concurred.
"And he's here?" Teda asked.
"Uh-huh. That's right."
"At the Eden Roc?"
"At the Eden Roc."
"I get those umbrellas a lot," Teda stated, almost to herself and not so much as a conversational point. In the same tone, Lilly quite agreed.
"He must have made a fortune, with those little umbrellas and all," Teda suggested.
"A fortune."
"A fortune?"
"A big one."
"A big fortune?"
"We should get lunch," Lilly suggested.
"Lunch?"
"Lunch."
"Now?" asked Teda.

Lilly nodded.

"Where?" asked Teda

"For lunch?"

Teda nodded.

"Wallace's?" Lilly replied, referring to a twenty-fourhour diner down Collins Avenue about ten blocks from Eden Roc.

"Walk?" Teda asked.

"Walk," Lilly returned.

"Walk, then?"

"Let's walk," Lilly affirmed.

"Now?" asked Teda.

"Now," Lilly replied.

The two ladies, each carrying an extra twenty or thirty pounds apiece, eased out of their respective chaises longue with noticeable effort.

"Diets," Lilly remarked. A mumbled statement.

"Yeah, yeah," Teda rejoined. In a mutter.

Once they were both standing, they each smoothed and patted their heavily hair-sprayed hairdos and sauntered across the pool deck to the entrance into the rear of the hotel's lobby. A thin-legged easel stood directly inside the rear doors that connected the lobby with the pool deck. On the stand perched a picture of the President-elect, John Kennedy, the man who inched to victory in the nation's election two weeks earlier. Both women had voted Kennedy and each took second glances at the handsome gent every time they passed to and from the passageway to the pool.

"Don't slip," Lilly cautioned Teda as she always did when they crossed the high buffed, shiny tiled floor. "Pool water!" Teda shook her head, scowling and scanning the lobby floor looking for errant drippings. They never found any during their stays at Eden Roc as the staff of regulars, a group of mostly Central American and Cuban immigrants, and a scattering of Jewish college age boys and girls working the holiday season, kept well-minded the gracious landings of Eden Roc.

Upon reaching the elevator, the women punched floor seven on the console and were back at their twobedroomed suite in little time. The ladies changed out of their lacey and ruffled bathing suits, reworked makeup and hair, and were ready to depart for Wallace's for lunch a little over an hour later.

"What's the time?" Lilly asked Teda as they adjusted hemlines in the sitting parlor of their suite.

"It's one o'clock, that's what it is."

"One o'clock?" Lilly sounded surprised at how much time they spent redressing and re-primping for lunch.

"One o'clock," Teda firmly replied, squeezing into a pair of size six shoes, two points too small. "My feet are swelling."

"They are not," Lilly retorted with an air of mild disgust. "They're the wrong size. You always buy the wrong size. You can't fit those sausages into a six, Teda Fineberg, or I'm Lauren Bacall."

"You're too old to be Lauren Bacall," Teda shot back.

"And your feet are too fat to squish in sixes."

As though none of the exchange had occurred, Teda happily said: "Ready?"

"Ready," Lilly replied.

228

The Shadow Cast

Teda wore a crisp, starched navy linen dress with gold buttons the size of small fists. Lilly chose a cotton two piece outfit, pale yellow with quarter-coin-sized dots in red. They each donned matching straw sunhats bought a couple of days earlier at a boutique on Ocean Drive.

"Where are we having lunch?" Teda asked as the two ladies made down the hallway to the elevators.

"We decided Wallace's," Lilly snipped.

"Well, that was an hour ago. I thought you'd change your mind like always," Teda snapped.

"Uh-huh. That's right," Lilly sarcastically rejoined. "It took an hour because of your fat feet."

"My feet?" Teda tersely queried as the lift doors slid open and the women joined two men inside, not pausing their conversation for a solitary pulse. "Uh-huh. That's right."

"My feet?" Teda repeated.

"If it weren't for your trying to shove your fat feet into those tiny, tiny shoes, we'd been ready to eat at eleven."

"Eleven?"

"Eleven."

"We weren't even in from the pool at eleven," Teda replied.

They reached the lobby where Teda asked Lilly if they were walking.

"Yes, let's walk."

"It's ten blocks," Teda reminded.

"Ten?"

"Ten."

They stepped outside and stood directly at the front of the hotel. A youthful bellman tipped his head towards the ladies with a smile.

229

The Shadow Cast

"What's the temperature?" Lilly asked the boy.

"Almost ninety." The smile he wore drooped in the heat the moment he uttered the mark.

"Ninety?" The ladies retorted together. "Oye Vey!" they exclaimed in unison. They asked for a taxicab.

"Right away," the bellboy responded, motioning for the first of four idling on the curb to pull into the hotel's roundabout to pick up guests.

"Tip him," Lilly whispered to Teda.

"Who?"

"Him." Lilly pointed at the bellboy.

Teda scrounged into her purse and pulled out a couple of quarters, which she handed to the eagerly helpful young man.

Inside the taxi they directed the Cuban at the wheel to ferry them to Wallace's.

"Da' stars, de' et der," he said, believing he was providing useful and tip enhancing information to tourists.

"What did he say?" Lilly asked Teda.

Word for word and syllable for syllable Teda precisely mimicked the man. Lilly groaned, irritated.

"Just go straight down Collins. We've been here a lot and don't need any running around. No foolishness," Lilly told the cabby.

The driver, whose English was limited, understood little of what Lilly said and responded with: "Yeah, yeah. Berry heated out, berry heated."

Teda began: "He said berry ..."

Lilly slapped her friend on the knee and scolded: "Quiet, just quiet down."

The Shadow Cast

In a few minutes, the yellow-colored cab pulled up next to Wallace's twenty-four-hour café, emblazoned with a neon sign that announced: 'Where The Stars Eat.'

Lilly and Teda piled out of the cab, Lilly grabbing the fare and tip on that trip. Lilly kept running calculations of who paid for what and when in an effort to keep balance between the two of them. Teda paid no never mind to who spent what for what.

The women had been seated a couple of minutes when a tall, silver haired gentleman, slim and trim and in his sixties, appeared at their table. Neither Teda nor Lilly noticed the gent's approach as they were well engrossed in another bout about Teda's feet.

"Miss Rosenthal?" the man interrupted.

She looked up, as did Teda, instantly. In a second the women locked gazes with each other, Lilly speaking as if no one stood next to their table.

"It's him," Lilly advised.

"Him?"

"Him."

"Who?"

"Him."

"Who's him?" Teda asked.

Lilly gritted her teeth, leaned in and whispered as best she could: "The umbrella-umbrellas man."

Teda's eyes opened wide as she knowingly nodded. Lilly blushed, realizing at the same instant that she'd forgotten the man's name.

"Hello," Lilly greeted, looking up at the lanky fellow.

"Hello," he gallantly replied. "And this must be your friend?"

"I'm Teda Fineberg," Teda responded. "Are you here for lunch?"

"Of course he's here for lunch," Lilly snapped.

"I meant," Teda retorted, directing her remarks squarely at Lilly, "Have you had lunch?" "I just arrived," the man explained.

"Join us, then," Lilly eagerly invited.

"Please do," Teda echoed. "Introduce us," Teda directed Lilly, near certain her friend did not recall the gent's name. An awkward silence followed during which the man extended his manicured hand to Teda.

"I'm Richard Therese," he said, speaking in the flat tone of a Midwesterner. Teda imagined Chicago, perhaps Omaha. Certainly not a Jew, she thought.

The women eventually ordered corned beef sandwiches and home fries while Richard Therese chose a patty melt with potato salad on the side.

"Lilly tells me you're at the Eden Roc," Teda said between bites on her corned beef on rye.

"I am."

"First time?" Teda asked.

"It is," Lilly responded for Richard, not wanting to get or even feel shoved out of the conversational flow for a moment.

"We go every winter. Five years now," Teda volunteered.

"Since both our husbands passed," Lilly added as Teda nodded.

"We both, with our husbands ... we all came to Miami Beach every winter for at least a month for years," Teda expanded.

"But since both our husbands passed, Teda and I come down together in November every year," Lilly continued.

"We stay through New Year's," Teda noted.

"We stay through New Year's," Lilly confirmed.

"Well, it's lovely here," Richard remarked. "Hot, but lovely."

"Today's especially hot," Lilly replied.

"Not normally so hot this time of year. Usually high in the eighties, but not ninety," Teda expanded.

"Not like today," Lilly remarked.

"Not like today," Teda echoed.

The conversation over the course of the nearly twohour luncheon at Wallace's meandered expansively. Richard ended up picking up the tab, over the firm and continuing protestations of both Lilly and Teda.

As they rose to depart, Richard explained that he planned to head down to Ocean Drive to do some window-shopping and invited the ladies along. They both declined in unison, bowing out because of their impending mid-afternoon naps.

"If we don't get our naps," Lilly whispered as if confiding a great secret, "if we don't get our naps, we can hardly move at dinner time, you see." "She's right," Teda concurred.

"Uh-huh," Lilly herself added.

"Well, then, how about joining me for dinner then, tonight at Eden Roc?" Richard invited.

Lilly and Teda looked at each other and shrugged, then agreed to accept.

"About eight then? At the hotel? I'll meet you both in the lobby."

The ladies again agreed.

"Then it's a date," Richard Therese said in parting.

Outside Wallace's, Richard first flagged down a taxi for his companions and then one for himself. During the cab trip back to Eden Roc, Teda asked: "When did you meet Richard?"

"Yesterday."

"Yesterday?"

"At the pool," Lilly noted.

"At the pool?"

"At the pool."

"I was at the pool," Teda remarked, a spritz of irritation in her voice.

"So was Richard."

"And why didn't I see him?" Teda asked.

"You went in."

"Went in? In where?"

"In the hotel," Lilly replied.

"Into the hotel? When?"

"Yesterday."

"Yesterday ... But when?" asked Teda.

"When I met Richard."

"I went into the hotel?" Teda did not recall leaving Lilly alone poolside. Before Lilly could answer, the taxi pulled up to the Eden Roc.

"It's your turn," Lilly sternly advised, referring to paying the fare and being the tab calculator.

Teda snorted, pulled some bills out of her purse and handed them to the driver. Entering the hotel, the ladies retired to the sleeping rooms in their suite.

Lilly covered her teased red hair in a navy blue scarf before lying back in her bed. Teda sheathed her coal

The Shadow Cast

black hair in a similar manner. Each lady kept the door to her room cracked open in case the other needed something during the mid-afternoon siesta.

Lilly and Teda were in the lobby a few minutes before 8:00pm.

"Eight o'clock ... awfully late for dinner," Lilly remarked, looking at her diamond encrusted watch, an anniversary gift from her late husband, given ten years earlier. Lilly was dressed in an orange summer dress that caused violence with her candy apple red hair.

"Oh, yes. Eight o'clock. Really, we've missed the good time to eat. We should have thought about that before," Teda agreed. Teda wore a similarly tailored summer dress, but colored in pale blue.

"And now he's late," Lilly remarked, still looking at her watch.

"Late?" Teda asked.

"Late."

"He's late?"

"He's late," insisted Lilly.

"What time is it?" Teda asked.

"7:58pm, on the dot."

"He's not late, then," Teda stated.

"He's late."

"He's not."

"He's late, Teda."

"It's not eight."

"He's late."

"Lilly ..." Before Teda could speak further she caught sight of Richard Therese stepping off the elevator. She glared at Lilly and pointed towards

Richard. Undaunted, Lilly mumbled something or other about their dinner host being late.

The trio adjourned to the dining room for their planned meal. Lilly and Teda rarely took their meals at the hotel, preferring to dine at the assorted restaurants and diners in Miami Beach that offered specially rated early-seating suppers. Teda figured the last time she actually had dinner at the restaurant at Eden Roc was with her husband before his passing.

During their dining the ladies learned more of their male companion. He explained that he had been born and raised in Kansas.

"Kansas?" Lilly replied, sounding as if Richard Therese had advised he was a Martian.

"Yes, indeed," he smiled.

"We've never been there," Lilly remarked.

"Not ever," Teda nodded.

"Well, I, of course, left after my bride passed on."

"Oh, my," Teda sighed.

"Yes, oh … my," Lilly remarked after her friend.

"We had a daughter and my wife died not long after that."

"Oh, my," Teda again sighed, as did Lilly.

"I raised my daughter … all on my own."

"How tragic," Teda remarked, catching herself by adding: "I mean, that you had to do it all alone."

Richard nodded. "Indeed."

"What was your wife's name?" asked Lilly.

"Hester."

"Hester," Lilly repeated, as did Teda.

"How …" Lilly said, meaning 'how did she die', which Richard understood.

"Cancer."

Lilly gasped, putting a hand to her mouth. Softly Teda said: "Cancer." "Yes, indeed," Richard confirmed.

"How tragic," Teda said a second time.

"Tragic," Lilly added.

"Tragic," Richard agreed.

"Where is she now?" Lilly asked, meaning Richard's daughter.

Richard, confused, did not respond at once. He finally said: "Well … dead," meaning his late wife, Hester.

Lilly gasped again. "Oh Lord!" She exclaimed. "Tragic."

"Tragic," Teda echoed, also believing, wrongly, that Richard was saying that his daughter had also passed.

Richard, realizing the mess, held up a hand as if to say 'halt'. "Now, now," he began. "I think I have confused you ladies. Hester, my wife, she's gone. But my daughter, she's quite well. She lives on Long Island in East Egg."

The two ladies prattled about how relieved they were to hear that Richard Therese still had his daughter.

"Would you dear ladies care for Champagne?" Richard eventually asked, seeming on the surface to want to divert the conversation from the wife he said had died and the daughter he said lived in East Egg.

"Oh my," Teda replied first. "No."

Shaking her overly coiffed head, her hair not budging with the movement, Lilly likewise said: "No."

"Ladies …" Richard tempted.

The Shadow Cast

"Oh, my, no," Teda repeated all the while Lilly continued to shake her head.

Teda averted her eyes from the table, looking around the Eden Roc dining room. Teda suddenly was awash with the memory of a quiet dinner years earlier with her husband and remembered the chilled, bubbling Champagne. At once Teda felt happy and ill, delighted by a light memory and pitted by the reality that the long ago night would never be repeated. An overwhelming desire to dash from the splendid eatery swelled over Teda, like the rush of breakers at the beach just beyond the walls of Eden Roc.

During Teda's wrenching introspection, Richard Therese continued to try and ply Lilly into concurring to a French bubbly order.

"Oh, what do you think Teda?" she asked.

"What?" Teda replied, far from the table in her lost thoughts.

"What do you think?"

"Think?"

"Think."

"What?" Teda asked.

Lilly nodded.

Richard said: "Champagne."

Teda responded with a vague "Oh." "So?"

Lilly asked, looking firmly at her friend.

"Oh," Teda repeated, still diffuse.

"Then it is," Richard definitely stated.

"What?" asked Teda.

"Champagne. Then it is," he said. He motioned for the server, quickly ordered and before long a bottle of decent vintage was tableside.

Before glasses were filled, Teda advised she needed to powder her nose.

"Me, too," Lilly chimed back and the two ladies adjourned.

"Hasn't this been fun?" Lilly twittered as they both stood in front of mirrors in the women's room. She rummaged through her purse as she spoke, looking for lipstick.

Teda, clutching onto a wash basin tightly with both hands, stared into the mirror directly in front of her tanned and freckled face. She did not respond to Lilly.

"Huh?" Lilly said, a lipstick pressed at her mouth, encouraging a response from Teda.

"Hasn't this been fun?" Lilly repeated, after spreading a rich red coat on her lower lip.

Nothing from Teda.

"Teda!" Lilly snapped, her upper lip without freshly applied color.

"Huh?" Teda responded, looking down from the mirror and into the basin.

"Teda, are you listening to me?" After making her terse toned query, she dashed the red stick over her thin upper lip.

"Yeah." Teda sounded noncommittal.

"Hasn't this been fun?" Lilly asked again.

"Yeah." Teda's tone did not change.

Lilly turned to face Teda directly.

"Well," Lilly stated.

"Huh?" Teda replied, keeping her glance turned down into the basin bowl.

239

The Shadow Cast

"Aren't you going to freshen?" Lilly waived her hands over her own face to indicate she meant 'retouch makeup.'

"I'm sick," Teda flatly responded.

"Sick?" Lilly immediately placed the back of her hand on her friend's forehead.

"You're burning!" Lilly exclaimed, blurting precisely what she would say whether or not Teda actually felt unusually warm to the touch. In Lilly's mind, a complaint of sickness coupled with a hand to a forehead always equaled imminent illness.

"Yes." Teda's inflection, tone remained flat, like morning grated and leveled beach side sand.

"Go to the room. You must go to the room. I'll come to the room. You're ill. You're sick." Lilly spoke with the clacking intensity and short flicks of a gambler's playing card clipped into bicycle spokes.

"No, you stay," Teda replied, looking at her lady friend for the first time since entering the women's room. "I'll go up, though."

"I'll come."

"No."

"I'll come."

"No."

"You'll need me," Lilly protested.

Firmly, Teda replied: "Lilly, go … go back and have Champagne. We can't just *both* leave Richard. He'll think we're rude."

"I'll come. You'll need me. You're ill."

"Lilly, I'll be fine." Placing her hands on Lilly's shoulders, Teda added: "I'll be fine. I just need to lie down. It's probably just something I ate, something not agreeing."

"I knew it," quipped Lilly. "I knew it."

Pulling back her hands, Teda asked: "What?"

"We ate too late, now you're sick."

In spite of herself, Teda smiled. She then led Lilly out of the women's room and motioned for Lilly to carry on back into the dining room. Before separating, Teda snugly hugged Lilly. "I'll be fine."

Lilly returned to the table the ladies shared with Richard as Teda walked from the restaurant into the lobby. Teda stopped short in the middle of the lobby, turning to look at the glass-paneled doors that led out to the pool. Beyond the pool lay the beach and the cool winter waters of the Atlantic. Shifting her direction, Teda walked towards the exit doors and passed through to the pool deck.

"Oye," she mumbled to herself, finding the evening air oppressively damp, humid, especially after the cool setting of the Eden Roc restaurant and lobby expanse. She shuffled across the poolside patio, populated by a couple of couples sipping wine and speaking at low pitch, the murmured, muffled sound of young lovers on holiday. In the dense night, and hearing the warble of the couples perched on the brink of adult life, Teda suddenly felt old. Plainly old.

Reaching an iron gate in a fence that separated the pool area from the hotel's claim of beach front, Teda sighed. She fumbled with the latch. She rarely walked out to the beach from Eden Roc, and always with Lilly or her husband; they had managed the latch before now.

The Shadow Cast

Eventually Teda succeeded in releasing the iron slider holding the gate in place but not before tears started pouring from her eyes and over her cheeks. She let loose with a deep sob, so significant that she snared the attention of the two previously preoccupied twosomes. Teda hurried off the patio and down a flight of wooden steps that led to the sandy shore of Miami Beach.

As best she could, she trotted across the sand away from the hotel, losing a slip-on shoe not far from the gate. Not bothering to stop and snare the errant footwear, Teda shook the remaining shoe off her left foot, continuing to move as quickly as her legs would allow. All the while, Teda continued to cry.

The winter swells of the Atlantic against the shore were particularly intense that November night. She reached the last slip of dry sand in less than a minute, trying to stop short to avoid hitting the beach at the breaker's edge and keep her feet dry.

The attempt to abruptly halt proved futile and resulted in Teda losing balance and toppling forward into the wet sand. She groaned at the impact, the force of the fall socking the breath from her lungs. She rolled over onto her back and rapidly panted trying to restore air to her chest.

The desire to fill her lungs hit up against her sobs, her real and plaintive tears fell in the sand.

Still struggling with air, a ripping breaker swung to shore, dousing her feet and legs with chilly night water. After being dampened by the crisp wave, Teda managed to pull herself to a seated position. At that moment, she heard the slap of bare feet, running on the

The Shadow Cast

wet sand, a growing sound heading in her direction. She looked to her right, in the way of the approaching runner. She barely made out a figure she thought to be a man.

A shiver went up her back, the result of the stranger closing in at her side. Before she could move any further, the runner, who indeed proved to be male, called out to Teda. "Are you okay?"

He repeated the question again in quick speed.

"Oh, well ..." Teda mumbled, planting her hands, palms down, onto the sand to push herself up. She was tottering to her feet as the runner slowed to her side. He reached out, taking hold of Teda by the arm to steady her.

Back inside Eden Roc, in the restaurant, Lilly and Richard Therese were well into the bottle of Champagne.

"So, you invent ... things?" Lilly asked of Richard.

"My whole life, my dear," he replied, with the dashing grace of a full gentleman.

"Oh my, how interesting," Lilly nearly gushed.

Richard leaned in closer to Lilly across the dining table. In a somber tone at low volume, Richard said: "I invented bouillon cubes ..."

"No!" gasped Lilly, her eyes splitting open wide.

"And cocktail umbrellas."

"No!" Lilly repeated her astounded rejoinder after which Richard once more nodded.

"I also invented the gas-powered Victrola years ago ... but that did not take off well."

The Shadow Cast

Lilly looked befuddled and uttered a baffled "Oh ... oh ... umm."

Richard carried forth with dribs and drabs of his life story, Lilly taking in less and less. She found her attention drifting to Teda. As the minutes ticked on, Lilly became preoccupied with Teda and her friend's wellbeing.

"Listen, Richard. I've had just a lovely time, really. Hopefully we can get together again, even tomorrow. But ... you see ... as I mentioned, as you know ... Teda's sick. I really need to get back, back to our room."

Richard smiled his understanding and gallantly bid Lilly goodnight with a kiss to her hand. Lilly scrambled out of the restaurant, took the elevator and made her way back to the hotel suite she shared with her friend. Lilly burst into the suite directly behind Teda, who had entered the room only a couple of moments earlier.

"Good heavens!" Lilly exclaimed, looking Teda over from head to foot. "You're wet, Teda, all wet."

"You must be spritzing something horrible," Lilly wrongly noted, bringing a slim grin from Teda.

"I fell," Teda explained.

"Fell?" Lilly asked.

"Fell, in the water."

"Fell in the water?" questioned Lilly. "In the bathtub?"

Teda's smile broadened, in spite of herself. "No, Lilly ... not in the bathtub."

Lilly's expression slipped from surprised to befuddled.

"I went outside ... to the beach ... to get some air," Teda explained. "I slipped in the sand, fell in the water."

"Your hip!" Lilly blasted. "You could have broken your hip!"

"Lilly, I'm fine," insisted Teda. "Fine."

Lilly fussed about Teda getting out of her wet clothing. "Put on your pajamas, your robe," she insisted.

In a short time, both ladies were wrapped in their bedclothes, covered with thick terry cloth robes, matching and rose-colored. The two old friends strolled out onto the balcony, overlooking the beach, and the black water of the Atlantic Ocean beyond.

"Lilly?" Teda asked as they both gazed out into the night.

"Yes, Teda?"

"What's to become of us?" asked Teda.

Lilly stood silent for a moment.

"I'm not sure, Teda," Lilly cautiously replied.

"Me neither, Lilly," Teda concurred, in a matching tone of voice.

"I do know one thing, though, Teda," Lilly remarked.

"What's that, Lilly?"

"You and I, Teda … you and I … we'll never be alone."

Teda and Lilly hugged and then turned back to look across the great sea.

Thanksgiving Callers

"Damn it, Ma!" I blurted at breakfast, sure that I sounded very adult.

"Kenneth Walker!" she shot back. I avoided her eyes and looked over to Pa who continued to shovel scrambled eggs in his puss as if Ma and I were not debating the merits of walking to Main Street to see the Thanksgiving Day Parade at noon.

Ma continued to speak, rapid fire, and directed her word flow squarely at my choice of language.

"A twelve-year-old boy does not use such language!"

When it came to Ma, a twelve-year-old boy like me pretty much did nothing, and anything I did was probably done incorrectly.

"Isn't that right, Russ?" she asked of Pa.

He obligingly nodded, continuing to stuff his cheeks with egg lumps.

"See, listen to your father," Ma said, referring to a man who never spoke. Listen to her, certainly, but Pa was a man of three words: 'Amen' at church; 'Yep' on occasion; and, 'Nope' once in a while.

"Why do I hafta go?" I asked, redirecting Ma to the real issue, lugging out to the parade.

"Your sisters want to go," Ma said, while three redheaded girls nodded madly at once. My sisters were all younger than me and looked like miniature versions of Ma. We had one older brother – Billy – who could not be home for Thanksgiving. Billy, the serviceman, was off in Viet Nam, some place a zillion miles from our town of Strasburg, Virginia.

"Your brother would go if he were here." Ma made her second point. When reasoning with me, when scolding me, Ma regularly pointed out what she imagined Billy would or would not do if present. I wondered …

"And, young man, we always go to the Thanksgiving Parade, don't we?"

I wanted to say 'damn it' again, or perhaps unfurl a new word I'd learned along the way in Junior High School. Instead, I groaned to make my point.

As it turned out, my point was not made as Ma spat out, just before sipping some homemade apple juice: "Good, I'm glad that's settled."

I matched my groan, to no avail whatsoever, finished my eggs, my sausage and retreated to my room for the inevitable trip up town for the parade.

The Strasburg, Virginia of my youth was a snug, homey hamlet nestled in the Shenandoah Valley. By the age of twelve I pretty much knew everyone in town by name, due in no small part to the fact that there were not many folks to name.

Truth be told, I enjoyed the Thanksgiving Parade. I liked all of our town's parades and the folk of Strasburg marched whenever possible: Memorial Day, Independence Day, Labor Day, Halloween, Thanksgiving, Christmas and, since I turned ten, even Easter. The parades were all about the same, only the colors changed. Marchers and floats, for example, were well decorated in red, white and blue on Independence Day; orange and black at Halloween; green and red at

The Shadow Cast

Christmas; and, most recently, pink and yellow at Easter.

Parade day gave me an extra chance to pal around with my chums up town when, otherwise, the entire day would have found me stuck at home with my folks, my sisters, and, by mid-afternoon, my grandparents in two sets and Pa's unmarried sister, Floreen.

Despite my actually liking the parade (if the truth was told, which I ensured would not happen), I was twelve, I was a boy. I felt in the same way Ma bitched over my language, Pa spent few words, my sisters giggled stupidly and served invisible tea to raggedy dolls, I was supposed to consistently gripe about family outings to civic events. We played our roles and life flowed smoothly through the valley, running evenly like the Shenandoah River in usually placid ways.

We ended up leaving home at 11:30 to make sure Ma was in plenty of time to glom onto her favored parade-watching spot at Main and Third. The parade route, always the same, ran from the post office at Main and First to the Cavendash Feed Store at Main and Eighth. Because the route was so short, the town fathers' – and in 1961 Strasburg like all of Virginia was tightly run by the men folk – horses trotted all through the marching line with rarely a mishap. My chums and I always hoped for mishaps. The best being when Old Man Twilliger's palomino pooped directly on Mayor Jeanette's wife's leg. Mrs Jeanette ended up screaming like a fright, so much so that the palomino spooked and bolted through the crowd and was not caught for two days. All this hoo-haw occurred at the first Easter

The Shadow Cast

parade, and I was amazed when another such event occurred the following year.

I spent the hour and some minutes up town during the parade festivities clowning around with my chums Shoe Landeau, Patrick Jonas and Clay Archer. We watched little of the marching and the floats and the Strasburg High School Marching Patriots.

I was home an hour before Aunt Floreen appeared on our doorstep. I answered her buzz on the doorbell and found her dressed true to form on the porch. She wore a red and black plaid skirt, like something I'd seen Catholic girls wear at the picture show in Richmond. Topping the skirt, Aunt Floreen wore a bright orange shirt with a strange tea-colored stain nearly covering one of the sleeves. Perhaps a coffee mishap, I thought. Or perhaps Aunt Floreen had some sort of run in with Old Man Twilliger's palomino.

On her feet, Aunt Floreen wore light blue shoes covered in sequins. She wore no stockings and her legs seemed nearly as pale blue as her shoes, absent the shimmer of the glittering pieces.

"Hello, Aunt Floreen," I greeted.

"Kenny, Kenny, Kenny," she said, poking me lightly on the tip of my nose each time she spoke my name. "How is my toodle-caboodle?"

I assumed she meant her butt and I was about ready to ask her to spin around so I could take a look when Ma appeared at my side.

"He's just fine," Ma replied, I guessed to the toodlecaboodle question. I did not figure out that I was the toodle-caboodle until Ma patted my head.

The Shadow Cast

"Damn it, Ma!" I blurted, intending to stand my ground and tell them both "I ain't no damned toodlecaboodle, and I ain't liking this head patting crap none either."

"Kenneth!" Ma immediately scolded, leaving me little time for anything else but speedy retreat into the living room where Pa adjusted the TV's rabbit ears to get ready for the football games to be shown. I escaped Ma, who fortunately was preoccupied with final preparations for dinner. My four grandparents, to a one, insisted that the holiday meal be served within a quarter hour of their arrival. They drove to our house together, both couples living about ten miles south on the Valley Pike in Woodstock, a town mostly like Strasburg.

I did not, however, escape Aunt Floreen. Off somewhere in the house I heard her calling, "Kenny?" and then again, "Kenny?" For a moment, I felt like we were playing 'Marco Polo,' but rather than respond "Polo" or "In here, in the living room, Aunt Floreen," I hung quietly with Pa who I knew would keep his lips zipped.

I wondered where my sisters had disappeared to. Before I figured out a destination beyond the living room where I could hide until dinner, Pa's sister entered the living room.

"There you are ..." she said, scratching her butt. If Ma saw that she would have made Aunt Floreen wash her hands before turkey. She plopped down on the divan, a heavy but not truly fat woman. She patted the divan next to where she took a seat.

"Come sit by me, Kenny-goo."

"Kenny what?" I asked, turning to Pa for relief. He seemed to be paying no attention, busy as he was with the rabbit ears.

"Come, come … my Kenny-goo." She patted the divan again.

Mumbling "ah, shucks" and "damn it," I slid in next to Aunt Floreen. "If only Billy was here," I thought. "If only Billy was home, he'd know what to do." Seven years older than I was, at nineteen, I believed Billy held all the answers to life's problems.

"So, Kenny-goo, how's school? Are you keeping with your studies?" Aunt Floreen's manner of speaking was classic Confederate or something of the sort.

"Yes'um, Ma'am," I replied, finding myself talking with a twang more distinct than my usual.

"Doesn't the house smell plum yummy, Kenny-goo?"

She was right about that, the smell of dinner in the making all over the house. Thanksgiving Day, and the smell of roasting turkey, fresh pumpkin pie, wheat flour rolls and everything else made me imagine what God's kitchen in Heaven was like everyday.

"Yes'um, Ma'am," I continued in my hypersoutherness, perhaps trying to match Aunt Floreen's own. "It all smells right nice." Deciding to try to draw Pa into my situation with Aunt Floreen, I asked over to him: "Ain't that right, Pa?"

Whether he paid attention or not to developments between Aunt Floreen and me, he said "Yep," and continued messing with the rabbit ears. They'd been adjusted once, but then he moved his chair and now the picture was fuzzy again.

The Shadow Cast

"Well, that's my special Kenny-googly-goo-goo-goo," Aunt Floreen blathered.

Aunt Floreen then asked me for a report on the parade.

"It was … nice," I said, not wanting to share with her the antics of my chums and me while folks dressed like gobblers strutted and clucked up Main Street.

"I didn't make it this year. I was occupied picking out my outfit for today," Aunt Floreen explained. Looking her over once again as she sat on the divan, I imagined a blind hobo could do a far better job of pulling together a wardrobe.

"And Billy? Have you heard from Billy?" she asked.

The mention of my brother's name brought a surprising "Yep" from my Pa who only just finished his fiddling with the television.

"Yes'um, Ma'am," I added, letting her know we got a letter from him on Tuesday. "How is he?" she asked.

"He's doing right well, Ma'am. Fighting the Gooks," I said.

Pa frowned at me, disliking my choice of language, I was sure. I muttered: "I mean the Viet Nam guys."

"Well, Kenny-doodles, Billy boy'll be home soon," Aunt Floreen said with the same tone of voice my math teacher used explaining fractions.

"Yes'um," I replied as the doorbell rang. Saved by the grandparents and a meal that would be served within fifteen minutes. Indeed, we were all around the table in just over ten minutes. Ma led us in a blessing.

"Dear Lord in Heaven, we thank You today. We thank You for our food, this meal. But mostly, Dear Lord, we thank You for our family gathered here today.

252

And, Lord, we ask You to watch over our Billy fighting for freedom and so far from home. Keep him safe, Lord. Amen."

The rest of us, Pa included, said "Amen."

About halfway through dinner, our doorbell rang again.

"Oh, heavens," Ma said, "I just bet that's Miss Grace. Who else could be calling on Thanksgiving?"

"Miss Grace" was Grace Plodden from next door, whose family ate Thanksgiving dinner in the evening.

"She said she was gonna bring over one of her gooseberry pies," Ma added. "You all just sit tight and keep on eating."

Ma got up and hurried out of the dining room to the front door. None of us paid any more attention to the doings in the entryway to our house, all of us preoccupied with the delicious spread in front of us.

A few minutes later, Ma walked into the dining room looking like a ghost with red hair. A couple of seconds later, a middle-aged man in a crisp army uniform came up from behind her.

Aunt Floreen was the first to start crying. My sisters and I looked at each other confused. The fellow in the army uniform softly said: "I'm so sorry."

And then I knew. For a fleeting moment before my eyes filled with tears, I thought of Billy at God's door like the Army guy calling at our own. I pictured Billy sitting in God's kitchen in Heaven having some turkey, some yams and a fresh piece of pumpkin pie.

Rocker Tales

As Randall Foster did each morning for nearly six months, he donned a broad brimmed straw hat, gathered his cane and walked up Collins Avenue. He slowly made his way up the bustling roadway until he reached 23rd Street. Turning left, he walked westward in the warm Miami Beach sun of late April.

Randall Foster was an old man, an ill man. Randall did not know of the brouhaha that the news reporters made over President Johnson picking up a beagle dog by its ears or that the man garishly displayed his appendectomy scar. Randall knew little about the President sending boys to rice paddies thousands of miles away to be shot in their heads and their hearts and to have their strong legs blown off.

It was not that Randall didn't care or chose to tune these occurrences and events out. Rather, he never tuned in at the first instance, at least not since his wife, Clarice, died a dozen years earlier. A wild eyed drunk cut through an intersection against the light, crushing and killing Clarice when she and Randall were out for a pleasant evening.

He and Clarice raised one child, a daughter they named Margaret. Only months before Clarice was killed, Margaret married a marine, a career officer, who eventually was swept up, shipped off to the war so far away. Margaret's husband was gone just two weeks when word came back that the good man was dead, killed by some sort of blast or bomb or explosion while scrambling over a flooded field.

Only days after the funeral, for which Randall traveled from Miami Beach to Atlanta, Georgia, Margaret learned she was pregnant. She begged her father to stay on in Atlanta. Randall begged Margaret to come with him to Miami Beach. Born and raised in Britain, Randall could never cotton to the American South. Despite its geographic position, South Florida was as far from the antebellum way as points north, New York City and Philadelphia and the like.

In the end, Margaret came to Miami Beach, sharing Randall's flat on Collins Avenue with him for nearly a year, until she gave birth and adjusted, a bit, to the prospects of new motherhood. When Eve, the baby, was four months old, Margaret and the baby moved to a peach-colored house about a mile and a half from her father's flat.

As Randall ambled up the walkway to Margaret's front door to spend the afternoon with Eve while Margaret went to work, Randall made a mental note to stop by one shop or another that dotted Collins Avenue to pick up a birthday gift for his granddaughter. Eve turned eight in a week.

Margaret opened the door before her father had a chance to press the buzzer.

"Hello, Dad," she greeted, looking and sounding tired. Margaret spoke in a voice dashed with a Bronx accent, coarse sounding and often strident. Unlike his daughter, Randall spoke in the fluid flourishes of his native London.

The Shadow Cast

Margaret was almost forty-years-old with coal black hair, cut in a simple bob and speckled with noticeable strands of gray here and there. Her skin was smooth, void of wrinkles, crow's feet and lines that might otherwise spill forth her age. Had she not had such dark circles under her eyes, nearly always, Margaret would look ten years younger than her true age, rather than the other way around.

"Love," Randall replied, crossing the threshold and giving his daughter a buss on her cheek.

"I probably won't be home until after midnight," she sighed.

"Well and good," Randall replied, smiling softly at his child. "We'll be fine, you know."

Margaret watched her father's loving expression, reached out and squeezed his arm. "I know, I know."

In the minute, the father and the daughter bid each other so long. Margaret, in a crisp white uniform, retraced her father's steps down Collins Avenue to 10th Street, crossing over one block east to Ocean Drive. Margaret, for several years, worked the tables as a waitress at the restaurant of the exclusive Tides Hotel.

With Margaret departed, Randall went to the small but nicely furnished and neatly kept family room next to the kitchen at the rear of the house. A more formal living room was situated at the front of the bungalow, furnished with lovely antiques of burled walnut and marble that belonged to Clarice, Randall's wife, and Margaret's mother. Margaret rarely used the living room, somehow concluding that disturbing the room might disrupt the memory of Clarice.

The Shadow Cast

A sofa with over stuffed cushions was centered on the far side of the family room, covered in green chintz with matching throw pillows. Under a pink flannel blanket, Eve was curled up on the divan, asleep.

Randall quietly took to the rocking chair, positioned next to the snug sofa. He picked up Bronte's Wuthering Heights off the coffee table in front of the couch. He had been reading it for a week.

After he had read for an hour, Eve awoke.

"Grandpa?" she said, sleepily.

"Love," he replied, returning the book to the coffee table, splayed open to keep his place.

Eve, keeping the blanket around her, over her shoulders, sat up on the sofa. Her towhead hair fell softly about her slender shoulders. Her delicate features, blue eyes, slim nose, reminded Randall of Clarice.

"Are you reading that book again?" she asked wryly, faking a tone that smacked of condescension.

"I am, indeed," Randall replied softly.

Mocking happily her grandfather's British accent, Eve remarked: "I simply don't see why you read such rubbish."

Randall laughed, reminding his granddaughter that Wuthering Heights was great literature, that she herself would enjoy Emily Bronte, perhaps all the Brontes, one day.

Keeping her faux-accent, Eve replied that she hardly thought so, after which she cut loose in a gale of merry giggles.

"Are you hungry, love?" Randall asked.

"Nope."

"Nope?" he mimicked. "That, love, is hardly a word."

She grunted, feigning disgust. "Tell me a story," she said before Randall remarked further about her language choices.

"A story?"

She briskly bobbed her blonde head.

"A story, love?"

"Yep."

Before he could correct her word choice, Eve stated: "Yes, Sir, please."

Randall glimpsed a fleeting image of a poor orphan in a Dickens tale begging for a ladle of gruel.

"Well, let's see," he replied, settling into a slow, easy tip in the rocker.

"Tell a story, from when you were a boy," she encouraged.

"From when I was a lad?"

"Yep ... Yes, please, sir." She smiled so broadly her grin seemed to stretch from ear to ear.

"Let me see ..." Randall continued. "Today instead of telling a story of when I was a lad, how about I tell you of when I met your grandmother, my Clarice?" Eve enthusiastically and sincerely agreed.

"I really was not much more than a lad when I first caught sight of Clarice, your grandmother."

Eve sighed. "I wish I'd known her."

"I know you do. And so do I." Randall looked into his grandchild's face and nearly saw Clarice, from another time, in another place, looking back. "How old were you?" Eve asked.

The Shadow Cast

"When I met Clarice, your grandma?" Randall thought for a few seconds, and smiled. "Just eighteen, just eighteen."

"That old?" the seven-year-old girl interjected.

"That's more than twice as old as I am." She added a quick "Sir" to ensure a smile on the old man's face.

"Ah, love, to be eighteen again, to be eighteen again," he replied, more to himself.

Randall went on to tell Eve of a dance, a festive event held every year when he was a boy.

"We lived in London, my parents and I, as you know, love."

She nodded.

"And every autumn, before the weather turned worse for winter, there was a grand dance ..." "Like Cinderella's ball?" Eve asked.

"You know, love, it was quite like the Prince's ball in your book, Cinderella."

She beamed brightly as if to encourage the old man to carry forth.

"Well, when I was eighteen, I went to the dance like always." Randall closed his eyes, tightly. "I can still see the beautiful gowns, I can. I can even smell the bouquets of flowers, even today. It seems only yesterday, love ... only yesterday."

Shaking his head slightly, Randall opened his eyes.

"And, love," he continued, "I had only been at the autumn dance just a few minutes, and there, standing not ten feet away, was the most beautiful girl I'd ever, ever seen."

"Like a princess?" Eve asked.

The Shadow Cast

"Yes, love, a princess. Just like a princess." He paused for a couple of beats and then told his granddaughter that the beautiful woman he spied at the dance – the princess – looked quite like her.

"Like me?" Eve asked excitedly.

"Your hair ... your eyes ... your cute little nose ..." Randall's voice drifted off as if he was carried off to sleep.

"And that girl ... she was my grandma?"

Randall nodded. "My Clarice." He continued, "At first, I was too scared, too scared to go up to her, to even say 'hello.' But finally, I summoned up my courage, you see ..."

A gay burst of giggling interrupted Randall; he knew the girl bubbled at his choice of words, natural to him yet foreign sounding to her.

"I walked up to her, told her my name. Before I realized what I was doing, I asked her ... asked Clarice ... for a dance."

"Just like Cinderella," Eve emphatically declared.

Over the next hour, Randall finished his story of the magical night, the cherished memory from an ocean away both in place and in time.

Randall and Eve spent the remainder of the afternoon and all the evening together. By ten that night, Randall tucked Eve into her bed and fell asleep in front of the television, not awakening until Margaret returned home from the Tides Hotel. She kissed her father on the cheek, which woke Randall.

"Everything okay?" she asked.

"We did just fine," he replied.

The Shadow Cast

"Why don't you just stay here until morning?" Margaret sternly suggested as Randall lifted himself out of the rocking chair.

"You know I can only really sleep in my own bed," he replied, referring to the stead he and Clarice had shared since their wedding night.

"Then, Dad, let me walk you home."

"Silliness, silliness," he rejoined. "I am a man quite capable of caring for myself, walking myself home."

"But it's late," Margaret protested. "I can get Carol to watch Eve for a few minutes," she added, referring to her neighbor, a woman normally awake all hours of the night.

"It's Miami Beach in the season. The streets are still filled with people and will be for hours to come."

He kissed Margaret on her forehead, collected his straw hat and cane and made for the door.

"Until tomorrow," he sweetly said, stepping out into the night.

Reaching Collins Avenue, bustling with lively people passing between bistros and bars, Randall casually strolled home at a sure and steady pace, firmly planting his oak wood cane into the sidewalk before pressing ahead with his unsteady left leg.

He passed the art deco buildings of South Beach, buildings like wedding cakes iced in pastel colored frosting. As was always the case, thoughts of Clarice invaded his mind. They had barely begun their life's chapter amidst the easy and the festive that was the southern tip of Miami Beach when the raging drunkard crushed Clarice at the busy intersection of Collins and 12th.

261

The Shadow Cast

Twice each day, both coming and going to and from Margaret's bungalow, Randall passed Collins and 12th. And on each and every occasion his stomach pitched and his sad, tired gray eyes blurred in tears. Each time drawing near the intersection, Randall necessarily stopped, leaned against a planter filled with brilliant seasonal blooms, and collected as best he could his wits, his bearings, himself.

The middle of the night proved no different, a shroud of darkness providing no cover, no relief. Through the happy gales of merry couples strolling the avenue in carefree abandon, Randall heard the screech and grinding of the careless driver's heavy auto even so many months turned years later.

In collecting himself at the planter filled with blossoms of gold, rose and snow, Randall thought of Margaret and became comforted by his daughter's strength. He thought of his little, blonde granddaughter, Eve, who needed him, needed her old Grandpa.

With his back against the stone planter, his head bowed down, he paid no attention to a young man, hardly twenty, and a young woman of the same age who stopped in front of him.

"Hey, Pops." The young man spoke out, his words slightly slurred from an evening in the drink. "Hey, Pops – are you cool, man?"

Randall raised his eyes, just taking in the faces of the couple before him. Rattled to be spoken to, he sounded harried, surprised when he replied: "Me?"

"Uh-huh, man. Are you okay?" The fellow asked of Randall again.

The Shadow Cast

Quickly standing erect, Randall told the couple shortly yet graciously that he was quite fine.

"Hey," the young chap rejoined, "you talk cool," he remarked, referring to Randall's full British accent. "You must be from France, huh?"

In spite of himself, Randall broke into a bright grin, a mischievous glint spiriting across his old face. "Yes, yes … France it is," Randall replied.

"Well, man, cool! You have a good one," the young man said as his pretty partner smiled sweetly and nodded.

Taking a deep breath of the warm night air, sea salt faintly tickled Randall's nose. He carried on the remaining paces to his flat, once shared with the late Clarice.

The next day and the day after and the one following that Randall repeated the stony routine. Friday as he sat in the rocker next to Eve, who rested on the sofa, nestled snuggly in the pink blanket, Randall's granddaughter asked of princesses and castles and knights – valiant in shimmering armor.

Randall chuckled and said he met a great princess, once, a Queen in fact.

"Silly, you did not," Eve, sounding wise, retorted.

"Ah, love, but I did," Randall replied, his gray eyes seeming to gaze off into the distance, not just in space, but of a time long since past.

Cautiously, thinking the old man was setting her up for a tease, Eve asked him to tell the tale. Pressing his shoes to the floorboards, he gently rocked the oak wooden chair.

The Shadow Cast

"You see, I was a boy, just about your age," Randall began.

"Almost eight," Eve boasted proudly and then fell into a fit of belligerent coughing. Randall comforted the child as best he could until the attack subsided.

"Are you all right, love?" he asked, a worried expression riddling his face.

"Shucks, yeah," she replied, hoping her improper grammar would not be corrected. "Tell your story, silly." She wiped her lips and forced a smile.

"Well, when I was a lad, my parents were in the service of the Queen ..."

"In England?" Eve cut in with a query.

Randall nodded. "Indeed. I, too, worked for Her Majesty ..."

"The Queen?" asked Eve, confused by the moniker used by the old man.

"Victoria, The Queen," he confirmed. "That's right."

"Victoria?" she repeated. "Why, that's Mom's middle name, Victoria. Margaret Victoria."

Feigning shock, Randall replied with a swift "Well, I'll be ..."

"Silly," Eve rejoined. "Just silly."

Randall continued. "My job, as a lad, was to tend to the stables. Not all together pleasant work, mind you, because the horses ... the horses could be rather ... dirty."

"Poop you mean," Eve interjected with knowing airs.

Hesitating a moment, mildly displeased with the girl's choice of words, Randall did agree.

"One night, I was at work in the stables, cleaning up after the horses," he carried on with the story from his youth. "I heard a sound, the noises of someone walking inside the stables."

"Were you scared?" Eve asked Randall.

"Scared?" he replied, thinking back on that night so many years distant. "I wasn't scared, love, as I think of it. Surprised, I suppose you'd say. You see, the person walking in the stables that night was Her Majesty ..."

"Her Majesty, that's the Queen, huh?"

"That's the Queen, love. You're right."

She beamed and asked Randall what happened next that night in the stables.

"The Queen," Randall continued, a misty smile crossing his face. "She and I walked through the stables, stall to stall, looking at her horses."

"The Queen's horses?"

"The Queen's horses, indeed," Randall confirmed.

Randall went on with his story of the stables at Windsor Castle, of his midnight encounter with the monarch, so many years ago when he was but a boy. Sometime during the course of the tale, Eve fell fast asleep, curled up on the sofa, snuggled in the pink blanket.

Randall finished his story of the British night before he realized Eve slept.

As the spring wore into the summertime and the Miami Beach weather became wilting, Randall found that although Eve still demanded stories and tales, she dozed off more and more often.

In the midst of June, the Floridian sun brutalized the realm. Even indoors, escaping the pulsing heat and swampy humidity was impossible.

The Shadow Cast

Rocking gently in his regular chair, wiping his damp brow with a handkerchief, Randall once more began the tale of Queen Victoria and the midnight walk through the stables. Eve seemed to enjoy the tale most of all, more than any other story he shared.

Midway through, Randall glanced at the sofa and saw that Eve was still, her eyes shut. She was seated, the blanket resting about her lap. Randall stopped speaking and looked at his little granddaughter long and hard. The sick little girl, Eve, breathed no more.

A tear rolled down the old man's cheek, then another. Sad though he was, in the depths of his tired heart, old Randall knew that somewhere, someplace his Eve walked hand in hand with his Clarice.

Leonard

"The lines are out," Martha, whose last name I could not recall, decidedly declared, flicking the toggle on the black colored telephone on the receptionist's desk at the Wayclocks Institute.

I moaned, sounding more like a gravely ill sort than merely a frustrated young doctor trying to telephone his newly wedded wife at home.

"The phone's down?" I asked, as if by phrasing the query, the transmission lines would blink back to life.

"Well, yeah ..." Martha replied, plopping the phone onto the cradle and looking back at me like I was a budding if not fully bloomed nincompoop.

I moaned, again, still sounding like a chap tapping at a grave's slippery edge.

"It's the ice," Martha flatly added, rising from the chair behind the desk. She rolled her eyes, intending the expression to communicate her annoyance with me and my growing agitation with being stuck at the Institute with no way to communicate with the outside world, most especially my wife.

As Martha prepared to take off down the hall, I groaned: "But its New Year's Eve ..."

With another roll of her eyes, Martha snorted and, with short and precise steps, made her way down the hall. After a dozen yards, Martha turned back to me and snipped: "At least our emergency generator works, Lance, and at least the furnace is going."

The Shadow Cast

Before I could respond, Martha carried on, the clickclick-clicking of her firm soled shoes echoing in the otherwise deserted corridor.

In fact, the day had not yet slipped to evening, but by three in the afternoon I had all but resigned myself to the creeping reality that, not only was I trapped at the Wayclocks Institute by the weather, but I was not even going to be able to telephone Mona, my new wife, on our first New Year's Eve as a married couple.

The entire Shenandoah Valley was gripped by the most wicked ice storm since the War of Northern Aggression some ninety years earlier. With the Valley frozen solidly still, I appeared wholly destined to spend the beginning of the new decade of the 1950's stuck, as quick as the ice outside, in the halls of the Wayclocks Institute.

The Wayclocks Institute was nestled tightly between the rises of two gentle mounts that contributed to the Massanutten range of the Blue Ridge Mountains of Virginia. As I was born and raised in the hamlet of Strasburg, at the northern edge of Shenandoah Country, the Institute, with its medieval spires, was a regular fixture during a good share of my twenty-eight years. An interruption of seven years occurred when I left the Valley for medical school at the University of Virginia, returning to do my residency at the Institute.

I was not entirely certain when the hospital of sorts opened its doors. I do know it was founded by one Hiram Wayclocks who ended up doing a modified swan dive off the north tower of the Institute, body slamming to his death in 1941. Since the suicide, the Institute had been overseen by his daughter, Priscella, who I long felt had less warmth than the presently frozen block solid Shenandoah River itself.

The site of my employment originally was called "The Wayclocks Institute for the Feeble Minded." Wisely, after her papa took his arcing finale, Priscella Wayclocks tidied up the firm's name to "The Wayclocks Institute."

Although the nature and scope of the Institute's operations changed through the years, it had ended up being a long-term care facility for persons with profound mental or physical conditions, often both.

Having plenty of time before I needed to start my late afternoon rounds, I plopped myself down into the chair at the receptionist's desk, the office furniture being well worn and obviously circa WWI. From the desk, I had a ready view outside the main entrance to the Institute, a clear vantage of the pounding winter sleet, tapioca sized pellets of ice raining down in terrific and grand cadence.

When I returned to the Valley just that past May to take up my residency at the Institute, Mona and I went house hunting. We settled on a farmstead with a 150year-old log house outside a tiny speck of a town called Toms Brook, five miles south of my boyhood home of Strasburg. We closed on the farmstead on June 1. After a stereotypical honeymoon jaunt to Niagara Falls, Mona and I moved into our house, our home, on June 15.

Looking out at the storm as the afternoon edged off into the night, I felt as if I had tumbled into grim, gray abyss. With the spitting ice, the dimming light of the cloud-obscured sun slipping from the sky, I could not

The Shadow Cast

even discern if I could see an inch or a mile from the door glass at the entryway to the Institute. Nature had created an impossible barrier, keeping me from my Mona, blocking my simple passage from the halls of the Wayclocks Institute.

While I was staring out of the glass of the doors, I heard the clacking of a woman's shoe heels on the corridor floor. I intentionally kept my eyes trained out, onto the sleet and ice and intense storm. Thinking I recognized the sharp clicks of the spiky heeled shoes, I hoped the walker would pass.

The stepping stopped exactly when a stern, familiar voice cut forth: "Priscella says you do floor five."

I did not move, kept my gaze and focus out of doors. "Hello again Martha," I retorted, trying my best to sound sarcastic.

"Did you hear me?" She demanded, leaving me to half expect she would stomp up and down like a naughty child.

"What? Hear what?" I replied, even though I clearly heard Martha advise that Priscella Wayclocks, the Institute's director, wanted me to take rounds on the hospital's top floor.

"You do floor five." Martha punched out each word with intensity born of well-rooted irritation. Her hands, fisted, were planted on her hips with the same firmness of her terse voice.

Still not looking at her, I rejoined with: "I never take floor five."

"Well, you do tonight. Priscella says so."
"Why?"

The Shadow Cast

"Doc Hollander can't get in, the ice and all."

"So?"

"So, Priscella says you're doing it, says you're doing floor five."

I sighed and shrugged, trying to appear cool, calm and completely collected.

Martha made some sort of disdainful snort, quite like a mouse sneezing, and clicked off down the hallway.

I shivered, perhaps because I was still looking out to the icy end of the day but more likely because I was directed to conduct floor five rounds.

"Food," I mumbled, determining I could put a top floor visit out of my thoughts by going to the cafeteria for an early supper.

I reached the cafeteria, picked up a molded tin tray and thought of prawns. My Mona intended to make a prawn stuffed pastry for our New Year's Eve dinner. Rather than my new bride's creation, I looked down the food line and saw I would instead have a murky stew, a corn kernel and carrot medley, over boiled new potatoes and an oddly tan-colored custard.

I took a table in the corner of the nearly vacant dining hall peopled only by a couple of staff members and no patients as yet. In the near still of the room, I heard the occasional clang of a pot or pan from the kitchen and the voice of President Truman on a radio somewhere in the vicinity.

My mama would not have been pleased. Rather then dive into my bowl of stew, I tapped the gray surface of the watery concoction with the tip of my spoon. With each tap of my spoon a little circular ripple spread out over the bowl like a pond splash from a tossed stone.

After fiddling with my supper tray for fifteen minutes, eating very little, I decided to make my way up to floor five for rounds. In my time at the Wayclocks Institute, I had not ventured to the top level, having no reason to do so. A long time staff psychiatrist, Doc Hollander, nearly always took care of floor five.

Occasionally, I heard rumblings and mumblings among the staff about the few patients that actually were housed on floor five. All I really recalled from the slanty gossip was that the small number of patients on the top level had been living at the Institute for years. They did not venture from the top floor.

I assumed the handful of floor five residents were particularly infirm, aged, crippled, incompetent or an unwholesome combination of age, ailments and afflictions, but I realized as I left the cafeteria that I had no certain idea what to anticipate and expect.

I collected my stethoscope and white coat and headed up the stairs. I diverted on floor three, my normal stomping ground, to let the charge nurse know I would be doing rounds a bit later than normal.

"Happy New Year," I sarcastically greeted Helen, a fifty-something nurse who had been at the Institute for over thirty years.

"Right-o," she replied, with equally dim dash, looking at me over the top of half-moon reading glasses on a rhinestone chain.

"I'm going to be a little late for my rounds," I said.

With a wry expression, Helen flatly replied: "I'll alert the newspapers."

"I'm doing rounds on floor five."

When she heard of my detour, Helen plucked the eyeglasses off her face. "What?"

"Floor five. I'm doing the rounds."

"You're what?" Helen sounded as if I'd told her I was headed outside to dance naked in the ice storm. I replied: "I'm going outside to dance naked in the ice storm."

"That's what I thought you said." Helen paused for a moment then added: "You're doing floor five rounds?" I nodded.

"You?" She sounded incredulous.

"What do you mean: 'You'?" I asked, defensively.

She waved a hand in front of me and explained better what she meant. "I am surprised that you got this assignment, really. I am surprised that anyone but Doc Hollander, Priscella or Nurse Kemp is taking floor five." I shrugged. "Just wanted to let you know." At a whisper, Helen wished me luck.

I continued my trek up to floor five, reaching a small staff station occupied by Nurse Kemp I presumed, although I realized I had never met that particular RN.

Nurse Kemp looked impossibly old and so wrinkled it appeared to me that all the skin from the back of her body had somehow been pushed to the front side. She was scribbling on a pad of paper and did not stop writing, let alone look up to acknowledge me at the station.

"What?" she sniped, carrying on in her preoccupation.

"Rounds," I replied, sounding like a worried schoolboy called on by a ruler-wielding teacher. "I'm to do rounds. Martha told me so."

The Shadow Cast

Nurse Kemp slammed her pencil onto the desktop and looked up at me with a frightful glare. "What?" she asked, sounding aghast.

"Rounds," I muttered.

"Who told you to come up here?" she demanded.

Before I could completely get out Martha's full name, Nurse Kemp sternly asked, with all the warmth of a stony nun: "Does Miss Wayclocks know of this?" I nodded.

Unsatisfied, Nurse Kemp yanked the phone off its cradle and quickly connected to Priscella Wayclocks. The conversation was brief and I was left with the clear impression that the Institute's director must have told Nurse Kemp I was the only one available to do floor five rounds.

"Be quick about it," Nurse Kemp directed, tersely, replacing the phone on its cradle with one hand while waving me off from her station with the other.

In short speed, and upon looking at the first patient, I discovered why floor five generally was off limit to most of the staff of the Institute. Pushing open the door of the room housing an eighty-year-old female patient, I found a frightfully wrecked human. The octogenarian had a solitary and oversized leg, no arms and a face and head that looked to have been mashed by some sort of immense roller.

Despite my training, I found it difficult to look directly at the woman, most especially her platter thick and moon round head. Indeed, I imagined I was taken aback by the woman's look, shape, condition precisely because of my training as a physician. A human woman should not look like the lady prone and unspeaking in the first room I visited on floor five.

After checking her vital signs and making due notations on her chart, I carried forth from room to room. In each instance, I came upon more peculiarly shaped, oddly constructed human creatures; all aged, non-speaking and staring remotely at the ceilings above their settled bedsteads.

The last room I had to tend was reached with relief on my part. I felt as if I had visited a carnival sideshow freak review without the hullabaloo of the barkers, carnies and crowds that made such obscene human twistings somehow palatable, at least for the moment of the exhibition.

Taking a stout inhale, I pushed open the door. The final room was more dimly lit than the others. Instinctively, I looked to the bed in the center of the room, finding it empty. Imagining this patient to be quite like all the rest, I immediately surmised he or she had rocked or slid from the mattress to the floor.

Before I was able to scout the obscured side of the bedstead, a smooth sounding voice etched out from a dark corner of the room. "Hello," the male pitched voice greeted.

Startled, I jumped back and towards the door to the room. In the faint light, I was halfway able to make out the shape of a small figure seated in a chair tucked snugly against the corner intersection of two of the room's walls.

"Hello," I replied, hesitating. "Are you ..."

Before I could finish by asking the patient, he spoke again. "I am. I am Leonard." "Leonard?" I asked.

The Shadow Cast

"Leonard."

My eyes adjusted a bit more to the low light and in a moment I took a better picture of the patient. He looked to be significantly younger than the other wracked bodies I had seen that evening. But had it not been for his soft, gentle tone of voice as my eyes focused on Leonard's person, I likely would have had to bolt from the room, his being so harshly alarming.

The man on the chair had a body the size of a stringed puppet, probably not more than three feet tall in all. His feet barely reached the edge of the wellcushioned chair.

However, it was not the size of Leonard that caused my alarm at the moment. Unnerving beyond anything I had seen that night was Leonard's head, as it were.

Connected to the man's shoulders was a foot long growth of flesh, cylindric in shape and looking quite like a neck, a very long neck. The expanse above his shoulders was flat at the top, and the whole portion devoid of hair.

Had it not been for some peculiar deviations in the flesh that looked most like a neck, I would have immediately thought Leonard actually was headless.

Pinching my eyes with one hand and grabbing my gut with another, I moved in closer to gain a better look.

Towards the top of the neck, I noticed a thin slit in the flesh that seemed to be upturned in a kind of smile. The gash seemed to quiver, slightly so slightly. While I tried to better examine the slit, Leonard spoke again and the gash opened as he formed words – his mouth, of sorts. "How are you?" he asked.

I nodded, speechless.

The Shadow Cast

Above his slit of a mouth, near the top of what could only be considered an elongated neck the more I examined it, were two round holes, bored in directly to the flesh without rise – his nose, I guessed.

And on either side of the makeshift nose, nostrils only really, were the eyes, Leonard's eyes. The one on his left was small, very small. Much tinier than a dime, the left eye was midnight black, as if entirely consumed by pupil.

As opposed to the left eye the one to the right was enormous, the size of an orange or an apple or some other hand-sized fruit. The right eye was rich green in color, lush like a valley alfalfa field in late spring.

Politely, because I really had not appropriately responded, Leonard asked me again: "How are you, Doctor?"

I managed a weak "Fine ..."

Leonard extended his right arm, which was very small, slight and disproportionate like that on an illdrawn stick figure by a scribbling grade schooler.

He wanted to shake hands, common enough. I struggled to raise my own arm, my fingers shaking slightly as my body continued to react to the person of Leonard.

Leonard's hand, so small, his bones so tiny, was only able to clasp onto a couple of my fingers, like a small child shaking 'hello.'

"Rounds," I muttered, as he said: "Good to meet you, Doctor."

"I imagined," he replied to my furtive mumbling.

I proceeded to collect Leonard's vitals, fumbling as I went.

The Shadow Cast

"New?" Leonard asked.

"What?"

"New? Are you new?"

In the instant, I realized my fumbling and groping about must seem the antics of a new physician. "No, no ..."

"I never have seen you here before. Of course, normally I only see only Doc Hollander, Nurse Kemp and Miss Wayclocks," Leonard explained. "Dr Wayclocks would call on me from time to time, before he ... died."

"Died," I repeated.

The slit on Leonard's neck turned upward again, apparently an understanding smile.

"Died, I suppose is the nice way of terming what poor Dr Wayclocks ended up doing to himself," Leonard noted.

I nodded, agreeing.

"He was not all that terrible," Leonard volunteered. "Oh, at first, I was more of a specimen to the fellow. But, in the end, he'd come up and play chess with me, play chess with me with good regularity."

The thought of Dr Wayclocks enjoying a chess game or any leisure activity, with anyone, let alone one of his patients, flummoxed me fully. "Dr Wayclocks ..." I began.

"Played chess with me, yes," Leonard stated, finishing my thought.

"I'm ..."

"Surprised that he would take the time?" Leonard again completed my thought.

I nodded.

The Shadow Cast

As I watched Leonard, and listened to him speak, I came to realize that only the very large eye ever blinked shut. The tiny one always remained open, wet and staring forth.

"The weather, it's bad?" Leonard asked.

I nodded, yet another time.

"Not a talker?" He asked me, looking to be smiling once more. His soft voice was lulling, almost calming.

"I'm sorry," I replied, shaking my head briskly as if to better collect my thoughts and myself.

"Not to worry. Your name?"

"What?"

"Your name?" he politely asked again.

"Jeannette ... Lance Jeannette."

"Dr Jeannette, good to make your acquaintance." I managed a feeble: "Me, too," gulping after I spoke.

"I've been here since I was a baby," Leonard stated, as if anticipating directly my own likely question. "Thirty four years, more or less."

"A long time," I remarked, my voice finally sounding a bit firmer.

"A long time, yes," he agreed.

"And you?" he asked.

"Me?"

"How long have you been at the Institute?"

"Not long, really. But I'm from the Valley."

"I hear the Shenandoah Valley, it's nice," he remarked.

"You hear? What do you mean?" I asked.

Again, Leonard's speaking slash curled into a smile, of sorts. "I've never seen it, except for what I see from my window here." "What?"

The Shadow Cast

"I've never seen it …" His voice trailed off.

"But, what do you mean?" I asked, glancing at his chart. "You've lived here for over thirty years."

Gesturing with his tiny hand at the end of his fragile arm, Leonard replied "Here, yes. Here." "You mean …" I started.

He nodded. "This room, it's my home. My place, you see."

"You never …"

"Never. I've never left this room. Not since I was a baby, that is. Not once."

A bundle of questions trundled suddenly through my head. I wanted to ask: "Did you learn to read … How'd you learn to speak, even … Where are your parents … Does anyone see you, come to visit you?"

Leonard spoke; again seeming to somehow nip at my very thoughts. "Dr Wayclocks, he taught me to read. My parents, I have no idea where they might be. I doubt they are alive any longer. I hear tell they were unusually old to have a small baby when they brought me here years ago. And, well … of course, Doc Hollander comes to see me. Nurse Kemp, too. And Miss Wayclocks, she comes by regularly."

"Why don't they take you outside?" I asked the moment I thought of the question.

"I expect they think my constitution can't handle the out of doors."

"Oh."

"You, Doctor … you should be home, being it's New Year's Eve and whatnot," Leonard said, shutting his large eye in a thoughtful blink.

"The storm …" I replied.

"Bad?" he asked.

"Yes, bad. Can't go anywhere." "Sad,"
Leonard remarked.

I nodded in agreement and told him I had only been married a short time and really wished I could be with my new bride.

"Of course … I expect so," Leonard replied.

"Do you ever …" I started to ask when Leonard completed my query.

"Want to go out, leave my room?"

"Yes."

"I used to want to leave, go out of my room," he replied, closing his large eye as if in thought.

Slowly, I eased down to sit at the edge of the patient's bed, just across from the chair in the corner on which Leonard sat.

"And you never did … could … go out?"

"No, Doctor, never did … never could. Eventually, you see, I never thought about the out of doors, not any more."

"Did Doc Hollander figure you'd become ill or something if you went outside?"

Leonard opened the large right eye. "No, you see, Dr Wayclocks, when I was just a child, he determined I would stay indoors."

"But …"

"Why?" Leonard finished.

I nodded.

"My constitution, I expect. Dr Wayclocks, and then the
others … they determined my constitution could not handle the out of doors."

The Shadow Cast

Leonard and I ended up spending nearly half an hour in conversation when Nurse Kemp barreled into the room, charging like a hunting horse onto a fox.

"Why are you in here still?" She demanded as I sprung to my feet from the bed.

"Rounds," I muttered. "My rounds."

"I am sure, Doctor, that you are done."

Leonard put one of his small hands up to and over his large green eye, the slit of a mouth turned down into what looked to be a frown. He seemed to slump in his chair.

"Out you go," Nurse Kemp shoved me, her tone terse and unyielding. Despite being the doctor and she the nurse, I obeyed, just as a primary grade student shuffles at a teacher's command.

I made off down the corridor with a dour Nurse Kemp directly on my heels.

"Tell me ..." I began, wanting to know more about Leonard.

"You're finished here, Doctor," she replied. "Your work on floor five is done tonight."

We neared the stairwell. "But, can you tell me ..."

She gestured at the stairwell. "Good evening, Doctor."

I wanted to stand my ground but from the nurse's sharp expression, I certainly knew that I would obtain no information from her about the oddly formed patient named Leonard.

Four days later, after the bitter weather cleared out of the Valley, more or less, I had occasion to visit the office of the Institute's director, Priscella Wayclocks. Well on my mind since taking floor five rounds was

282

Leonard, more so than the other patients I had encountered on New Year's Eve.

As is the norm on the occasion of my trips to Priscella Wayclocks' office, I found the director behind her desk scratching on a sheet of paper, with a substantial mound of documents and forms requiring her attention piled in front of her.

"Good morning, Miss Wayclocks."

"Hello, Doctor," she replied, at a monotone and not looking up from her work. "Sit, sit," she added and I took one of the chairs in front of her desk.

"What do you need, Doctor?" she asked.

"Need?"

"Uh-huh."

"Well ..." I hesitated. "It's not that I really need anything." I did not really know what to say.

Priscella Wayclocks pushed out air, a gesture that could only be pegged as a thoroughly exasperated sigh, bordering close to a groan. She looked up, glared, from her work.

"A social call, then, Doctor?" she asked.

I realized that despite what I imagined her age to be, somewhere in the seventies I guessed, Priscella Wayclocks had a remarkably smooth face. I rather thought she must have dyed her hair, given the black hue. But, Priscella Wayclocks never seemed one to succumb to the vanities and perhaps her hair preserved like the unwrinkled skin of her face.

Had she not been afflicted with what seemed to be a permanent glower, Priscella Wayclocks might be considered attractive, in a chilly, Virginia winter sort of way.

The Shadow Cast

"Social?" I stammered. "Well, no ... not that."

Tapping the tip of her pencil on her desktop, rapidly, she replied: "Really, Doctor, I have work."

"I'm sorry," I said, and I was sorry for making the decision that propelled me into her office.

"You see ... it's this ..." I tried.

"It's what?" she snapped, hardly amused with my near boyish banter.

"You know, I did rounds on floor five."

She nodded and added: "New Year's Eve."

"Right."

I did not continue speaking quickly enough, allowing for Priscella to speak out with: "So?"

"Well, it's like this ..."

Lagging again verbally, I did manage to speak just as Priscella opened her mouth but before she verbalized.

"There is a patient up there," I continued, after a bracing inhale, "Leonard, the patient, he never gets out."

I stopped speaking. She said nothing, her typical and usual scowl in place.

"And?"

"Like I say, he never gets out. Even from his room. I think he could, you know, go out."

"Yes, of course, physically Leonard can leave his room. But, Doctor, the emotional toll on Leonard should he leave his room would be too great for the man to bear."

The words flowed from Priscella Wayclocks' lips with precision, as if a prepared statement.

Again, I did not carry on quickly enough.

284

The Shadow Cast

"Doctor, is there a point?"

I shifted my weight from side to side in the chair and then back once again, feeling all the more like a school boy at teacher's desk. "I was just wondering, with Leonard … can he go out?" And, in my mind, the pangs of youth cemented with the "Can Leonard come out" phrase.

"Out?" Priscella asked, a baffled tone.

"Yes."

"Out?"

"Yes, ma'am."

"What is 'out,' Doctor?"

"Out, out. Can Leonard go out … from his room?"

"You mean into the hallway, the corridor?" she asked, her confused sounding voice unchanged.

"Or outside … outside." The words rushed from my mouth.

Instantly, Priscella looked at me as if I had grown green horns while I stood in front of her desk.

"Outside?" incredulous, Priscella Wayclocks asked.

I nodded, barely.

"Out of doors?" she asked, enunciating each word with drilled precision.

I nodded, barely, once more.

She laughed. Priscella Wayclocks spat with brittle laughter, a crackling rife as if jocularity in any form long ago abandoned her being. She finally managed a barely decipherable: "You're kidding, right?"

I replied by asking the Institute's matron if Leonard of floor five was too ill to be out of doors.

"What do you think, Doctor?" she queried, posting her words in thick disdain.

The Shadow Cast

"Think?"

"Think, Doctor. Perhaps if you thought before blabbering you'd not come up with such nonsense at all. At all."

Suddenly, I felt emboldened, oddly so. "Well, why can't Leonard come out, go out of doors?"

Before Priscella could rejoin, I forged ahead. "I saw his chart. I can see no reason why Leonard can't come out of doors. I've seen his chart and ..."

Priscella Wayclocks cut in with a tough and terse: "And, Doctor, you've seen Leonard."

I stood, my mouth agape and speechless. Eventually, Priscella spoke. "You see, Doctor, it's not a question of whether Leonard's capable of being out of doors. Surely, he is capable. I don't know of any health consideration that would prevent Leonard from going out of doors. But Doctor, you see, the out of doors, what lies outside this building, Leonard does not belong there. The people who live out in the world, they do not want Leonard nor any of the others on floor five near them. The people who live out in the real world, Doctor, they have a right to take their walks, go to market, worship at their churches, without the likes of Leonard intruding on their respectable view."

Statement made, Priscella mechanically returned to the paperwork on her desk. Without a specific directive, I realized I was dismissed. Slowly I shuffled from Priscella Wayclocks' office.

For the rest of the day, I found it impossible to relieve my thoughts of Leonard. I began to plot courses by which I could return to floor five and pay a visit to the little man. No matter what I mentally planned, however, my designs were quickly dashed. Absent an assignment to carry out rounds like on New Year's Eve, I knew gaining access to floor five through the centurion that was Nurse Kemp would prove impossible.

Six days later, in the night as I lay asleep with my young bride at my side, the phone rang in the kitchen. I am not sure how long the phone jangled, the kitchen being downstairs from the bedroom my wife and I shared.

Death. Someone had died. One of my parents. Or one of my wife's folks were dead.

Barefoot, I hurried down the stairs, across the lower floor of our house and into the kitchen. Snatching up the phone, I certainly sounded frazzled.

"Doctor? It's Priscella Wayclocks," the caller advised.

"Thank God," I gasped.

Obviously understanding or at least anticipating the sort of greeting she received, Priscella made no remark.

"We have troubles here, Doctor," she said, her voice astoundingly even-toned and paced for a person facing problems. Before I could ask "what" or say "Oh, my," Priscella Wayclocks continued. She explained that Doc Hollander had died.

'Death,' I thought. 'Someone really had died.'

"He lived in Winchester, you know," she said, referring to a community North of the Institute.

I did not, but said "uh-huh" anyway.

"We need coverage, temporarily, for floor five. Doc Hollander did all regular checks on floor five." She paused for a moment and then asked if I could come in.

The Shadow Cast

"Now?"

"Please," replied Priscella. Never had I heard stony Priscella Wayclocks say "please", "thank you" or any words of the sort.

"Okay," I replied. "Of course."

Clicking off the telephone, I hurried upstairs and told my bride I was off to the Institute. While I threw on my clothes, I told my wife about Doc Hollander's death, Priscella's call and the need for "coverage on floor five."

"That's what she said?" my wife asked.

"Right." And with a kiss to her cheek, I was off.

Reaching the Institute about half an hour later, I found Priscella Wayclocks waiting for me at the main entrance, standing in the lobby illuminated only by a red glow from a couple of directional exit signs. The director looked as well molded as if the hour were three in the afternoon rather than the same clock twist in the morning. I realized at that instant that Priscella Wayclocks was a formed creature as opposed to a styled and daily reconstructed person.

"Doctor," she greeted.

"Morning," I replied simply.

"You've done floor five once before, so I guess you know the routine."

I nodded and asked who else would be responsible for rounds on the top floor.

"For the time being you and I," she explained. "We'll make do."

"Do you want me to check on things now?" I regretted my turn of phrase. Priscella Wayclocks was not one for casual reference. I imagined because of the odd hour she allowed my verbal sloppiness to slide and only nodded in reply.

I went up to floor five, half expecting to find Nurse Kemp posted at the nurses' station, a part of me imagining she never left. An equally stern, dour looking woman in crisp white, a nurse I did not recognize, was seated at the station. She only nodded, once, and did not speak, at all, when I walked near the station.

I hurried through rounds, saving Leonard's room for last. Entering into the little man's chamber, the place of the patient with the queer, narrow neck-like expanse between his shoulders that made for a head, I well expected to find Leonard asleep, in bed. In fact, I jumped back and felt my blood surge in shock when an even voice greeted me as I slowly, delicately, opened the door. "Hello, Doctor."

I imagined I noticeably started, a flinch noticed by Leonard. "Oh, my," Leonard went on to say, "I alarmed you. I startled you. I'm sorry."

The diffuse light slipping in the room glinted off Leonard's large eye. I could not make out the small, black eye in the near darkness. Leonard sat in the same chair I'd seen him in on my first visit to floor five.

"Leonard," I sighed, regaining my calm, my composure. "I'm okay."

"I'm sorry … I did not intend to alarm." Looking at the oddly shaped man, I wondered if he could blush. I often saw a person's cheeks become ruddy in situations like this. But Leonard, he really did not have cheeks, even really a brow let alone a chin. "I'm fine."

"Good, then," he said, sounding satisfied.

"Rounds," I sputtered, more to direct myself than to inform the patient.

The Shadow Cast

"Of course, yes," he knowingly replied.

I walked to Leonard, took his arm to take his blood pressure and check his pulse rate. As I worked, I inquired as to why he was awake.

"I sleep only a little," he replied, a sad glint in his voice.

"A little?"

"Yes."

"A few hours?"

He chuckled. "A few hours and I might even have a real dream ..." His voice trailed off. He mumbled something I did not catch when I finished with his vitals.

"What?" I asked. "I'm sorry ... I didn't hear what you said."

"Nothing." His inflection was such that I imagined Leonard would have been pouting if his features allowed.

"You sound ..." I started to speak but did not know precisely what to say. "Sad?" I thought Leonard sounded sad.

"I'm well," he volunteered.

"So, you don't sleep more than three hours?" I asked.

He twisted his elongated head, as if to shake "no." He said: "less than three, most often."

"That's not enough," I advised.

Ignoring my remark, Leonard asked me what I dreamt of when sleep came.

"Dream about?" I asked.

"Yes," he replied.

"What do I dream about?" I asked, mostly of myself as I rubbed my chin for a moment. I quickly dropped my hand to my side, pulling it away from my face. I realized I should have no more stroked my chin in front of a man without one than I should have wiggled fingers in front of a person lacking digits.

"I guess I dream of many things," I finally, generally, responded.

"I dream of little," Leonard remarked. "All I see, ever, in all of my dreams is this room. All of my dreams play out … play in … this room."

Confused, I asked Leonard what he meant.

"You see, Doctor, you take in different sights every day. You don't even know you do this. Different sights you see every day."

I nodded, suddenly feeling bad about bobbing my head in front of Leonard in the same way I earlier regretted rubbing my chin. With nothing separating what made for Leonard's head he certainly could not nod even though he struggled with a stiff twist intended as a shake earlier.

"I see only this room," Leonard said without a tinge of bitterness or anger or frustration in his voice. He spoke nonchalantly, remarking in a tone I would use if I noted the obvious that I did not stroll about on planet Venus.

"I'm not sure I understand," I finally conceded.

Leonard replied:

"Consider the blind man, Doctor." He paused, obviously leaving me an opportunity to reflect on a blind man. He continued:

"A blind man, a man blind from birth … when he dreams, Doctor, he doesn't actually see anything in his sleep. He hears his dream, of course. But when all is

The Shadow Cast

done, a person can only dream about things he has actually seen or heard." He took a deep, labored breath. "I see this room, Doctor. And my dreams ... they are limited to this room."

I understood. Dreams were fanciful, naturally. But dreams were built on what we see in the light of day.

Whispering, I said "I'm sorry" to Leonard.

"Sorry?" he asked.

"I'm sorry," I repeated. I wanted to explain that I was sorry that we, his doctors, his nurses, that we stole his dreams, literally snatched away Leonard's dreams. I guessed that we took care of his body as best we could, but what had we done to Leonard's soul? Or his dreams, his only means of escape from that room? All I could manage, again, was a feeble "I'm sorry."

"Doctor, here there is no fault. Within these walls there is only reality."

With my new duties, I would see Leonard a few times every day after the wintry night in January when I was called to the Institute. I never broached the subject of dreaming again with Leonard, although I think it was always on my mind during my thrice daily trips to floor five.

Spring came to the Shenandoah Valley early that year, pleasant weather pushing away winter's chill by the middle of March.

Crocuses, tulips and daffodils were in glorious bloom, around my house and at other well tended plots over Shenandoah County. Luscious sprays of red, pink, orange and yellow, clipped and snipped from beautiful gardens were everywhere. These colorful greeters called in the parlors and foyers of nearly all homes.

The Shadow Cast

Despite the spring-burst of vibrant hues, I easily noticed that the Wayclocks Institute remained steely gray, the somber tone of winter, the funereal shade of the tomb.

Although I often considered asking Priscella Wayclocks if I might take Leonard out for a stroll on the grounds, I knew her answer would be a firm and definite "no." Instead, I asked Priscella if I might, from time to time, bring a bouquet of flowers from my wife's garden to place in a vase in the lobby of the Institute.

"What?" she asked, not angry or threatened, but confused by my suggestion, my request. "Flowers," I said again.

"Flowers?" she asked, seeming to have trouble with pronunciation as if I had uttered an exotic word in a foreign tongue.

I stammered, as I often did when with the director. "Well, yes. From my wife's garden. I thought I'd put them in the lobby. I thought it'd brighten the place up, it being springtime and all."

She looked at me for nearly a minute, a quizzical glint to her eyes. And then, I actually thought I detected a shiver of a smile slipping over her lips.

"Yes, then," she said. "Flowers in the lobby. I think that might be fine."

And so, every couple of days, my wife would snip a fresh clutch of blooms from the garden and I would take them to the Institute. After a couple of weeks, Priscella Wayclocks stopped me in the corridor when I was on my way to floor five.

"You know, Doctor," she began, hesitating. "Those flowers, in the lobby … those flowers are really quite nice."

293

The Shadow Cast

She walked away without another word and I carried on, ending up in due time once more in Leonard's room.

I surprised even myself when I blurted out upon entering the room words that sounded especially stout. "You know, Leonard, I'm going to get you out of this room. It'll do you good."

Leonard sat silently, awkwardly. In a couple of beats I apologized for sounding so rash. He assured me he was not offended or upset. Although I verbally backed off my firm proclamation, in front of Leonard I silently vowed to follow through on getting Leonard out of his room. Somehow I built a flimsy connection between Priscella Wayclocks allowing flowers in the lobby and the possibility of obtaining her permission to escort Leonard from his closed room.

All the following week I stewed, devising scenarios by which I could get little Leonard from his room. I found myself thinking of Leonard and the world outside his room often. At Sunday church services I dashed off mental scripts I might use on Priscella Wayclocks to convince her to allow Leonard a respite in the corridor or even out of doors.

Sitting in the snug confines of River's Edge Baptist Church, I let my schemes wander to the more obstinate. I envisioned sneaking Leonard out of his narrow room and into the bright light of the Shenandoah spring. With most of my week far afield from Pastor Wanamaker's pulpit, I often contemplated Leonard's stealthy exit from the Institute's stony walls.

I discussed my ruminations with my bride. Mostly she called me silly, and giggled.

The Shadow Cast

Finally, on May Day, I had occasion to go to Priscella Wayclock's office to discuss a new admit to the Institute. The day dawned spectacularly, not a cloud in the sky and a gentle, soothing breeze wafting down the Valley.

When I reached Priscella's office, not long after arriving at the Institute, after coming in from the out of doors, taking Leonard beyond the walls was well on my mind.

"Tell me something," I eventually and politely requested of Priscella, after we had discussed the new admission to the Institute.

"Yes, Doctor?" she replied, sliding a couple of sheets of paper across her desk, a movement that I took as a sign that the director was ready to end my audience.

"I was wondering ..." I began, then improvidently faltered. Priscella waited in silence for several beats, finally repeating "Yes, Doctor?"

"I was wondering ... about Leonard."

She nodded, pushing a couple more pieces of paper over desk.

"What do you think about me taking Leonard out on the lawn? It's such a pleasant day and all."

Priscella commenced the movement of another two slips of paper as I began my query. She stopped halfway across her desk when I completed my statement. She responded, looking me directly in the eyes.

"What, Doctor?" she asked, her voice maintaining her standard lack of inflection.

The Shadow Cast

"I mean," I stammered, "Would you think Leonard might be able to come outside?" In an instant I felt again like a schoolboy asking a neighboring mother if Johnny, Tommy or Timmy could come out and play again.

Priscella pursed her lips and scowled. She said nothing for nearly a minute.

"Well, then," she finally flatly stated. "Leonard ... out of doors?"

I posted a feeble head bob.

"I see," she said, her expression remaining unchanged.

Priscella rose from her desk, turned away from me and walked to a window to her right and a few yards away. In the meantime, I fidgeted nervously in my chair, wanting to bolt from the director's office. I knew better than to speak any further.

After a couple of minutes, Priscella retook her seat behind her desk. "Doctor ..." she said, reconnecting to me with a dead on stare. "Yes."

I sat stone still, not understanding Priscella's conclusion.

"What?" I asked, my own tone belying my true confusion.

"Yes, then," she replied. "Leonard ... out of doors. I think that might be fine."

In spite of myself, my jaw dropped. Priscella kept her eyes well locked onto my own. Before I spoke, moved or even properly closed my mouth, a queer little smile wafted across Priscella Wayclock's face.

"Doctor?" she said.

"Yes ... Yes ..." I fumbled.

The Shadow Cast

"Go on, then," she said. "Get Leonard. And take him out of doors."

She broke her gaze with me and recommenced the movement of papers to and fro about her desk.

Upon leaving the director's office, I found myself sprinting down the corridor and up the stairs to floor five. Out of breath, I reached Leonard's room in little time.

"Leonard!" I excitedly greeted to the little man seated at his chair.

"Good morning, Doctor," he replied.

"Leonard!" I said, fighting to catch my breath. "We're going outside! Right now! We're going outside."

I drew close to Leonard with the intent of helping him up from his familiar perch. Bending down, I immediately saw that tears were welling up in both of his eyes, the large one and the small one. "Leonard," I said. "Are you … all right?"

"Yes, yes, Doctor … I am."

"But, why are you crying, Leonard?"

Several seconds passed before Leonard spoke. "You see, Doctor …" he replied, "tonight … tonight I'll be able to dream … I'll be able to dream of the sky, the sun … I'll be able to dream of the grass … and of the flowers."

Umbrella Man

I wandered the long, winding rural road alone. The crisp April morning air was bracing and pleasant. Off to my right and off to my left, as far as I could see, were fields of green, inch high growth just pushing through the black Kansas soil.

The green expanse, from horizon to horizon, met with the rich blue of the early morning sky. Not a cloud, not a sprinkle of white, did I see anywhere.

I landed as the pastor of the small Catholic parish in Rossville, a small town nestled just west of the Kansas capital city of Topeka, two springs earlier in 1948. I hailed from a small Iowa berg, Otterville, and went from my boyhood home on a farm to Saint Meinrad's Seminary in Indiana then on to Saints Peter and Paul Catholic Church in Rossville.

Mondays, from the end of March until mid-October, I reserved for long early morning walks along the meandering dirt and pea gravel roads running away and around Rossville. The roads ran out of town like a dusty spider's web knitting through the green fields and pastures.

About an hour deep into my walk-about, I caught a glimpse of an unexpected dash of color different from the green and blue all around. I caught sight of a glorious glow a good hundred yards from my path on the roadway. Up next to a farmhouse, a rambling, white place with neatly trimmed green shutters that matched the hue of the encompassing fields and dales, was cut out a large garden plot.

Up and down over about a third of the garden patch was a burst of color – pinks and blues and violets and oranges. I squinted my eyes to try and get a better look, never having seen such a wild flush of blossoming blooms so early and so thick at that time of year.

In my two years in Rossville I came to know or at least know of most of the folks who lived in the area. But as I looked upon the busy, bursting strip of bright color, I realized that I did not know who owned that particular farm, who was responsible for planting and tending what looked like thick, healthy growth. I lost track of time, staring at the garden off in the distance. I did not hear the rack and rattle of the old Ford pickup truck making down the road, coming from the same direction that I had walked.

The rickety Ford slowed and stopped at the same time I paid attention to its appearance.

"Father White?" the driver, a sixty-something farmer, called out from the rusted cab.

I turned away from the garden patch for the first time since my discovery of the gaily growing blossoms.

"Hello, Warren," I greeted. I asked him at once who lived at the farm at which I was stopped.

Warren Rogers chuckled and shot me a look like I should know better. "It's those looney birds," Warren replied, looping a forefinger around his head.

"Those what?" I asked, having no idea what the good old fellow meant.

"Looney birds," he repeated, his finger still orbiting around his right ear. "Couple of looney birds, they is.

That's who's livin' there ... a couple real looney birds, that's what."

Warren finally rested his twirling hand, dropping it to his side.

Mustering a smile, not wanting to sound as if I was chiding Warren Rogers, I asked if he knew their names.

"Sure do," he proudly boasted, but said no more.

Keeping what I hoped was a pleasant, safe smile I asked: "And they are?" "What?" be asked.

"Their names," I replied.

"Who?" he asked, looking befuddled.

"The names of the people who own this farm." I pointed at the bright patch of color.

"Oh yeah, them looney birds. Not even sure if they're actually hitched up," Warren explained.

"Hitched?" I asked.

"Married ... married up," Warren replied. "I'm not sure certain they'd even done got married up together to the other."

I nodded, still smiling. "So," I continued, "their names. What are their names?"

"Oh, sure," Warren responded. "They be Hester, she's the woman. Her father used to be a doctor some thirty years back, down the road in Topeka. He's gone now, 'course. Old Doc DeWayne. And the fellow who lives there ... some fellow called Handy Weather. No idea where that fellow's come from. No idea at all."

"So, the people who live here are named Hester DeWayne and Handy Weather?" I asked.

Warren shook his head and said: "No." My smile slipped and I knew I looked hopelessly puzzled in spite of my best efforts.

The Shadow Cast

"You lost me, Warren," I confided.

"You see," he replied. "Doc DeWayne's girl ... that's Hester who lives here. She once got hitched up to a fellow named Therese, Richard Therese. He got himself killed sometime after they got married up ... or so they says. But, no one ever come up with no body, you see. So I expect if Hester ain't married up to this Handy Weather fellow, she's still to be called Hester Therese."

"You're probably right," I acknowledged, my smile returning as my confusion passed.

"Need a ride somewhere, Father White?" Warren asked.

"I'm just out for a walk. But, thanks," I told the old farmer.

"A walk?" Warren asked me like I told him I was planning an outer space trip to the moon.

"Right." I smiled.

"Whad' ya' mean? A walk?"

"I'm just out for a walk, that's all," I replied.

"But where ya goin'?" he asked.

"Nowhere special. Just out for a walk."

At that remark, Warren Rogers looked at me with the same expression he used when he described the owners of the house with the peculiar garden plot as being "looney birds." I thought I needed to accept a ride from Warren to avoid having the farmer say about me: "Father Al White? I reckon he's a looney bird. Just wanders around, going nowhere at all."

But, I decided to risk it and bid the skeptical farmer a good day and continued my walk down the road.

I returned to the rectory house, directly next to the church, in time for lunch. The parish housekeeper, a plump, Berlin-born woman of sixty who'd served the parish's pastors for forty years, had a hearty lunch prepared and waiting for me upon my return. As was our custom, except on Sundays, Hilda joined me for the noon meal.

Having been in the United States for over four decades, on the plains of Kansas where speech was as flat as the prairie, Hilda's voice bore only a trace of her Germanic birth.

As we ate, I mentioned coming upon the house with the odd, early blossoms.

"It was strange," I said in summation of my morning trek. Hilda chuckled.

"What?" I asked, imagining she chortled at my rambling, weekly morning walks, as she did from time to time.

"Strange?" she asked, still alight with laughter.

"I didn't get close, but the patch was already blooming. All colors. Pink. Red. Orange. Purple." "You said 'strange'?" I nodded.

"The people or the flowers?" She laughed again, at what was a joke she alone understood at the moment.

"Meaning?"

"The people ... who live there." Hilda mimicked the twirling finger I saw earlier that day, performed by Warren Rogers. "Yonky-bonky," she said.

I chuckled myself at her terminology. "Yonkybonky?" I asked.

"Those people, at the house you saw."

"Yonky-bonky?"

"Crazy," she clarified.

The Shadow Cast

"That's what Warren Rogers told me." "Warren Rogers?" she asked.

Between bites of Hilda's tender pot roast I explained that I saw the old farmer that morning while walking about.

"Oh, Father, I don't mean to be foul-mouthed. But old Hester and that Handy ... They're quite a crazy pair."

I smiled and teased my housekeeper with the prospect of her walking across the lawn to the church for confession.

"Really ... I don't mean any harm. Really, I don't."

Although I was more and more intrigued about hearing more of Hester, Handy and the garden patch, I knew Hilda baked a German apple pie that morning.

"Know what?" I said, shifting gears.

"What, Father?"

"I can still smell the pie you baked."

"Whipping cream?" she asked, adding: "It's fresh."

"On the side."

In a couple of minutes Hilda served up triangular slabs of still warm pie with healthy scoops of whipping cream to the side.

When Hilda and I nearly finished our pie slices, she reminded me of an appointment I had that afternoon with a young man from town, a dentist who settled in Rossville and hung a shingle at about the same time of my own arrival. I excused myself, telling Hilda I would be in my study.

"Just bring him back," I instructed, referring to my appointment.

The Shadow Cast

I settled in behind my desk, which belonged to my father, a piece of furniture that stood at the edge of my family's parlor in our farmhouse in Otterville when I was a boy. When my father passed in '49, Mom thought I might like the desk. With great effort, I managed to get the desk from Northeast Iowa to Northeast Kansas, glad I arranged for the move.

In the very left corner of the aged desktop was an indentation of perhaps half an inch – a smooth, worn spot. My father had one nervous habit, a tic so constant that the gentle curve down in the wood at the corner was created.

I can rarely remember a time when my father was posted at his desk that he did not clutch the corner of the desk, rubbing his thumb on the top. Slowly, very slowly, he wore the groove.

Since the desk arrived in the study at Saints Peter and Paul Catholic Church rectory, I had developed my own habit whenever I sat at the desk of resting my thumb in the niche created by my father.

Eventually, after taking to my study, Hilda poked her head through the open door and announced the arrival of my afternoon appointment, the young dentist. A regular Sunday church-goer, combined with two visits of my own to his professional chair, I felt pretty familiar with the fellow. When he arrived at the rectory study that Monday in March, I immediately noticed that the young dentist did not look exactly well; he did not look quite right.

The man's hair was disheveled, his face ashen like dust from burnt coal pieces. He looked oddly unfamiliar to me despite my knowing the man rather well. At the instant, I even forgot his name. I frowned, not wanting to say "What happened to you?" Let alone "What in the world is your name?" I managed: "Tea. Let me fetch us some tea."

I motioned to the chair in front of my father's desk and made a quick exit from the study. I retreated to the kitchen, finding Hilda chopping carrots for supper.

"Hilda," I said, entering the room, "he doesn't look well at all."

"Not at all," she agreed.

"Hilda, I forgot his name. I know it as well as mine. But, what is it?"

Grinning, with a spray of mischief, my housekeeper responded: "Yours or his?

I laughed, a bit. "Hilda ..."

"It is Dr Rydel," she began, when I interrupted with: "Clinton?"

"Clinton Rydel," she confirmed.

I started from the kitchen, stopping short just at the door. "Tea, Hilda. Do you have some tea?" "Hot or iced?" she asked.

"Either."

"Iced, yes. Hot, Father, I'd need to brew."

"Iced, then."

Without a pause, Hilda prepared a serving tray with a pitcher of tea and two glasses. Armed with the beverages, I returned to the study.

Somehow in my brief absence Clinton Rydel managed to look even grayer, his hair more messed as if he pulled at his head. Depending on what was on his mind, I imagined hair yanking might be a possible response. He seemed to crumble before my eyes, like a nearly spent chunk of furnace coal.

I did not bother pouring glasses of tea, figuring that if Clinton Rydel wanted refreshment he would pour on his own accord. Armed with his name, my memory itself refreshed, I felt it best to carry on with the appointment without an obvious interruption for drink service.

"Well, Dr Rydel … Clinton … how have you been?"

"Father, can I ask you something?"

His voice sounded surprisingly strong considering his outward appearance, his speech most direct. However, he looked to the floor and not at me when he spoke, all the while kneading his hands.

I rested my own hands on the desk, my thumb naturally sliding into my father's groove. "Of course." I nodded in what I hoped to be a reassuring fashion. "This isn't confession, though, right?" "What do you mean?" I asked.

"Well, Father, I know in confession, what I say is private … secret."

"I see," I replied. "Consider what you say here today the same. Private. Secret. Between us."

He slowly nodded, still looking at the floor but somehow seeming to be weighing my words, my promise of confidentiality.

"Father, you know my wife …" His voice trailed off leaving me uncertain as to whether he expected a response from me at the moment. I nodded, but realized he still was not looking at me, his face averted downward.

"Yes, of course. Mary Kay."

The Shadow Cast

I found no problem recalling her name, unlike my earlier difficulties with her husband's moniker.

He nodded after I spoke his wife's name and then continued. "We've been married for five years."

"I didn't know that," I replied, more to fill what became an uncomfortable and soundless gap in the conversation.

"We're from Virginia, you know."

I did not, or at least did not recall, that geographic detail. I said "Uh-huh" nonetheless.

"Well, I'm from Virginia, I mean. She's from ... my wife's from Topeka, from right here in Kansas."

"Yes," I finally said, filling another awkward break.

"We met in Virginia Beach."

"I see."

"Got married. I came here. She wanted to live near her family and all that."

"I see."

"They needed a dentist here in Rossville. So it all worked out pretty well, I suppose."

"Yes, I suppose so."

Clinton Rydel carried on for a quarter of an hour, prancing about details relating to his wedding and move to Kansas and early life with Mary Kay, his wife. His eyes never left the floor and then he said: "I killed her, Mary Kay."

I gripped onto my desk so hard that a part of me actually was surprised that I did not poke through my father's worn spot with my thumb. I nearly gasped, but did not and not because of self control. Rather, my lungs, indeed my entire body, felt frozen. I could not

The Shadow Cast

move. I did not speak and probably could not have even if I was determined to do so.

"I did," Clinton eventually muttered, speaking as if his stony announcement of homicide required verbal confirmation.

Finally, words began to form, at least within the confines of my own head:

"When? Where? Why? How?" I thought. I knew the answer to "what" at that juncture, obviously. Despite appreciating that one of perhaps another of these possible single word queries was better placed, more appropriate that the others, the first that tumbled from my mouth happened to be the least acceptable, I imagined.

"How?" I asked.

I regretted the question the moment the lonely syllable slipped from my lips.

"Gun," Clinton replied.

"When?"

"This morning."

"Where?"

"At home," he responded, adding: "I called in sick to the office."

"Why, Clinton? Why?"

With that asked, the homicidal dentist finally removed his gaze from the floor.

"Father, she deserved it."

Although I thought the "what" question was answered with the knowledge that Mary Kay Rydel was killed by her husband, I asked "What?" instinctively to Clinton's matter-of-fact reply to my question of why.

308

The Shadow Cast

Speaking louder, almost as if he thought I did not hear well, Clinton repeated: "She deserved it, Mary Kay did."

Aghast, I asked: "What in the world do you mean?"

Clinton furrowed his brow and tossed my question back at me, speaking in what seemed a close to flippant tone. "What do you mean?"

"How in God's name could Mary Kay ... your wife, Clinton ... how could she deserve to be shot ... by you?"

I half expected the thus far casual and cool sounding fellow to shrug his shoulders and say: "Gosh, priest-man, beats me. Beats me."

He said only: "She just did." The three words fell like cats-eye marbles onto a wooden floor.

I felt a tightening in my stomach. My immediate desire was to push my father's desk out of the room, away from this man. I felt that the presence of Clinton Rydel defiled the old desk, my father's memory.

I wanted Clinton Rydel gone. I wanted to take a long, hot shower. I wanted to be a boy back home in Otterville, Iowa. And, at that precise moment, I shuddered, I obviously shuddered. My brain flashed a long buried memory from back when I was just a boy, gleaning a corn field at harvest time.

Two of my childhood friends and I stumbled upon a body, a dead boy's body, in a little patch of woods near the field in which we scooped together errant ears of corn. I felt my gut tighten, knot up horribly.

"You need confession," I managed to say, grimly.

Clinton did not move, his pale green eyes looked into my own. I broke the stare, turning my own gaze to the worn spot on my desk top. "And you have to go to the Sheriff."

Clinton jumped to his feet, his face flushed red before he was fully standing. "You said you could not tell anyone anything I said!"

I did not know whether I should stand or continue sitting.

I definitely worried about what a man who killed his wife was capable of doing to another person to whom he was never wed. Certainly, in my mind, it was not beyond the realm of possibility for such a man to turn on his parish priest and unsuspecting housekeeper.

"Calm down," I retorted, a surprising amount of authority in my voice. "I can't tell anyone what you've told me, that's true. And I won't. But you … you need to – you have to go to the Sheriff."

"I do not!" Clinton shouted and I was certain he was heard by Hilda off in the kitchen. Under the circumstances, I hoped she would stay put and not wander back to see what developed in my study. How I would explain the situation to a curious Hilda I certainly could not imagine.

"Clinton, try and calm down," I said, having no idea what else to say or do with the crimson faced dentistturned-murderer hovering at my desk flexing his fingers in and out, forming fists and releasing. I realized saying anything further about the Sheriff at that time would be pointless, counter productive, perhaps even dangerous.

"Do you want confession?" I asked.

"I don't know," he replied, using the same harsh, nearly fierce inflection. He repeated "I don't know," the second time, his tone a notch lower but far from calm.

"I think you should," I stated with all of the certainty I could muster on the moment.

Over the course of the next quarter of an hour, Clinton Rydel and I fully reached an impasse. I gained only one concession; an assurance from Clinton Rydel that he would return to see me at the rectory after supper. I hoped giving him some time to consider his situation and his murdered wife would result in Clinton reaching the decision to face the Sheriff at the Courthouse and his maker at the Church. But, I had no illusions about the dentist actually reappearing at the rectory.

I ushered Clinton out the front door, wondering of the propriety of freely bidding adieu to a self-declared wife killer. After shutting the dentist out of the rectory I made my way to the kitchen to see what Hilda had or perchance had not heard of my visit. I entered the kitchen as the housekeeper finished putting up the lunch dishes.

"So?" I asked upon walking through the door into the room.

"Doc Rydel gone?" she returned, not turning from the cabinet at which she struggled to return a serving platter to the top shelf. Her back turned to me, I could not make out her expression. However, the unemotional tenor of her voice led me to conclude she heard nothing of importance. On some level, I wished Hilda had heard all. I badly wanted to talk.

The Shadow Cast

"Need help?" I asked, regarding the platter exactly at the moment she managed to get it into place.

"Got it." She turned around and belied no expression that suggested she heard the discussion in the study.

At that moment, I found myself terribly torn. I had met with a murderous parishioner that I sent on his own way. I wanted to unbridle myself with the housekeeper, but my vows prevented me from gut spilling, from human contact. On the whim I announced: "I'm going for a walk."

"Again?" she asked, surprised.

I nodded, turned and exited the room, uncertain as to whether I could dutifully survive further questioning without slipping and spilling the secrets of my study.

Never before having taken to the lonely rural roads around Rossville after noon, I immediately was stunned at how very different the scene looked in the glow of the westerly sun. Places I had only before seen veiled in shadow were beautifully lit with the soft rays of spring, other spots that shone brilliantly in the morning light seemed all but gone.

Despite the pretty afternoon, and a near perfect temperature, the visit from Clinton Rydel remained well affixed at the tip of my thoughts. Death was commonplace enough of an occurrence in my profession, an integral part of my vocation. But murderous dentists who slay wives seemed unique. Only one other fellow in my seminary class had faced a confession of homicide since our ordination, that I knew of at least. And his case involved a man who clubbed another man with a table leg in a riotous bar brawl, not a husband against his very own wife.

The Shadow Cast

Although I was not conscious of setting a true course for my irregular afternoon stroll, I ended up for the second time that day standing on the road in front of the peculiar patch of early bloomers, in front of the farm that belonged to the apparently uneven folk called Handy and Hester.

Gazing upon the pastel colors of the garden patch, I quickly realized that it looked different from how it had appeared just that very morning. Immediately, I chalked the changed appearance to the different slant of the sun. But shortly I determined the alteration in the patch was not merely the illusory workings of bright light and veiling shadow.

Standing roadside and looking across the green pasture over to the farmhouse and on to the garden, I thought with near certainty that the flower patch had grown, grown wider. There appeared to me to be even more rows of pinks and blues and violets and oranges. What in the morning appeared to cover no more than a third of the garden seemed to have spread to over half the plot. Mysterious blossoms magically spreading, I thought. I wondered, for the moment, whether if I stood very still I might witness new, pretty colored blossoms open over the garden patch, bettering the glorious carpet of spectacular hues right before my eyes.

I lost track of time, just as in the morning.

And, somehow and someway, thoughts of Clinton Rydel and his unnecessarily deceased wife slipped away. I toyed with the idea of walking across the pasture and over to the farmhouse and the brilliant blooms, to pick a flower or two. But, just as I was about to make across the tender spring alfalfa that grew inch high in the pasture, the door to the house swung open

313

and out walked a thin man, who looked to be middleaged or perhaps just a tad more. He did not seem to notice my presence.

I watched the man, secure at my distance in knowing I could merely begin walking down the road again should he glance my way and he would be none the wiser about my gazing at his beautiful flower patch. He would not know that I gaped and gawked at the pretty creation next to his house.

I assumed the man to be Handy Weather, of offbeat character and unbalanced nature according to the old farmer and my faithful housekeeper.

The fellow, Handy, strutted over to the garden patch, hoisting up his britches as he walked. He likewise scratched himself most indelicately, a sure sign – or so I believed – that he knew not of my nearby presence and directed gaze.

At the garden's edge, Handy plopped down to his knees and quickly bent over further still. From my vantage point on the road, the odd fellow appeared to be looking under the brilliantly bright blooms, to be peering under the glorious and queer flower buds of the early season.

The words of Warren Rogers, the farmer, quickened in my thoughts: "Those looney birds." The comments of Hilda reverberated as well – "Yonky-bonky."

I thought, in spite of myself: 'Oh, yonky-bonky looney bird, how doth thy garden grow?'

As if in some sort of sudden retribution that caught me so off guard, I nearly tripped to my knees when the fellow at the garden, that Handy Weather, bellowed at the tip top of his lungs: "Hester!"

The Shadow Cast

He shouted again: "Hester!" His voice bore a youthful eagerness. Simply put, his was a happy voice.

Once more the door to the house opened and out trundled a stout woman who managed lumbering steps. Reaching the garden patch, with great effort she joined Handy on her knees next to the flowerbed. She too crouched further and appeared to be looking underneath the blooms.

A guilty rush invaded me not long after the woman joined the man. I felt as if I wormed into something special, something private, by peeking at the doings of Hester and Handy from the dirt road. Flooded by such feelings, I hurried home.

The closer I drew to the rectory, the more a dreadful feeling of gloom stifled my senses. Clinton Rydel and his murdered wife, a most hard and harsh reality, returned full force to my thoughts, quite like the mad rush of freezing water from a well-primed pump.

I returned to my study without so much as a "hello" to Hilda in the kitchen. Faced with the prospect of another possible and at least planned visit from Doc Rydel, I knew the remainder of the afternoon would grind miserably slowly.

My thoughts became jumbled fare, mixed images of Clinton Rydel and the blooming garden patch, of an Iowa cornfield and a dead boy's body so many years earlier, all mingled and meshed. The horrors that life can bring blended with the beauty that living can many times bear.

I slid my thumb onto the worn spot on my father's desk and with my other hand began making a round of my rosary beads. I was halfway through the circuit of

"Our Father's" and, mostly, "Hail Mary's" when Hilda entered the room.

"Father?" she softly said, obviously not wanting to disturb me. I looked up.

"Father," she continued nervously, once gaining my attention. "Sheriff Menely ... he's here."

"Here?" I asked, knowing the man, but also knowing him to be a Lutheran.

"Here."

"Now?"

"Now."

"Oh," I said.

I naturally imagined the visit was related to Clinton Rydel and asked: "Troubles?"

Hilda nodded, wiping her dry hands on her apron, a nervous habit.

"Yes, then," I replied. "Well, bring him in, then."

She nodded, hurried away, and in a moment returned with the Sheriff at her heels.

I stood, greeted the lawman and offered him a seat. He was tall, prematurely graying and tan despite the early time of year.

"How are you?" I asked.

"Oh, no complaints," he replied in a voice that seemed tinged with the round accent of the Ozark Mountains some four hours southeast of Rossville. Hilda managed to vanish, rather like a magician's assistant stashed in a tricky box.

"Seems this isn't a social call ..." I suggested.

"Oh ... no," he replied, nonplussed.

"How might I help you?" I cleared my throat.

"You know of Tim Fellows?" he asked.

A parishioner, so I nodded.

"An' his wife, Rita?"

"Louise."

"Louise?"

"Louise."

"Oh," he replied, pulling a tiny notebook from the breast pocket of his navy blue uniform shirt. He scribbled a note.

"Mrs Fellows, she tells me you may have seen Doc Rydel today ..."

I sat still. I recollected that the Fellows lived next door to the Rydels.

"Seems ole Doc Rydel, seems he told ole Mrs Fellows he was headin' here to see you."

I did not move.

"Anyways, like it is, of Doc Rydel ... looks like he done an' gone shot up of Mrs Rydel. Just this mornin'. An' now he's gone a-missin'. But Mrs Fellows says she heard the commotion over to the Rydels. She was out waterin' her 'tunia plants, I guess. Ole Doc Rydel comes outta his house and tells of Mrs Fellows he's comin' on down to see you. Says it after Mrs Fellows asks about the commotion and all." "Oh," I managed.

"Course, Mrs Fellows, she telephoned us up, reportin' the commotion and all."

"Oh."

We sat in silence for what seemed a full season on the Church's calendar. Sheriff Menely finally spoke. "So, you seen him or what?"

"Clinton Rydel?" I asked, buying a slip of time to think.

"Yep."

"Yes." "You did
then?"   I
nodded.   "This
mornin'?"   I
nodded.
"Here?"
I nodded.
"Know where he's gone off to?"
I shook my head, honestly.

The Sheriff rose, seeming satisfied with what he obtained from me, a surprise in my mind. I imagined a long interrogation, me continually invoking the privilege of the confessional, a scene from a John Ford motion picture.

"You know," Sheriff Menely boasted, "I've been to them training sessions off in Kansas City. I know all 'bout that priest and convict confession thing."

In spite of myself I slivered off a grin at the Sheriff's quick move to place Clinton Rydel in convict status.

I rose and replied: "Of course. I knew you would have."

"Can you telephone me if you see him?"

"I suppose I can. I'd tell him I was doing it though."

"Seems fair enough."

I walked the Sheriff to the front door of the rectory, neither of us speaking. In the foyer, just before he departed, Sheriff Menely remarked: "Sad business."

"Yes."

"He's the only dentist we done got."

With the Sheriff gone, I walked back to the study and settled in behind my desk to finish the rosary. Once more, Hilda was at the door to the room. "Father?" Her voice was soft.

"Hilda, yes?"

"Father ... Gwen Mersh ... she's here."

"Who?"

Hilda apologized and explained that Gwen Mersh was the late Mary Kay Rydel's sister from Topeka. "Oh Lord," I muttered. "Will you want tea?" I shrugged, myself at a loss.

"I'll get her," Hilda advised.

I stood up from my chair and remained standing until Gwen Mersh entered.

"Hya Father." The woman, looking to be in her midthirties, had a peculiarly chipper voice, I thought. Except for red rimmed eyes, tell-tale signs of crying, she appeared perfectly at ease, strangely composed and oddly content. "May I?" she asked, pointing at a chair in front of the desk.

"Please."

She propped a huge, shiny black leather handbag on her lap. She was a trim woman in a powder blue suit with large, oversized brass buttons in the shape of anchors. Her chestnut brown hair was pulled back in a most efficient bun.

"I'm Gwen Mersh," she introduced, looking dead on into my eyes, firm and unblinking. I introduced myself.

"So good to meet ya."

"Tea? Would you like some tea?"

She seemed to consider my offer of refreshment for a moment and then declined.

"I expect you've heard?"

I grimaced reflexively and slightly nodded with my eyes closed.

"Oh, yes, my sister ... she's done got herself murdered."

At the strident remark, my eyes popped open, just as Gwen Mersh reached into her handbag.

"I've made lists ..." she continued with the same efficiency she must have used in styling her hairdo. She pulled what looked to be a half dozen sheets of paper from the large purse. Setting the handbag on the floor she rested the sheets on her lap, plucking one off the top of the stack, setting it on my desk.

"Obituary. Wrote it myself. Can you see the newspaper gets it? I don't mention Mary Kay going and getting herself murdered, of course."

Before I could respond, perhaps comment on the concept of Mary Kay Rydel "going and getting herself murdered," Gwen Mersh was on page two with all the sure swiftness of Mr Paul Harvey. In fact, she said: "Page two."

"List of ushers, altar boys. Can you get a copy of this over to Brennan's Funeral Home? They'll handle things, of course."

Even though Gwen Mersh appeared to be paying little attention to me, I made an effort to nod my head. I knew people handled grief differently. But, Gwen Mersh marked the first occasion in which I confronted a person seeming to deal with grief with efficiency.

"Songs," she said, laying page number three upon my desk. She smiled and added almost coquettishly: "I'll do the solos, of course." "Of course," I muttered.

The Shadow Cast

Plopping page four on my desk, she explained that the paper contained a list of suggested Bible readings for the funeral Mass.

"Okay." I barely managed a whisper.

Gwen Mersh ended up placing a few more sheets of paper in front of me, briefly explaining each in turn. When finished, she collected her handbag, rose to her feet and brightly advised: "I'm off to Brennan's. Need to pick out a casket, don't ya know."

And with that Gwen Mersh was out the door, showing herself the way out of the rectory.

Picking up my rosary to finish my prayers, the telephone clanged to life.

"Hello?" I greeted.

"Father?"

"Yes?"

"Sheriff Menely here. Hey, we done got ahold of Doc Rydel. We done arrested the fellow." "I

see."

"So then, just wanted to let you know and all after our meetin'. One of my deputies done snatched the Doc while you an' me was a-meetin'."

"I see." Taking a deep breath I then asked if Clinton Rydel mentioned wanting to see a priest, to see me.

"No he ain't done nothin' like that."

"Thank you, Sheriff."

I disconnected the call and, as if on cue, Hilda entered the study with iced tea and fresh, frosted sugar cookies. She brought a glass along for herself and took the chair occupied by Gwen Mersh only a few minutes earlier.

"A long day, Father?"

"Do you know what happened?"

She blushed and admitted to hearing some of what Clinton Rydel had all but shouted that morning. "And, of course, Gwen Mersh told me on the stoop the second I opened the door that she was here to see you because her sister's 'done and gone got herself killed.' I guess she actually said 'got herself murdered'."

"Clinton needs confession."

"He'll call for you, Father."

"You think?"

"I do."

We finished our glasses of chilled tea and ate the still warm from the oven cookies, speaking very little.

The next couple of days passed in a flurry, the township all abuzz with the news of Mary Kay Rydel's murder, Doc Rydel's arrest and the victim's efficiently arranged funeral at Saints Peter and Paul Church, my parish.

The funeral Mass, held on Thursday morning, brought a packed church. Gwen Mersh commanded the memorial service like a stockade matron and sang the 'Ave Maria' at the end with efficiency and no seeming regard for musical niceties.

On Friday Sheriff Menely relayed a message to me from Clinton Rydel; the dentist sought confession. I obliged in haste, worried all week that Clinton Rydel would face his maker by some fluke of dire fate before he took occasion to address his state of mortal sin.

Never having to take the confession of a self proclaimed killer, I was nervous, anxious. Hilda drove me to Topeka, some ten miles east, to the county lockup. She volunteered to drive as she was convinced that in my distracted state I would poorly navigate the paved although winding road to the government seat.

Arriving at the jail on Friday morning, the guards on duty quickly arranged for my session with Clinton Rydel. In the absence of a confessional, Clinton decided that he preferred our chairs to be set back to back so that he would not have to look at me, and me at him, while he confessed to the sin he previously told me about face to face.

Had I not known what was coming next, considering the tone of the initial words Clinton Rydel uttered in his confession, I would have thought I was about to hear the naughty disclosures of a teenaged boy or another such minor league n'er do well.

"Bless me father, for I have sinned ..." the dentist began in a sort of sing-song voice. "I made my last confession about one month ago."

He paused at that point as if expecting an accolade from me for being a regular recipient of the Sacrament. I sat quietly.

"My greatest faults are ..."

As he continued, I found myself gripping the edge of the seat of my chair tightly with both hands, my knuckles white from the intensity.

The dentist carried on: "I took the Lord's name in vain ..."

I released a hand and scratched my head, not expecting heavenly cursing to be the first transgression out of Clinton Rydel's mouth. Nevertheless, I thought of the penance I usually assigned to that sin; the Hail Mary, four times.

The Shadow Cast

And, at that instant, I broke into a cold sweat. 'Thank God, literally,' I thought. 'Thank God that we are not sitting face to face.' I realized I had no idea what penance to give to a man who murdered his wife. I immediately became so wrapped up in that point, I paid little attention to Clinton Rydel's litany of venial sinning.

I forced myself to redirect my attention to what the dentist was saying after almost a minute passed. If nothing else, Clinton Rydel was a thorough confessor, or so it seemed.

"And I had lustful thoughts about Roxie Spish ..."

Not a parishioner, so I did not form a visual image.

"I swiped a newspaper, a Topeka Capital, off a table at Peg's Dinette ..."

Peg's Dinette, I reflected, great chicken fried steak sandwiches.

"And, oh yeah, I shot Mary Kay."

The words echoed in my head: *"And, oh yeah, I shot Mary Kay."*

The words sounded in tone and cadence like he said: "And, oh yeah, I fibbed on my time card at the plant."

Or: "And, oh yeah, I fiddled with my privates."

Not: "I shot and killed my wife."

I responded: "Well ..."

He said: "Yeah?"

Clinton sounded impatient, as if he expected me to say: "Well, Doc, thanks for the swell confession. For your penance, light a candle and say a Hail Mary."

I must have sat quietly for longer than I realized because Clinton, sounding irritated, said: "Father, can we get on with this?"

The Shadow Cast

"Right," I said with no penance coming to mind.

"Well, then, Clinton ... are you sorry for your sins?"

"Yeah."

'Yeah ...' I thought, parroting the penitent to myself.

"Well, you know this is serious?" I asked.

"You mean the part about Mary Kay?"

Dumbfounded with his placid sounding statement of the most obvious, I snapped back: "Well, of course that part about Mary Kay."

"Yeah ... that ..." he replied.

"Say one thousand Hail Marys," I blurted, the words tumbling almost uncontrollably from my mouth.

"Say what?"

"The Hail Mary ... one thousand times."

"One thousand times?"

Firmly, I advised that saying the Hail Mary a thousand times was a fair trade off as a penance for wife killing.

"All at once," he asked, as if negotiating the price of sheep.

"Finish in two days."

Personally not wanting to, I nonetheless gave the man absolution. I hurried from the jailhouse, prodded Hilda to best the speed limit on the way back to the rectory and, upon arriving, dashed to the bathroom upstairs next to my bedroom. After vomiting, I drew a hot bath and soaked in the tub for over an hour. On my own, I said one hundred Hail Marys.

After the respite in the soothing water, I redressed and went downstairs, joining Hilda in the kitchen for lunch.

"Are you okay?" she asked.

"It was hard." She
nodded.

"Has this happened before? Here?" I asked.

"One time, a dozen years ago." "A
parishioner killed someone?" She
nodded.

"What happened? Who?"

"Oh, they're gone now." Her face flushed. "I mean,
the whole family's gone. The husband dead. The wife
shot the husband. A shooting, just like with the Rydels."

"I see."

"Father Rice, he was the pastor here then. He had a
hard time with it, just like you. A hard time with the
whole mess."

"I'm sure."

Hilda spent a bit more time filling in a smattering of
other details relating to the prior incident of intra-family
homicide. When she finished, she suggested I take a
walk.

"But it's not Monday," I responded, referring to my
normal strolling day.

"Oh, be untamed Father," she smiled.

"You know, Hilda, a walk sounds like just the right
thing for me."

"Off you go, then."

Leaving the rectory, I guessed the temperature out
of doors to be somewhere in the seventies that Friday
afternoon. The sky was a deep blue with a scattering of
small and fluffy white cloud puffs. The little clouds
looked quite like young lambs flirting about in a mellow
pasture.

326

The Shadow Cast

The sun had just slid over to the western half of the sky, bright, golden and reassuring.

I wondered if I had become something of an automaton because I ended up back square in front of the farmstead that was the home of the allegedly peculiar couple of Handy Weather and Hester Therese. On the occasion of my third visit, I knew absolutely that the colorful blossoms of the garden patch had spread even further, covering nearly all of the tended area.

As I looked upon the ever spreading blooms, Hester and Handy walked into my view from the backside of the farmhouse. On this occasion, they caught sight of me and each waved in friendly fashion. I did the same and then decided to walk across the trim alfalfa pasture towards the house, the couple and the garden.

Wearing my Roman collar, which I forgot to remove after my visit to the jailhouse, Handy and Hester easily identified me both as a Catholic priest and as the local pastor, Rossville being a small town.

"Hello, Father." Handy spoke first, Hester immediately repeating the hospitable greeting.

"Hello there."

Reaching the yard and standing only a few yards from the garden, my eyes were diverted from the faces of the welcoming hosts to the brilliant patch of color that had engaged my attention and regularly invaded my thoughts for days. Before I really could think, the words slipped from my mouth.

"What in the world?" I exclaimed.

Both Hester and Handy beamed proudly, like pleased parents.

The Shadow Cast

I squeezed my eyes shut not one but three times, trying to adjust to what actually lay in front of where I stood, the gaily colored garden patch.

Clearly noticing my incredulous expression, Handy spoke. "You know, Father, Hester was married once before and her husband came up with these. He was an inventor, of sorts, I expect you could say. He invented these."

Handy broadly gestured with his right hand, a sweeping movement over the garden patch.

"He did," Hester confirmed.

Before me lay not a bed of unusually early blooming flowers. Rather, a clutter of what looked like tiny umbrellas covered nearly the entire expanse. Dainty parasols of thin paper on slender sticks poked into the garden's soil.

"Umbrellas?" I asked, confused and yet delighted by the scene.

"Oh, yes," Handy replied. Hester, smiling broadly, nodded along. "Made of paper."

"But why?"

"Oh, silly," Hester rejoined. "To block the sun."

"Block the sun?" I was puzzled.

"Oh, yes," Handy replied once more. "This is our cabbage patch."

"And our cabbages are just sprouts," Hester interjected.

"Sprouts," Handy agreed. "And we don't want them to get scorched ... scorched by the sun, don't you know."

"That's right," Hester affirmed.

"So little paper umbrellas ..." I remarked.

The Shadow Cast

"That's what Hester's husband ... well, her long ago husband ... that's what he invented," explained Handy.

"To cover the cabbage sprouts, to keep them safe," Hester remarked.

I spent the next few hours with Hester and Handy, sitting beside their cabbage patch. I listened to their stories. How they met, where they met. I heard about Hester's sad past, losing her first husband and her child in such a strange way and it brought me back for a moment to the evil in the world and the sad couple whose fate had made me want to escape for a walk that day. Hester and Handy both spoke of the famous actress that brought them together and they still praised her and mourned her passing.

As they reminisced, I thought about the colors in the garden, and the shades of gray in life itself. People thought this couple crazy and further proof of it was before my eyes in those little, colorful umbrellas protecting those cabbage sprouts. But what was truly crazy or evil was a man killing his wife in cold blood. To all the world my penitent and his wife looked perfectly sane until their awful tragedy became the source of town gossip and hit the papers across the state.

I felt a sense of peace knowing that there remained a place in the world where a man loved a woman, where a woman loved a man, and where little cabbage sprouts were kept safe beneath paper umbrellas. If this was crazy, then perhaps I was crazy too.

Straw

I looked into the cracked mirror on the wall next to the churning wood burning stove in the kitchen. I focused on my lips as I spoke: "I pledge lee-gents ..." Mama cut in. "I pledge allegiance. Allegiance."

"Allegiance," I repeated, getting the word right.

"Good," she encouraged. I did not turn around to look at her as she sat at the square table in the center of the small room. If I tilted my head a bit to the left, I could snatch Mama's reflection in the little mirror.

"I pledge allegiance," I continued, smiling when I managed a correct pronunciation yet again. "To the flag of the United States of America." I twisted my neck, caught a glimpse of Mama, saw she smiled. I continued. "And to the public ..."

"*Re*public."

"Rep-ub-lick."

"Republic," Mama repeated.

"To the Rep-ub-lick ... Repub-lick ... Republic ..."

"Good. That's right."

"And to the Republic for witches stand."

Mama laughed in spite of herself, I was certain.

Slightly discouraged, I did turn around to directly face Mama seated at the table.

"What?" I moaned.

She spoke, kindly. "And to the republic for which it stands."

I cut her off with a plaintive "That's what I said."

She shook her head.

"And to the Republic ..." I stated, keeping my eyes on Mama. She nodded to let me know so far, so good.

And then I blew it. "For witches stand."

Mama stifled a snicker as best she could as she shook her head. "For ... which ... it ... stands," she stated very slowly.

Together, we said: "For which it stands." Once again. "For which it stands." "See? You got it," Mama extolled.

I returned my attention to the mirror and began from the top.

"I pledge allegiance to the flag and to the ..." I paused and inhaled deeply "... Republic." I smiled. "For which it stands, ind ... ind ... indivisible and with liberty and justice for all."

Mama stood, clapping. I spun around and hugged her tightly. I noticed a tear in Mama's eye, even though she smiled.

After a minute, Mama told me: "You'd better be going. Before things get too busy."

I wanted to stay in our little house with my Mama where it was warm. But, with Papa gone, Mama always told me I was now 'her little man.' I was ten, but whenever Mama called me 'her little man' I felt bigger.

Mama helped me bundle up in a ragged coat and a worn woolen muffler and stocking cap. I pulled on mittens, each with a hole at the tip of the thumb.

When I was ready to go, Mama kissed me on the cheek, told me to be careful, and I was off.

Our little house, my Mama's and mine, was on a narrow strip of a street near a row of livery stables. School was out of session for the Christmas holiday.

The schoolhouse was down the same street as our house and the livery stables.

At the side of our house, I kept my Radio Flyer Wagon, built up with wooden slats so that I could load more stuff than if I just had the plain old low-lipped version. I gathered up my wagon and headed off down our street to the first livery post.

Not much snow fell in Denver that December. The street was clear but the dirt roadway was hard from the winter frost, making the pulling along of my red painted wagon easy.

About once a month, Mama let me pull my wagon down the street from livery stable to stable. Having me go to the stables was not my Mama's idea. I spent four months convincing my Mama that I could handle the job of going to the stables. Plus, I had a wagon of my very own that could be very useful on trips to the stables.

Mama finally relented, and I happily took on the task, a chore that I undertook once a month, more or less, since I was eight.

I enjoyed my trips to the stables, for the most part. I liked looking at the big horses, nearly all of them having brown hair. Some I saw were black. Once in a while, I even saw an all white horse. But most of the horses at the livery stables in Denver were brown colored.

I was able to go about my business pretty easily at all the stables, except for one. Altogether there were five livery companies down my Mama's and my street; Shram, Eden and Ricketts, Denver Livery Company, Morgan and Humber's Livery, Snyder Stables, and Gitano, Tulareo and Puleo.

Shram, Eden and Ricketts was the oldest livery company in Denver. I heard over 100 years, but that could have been puffing. Even though Shram was the oldest, when President Coolidge came to Denver that summer he had horses from Morgan and Humberts in his parade down Colfax Avenue right by the Statehouse.

Mama took me to see the President and the parade. I was disappointed when he went by in a motorcar because I expected him to be on a Morgan and Humberts horse. They must have been the biggest and best, after all, to be in a parade for the President.

Denver Livery was the smallest operation, run by two Irishmen who spoke with hearty brogues. Mama liked them especially because her own parents came from Dublin. Gitano, Tulareo and Puleo was owned by Italians. Mama and I really knew nothing of any Italians except for Pius who was the Pope off in Rome.

I looked forward to going to the stables on my almost monthly outings, all of them except for one that I always did my best to avoid. Snyder Stables was located smack dab in the middle of the four other operations. I only went into Snyder's one time on my business and after that vowed never to return, not ever.

Snyder's was owned and run by a woman I'd guessed to be near fifty, named Martha, Martha Snyder. After my first and only intentional visit to Snyder's, when I ended up running all the way home in tears even though I was my Mama's 'little man,' my Mama explained to me about Martha Snyder.

First of all, Mama said, we needed to feel sorry for Martha Snyder because her own Papa died, just like mine had passed. On top of that, Mama explained, Martha Snyder was a spinster woman.

"A what woman?" I asked at the time, flummoxed to be sure.

"A spinster woman," Mama repeated.

"What in a frog's eye is a splinter woman?" I asked.

Mama chuckled, corrected me by slowly stating "spinster woman."

"Spinster woman?" I asked, accurately.

"Yes, Herbert," my Mama replied. Only Mama called me Herbert. Others just called me regular Herb.

"Well, what's that then?" I asked.

Mama sat down at the kitchen table and patted her lap for me to take a seat.

"I'm too big for that," I protested, even though I was not and was small for my age.

She smiled and allowed me to pull up a chair like a full-fledged man would to sit and visit.

"You see," Mama continued, "we need to feel sorry for Miss Martha Snyder."

"We do?" I asked, astounded by the idea.

"We do."

"Why's that?" I asked, sure that my eyes were bulging from their sockets at hearing such a proposal. "Because she's all alone."

"So?" I was not persuaded.

"She's all alone. That's why she's a spinster woman."

"Because her Papa died?"

"Well, yes, that," Mama agreed, "but, Martha Snyder, you see, no one ever married her."

I eyed my Mama as if to say "Well golly, who would marry such a cow anyways?" Mama knew the look.

"Now, Herbert. If you were all alone in the whole wide world, how would you feel?"

I thought for a moment and then replied: "Well, I expect those horses she's got don't like her a lick anyhow."

Mama turned away, I knew to hide a smile. Not looking at me she forced a "Herbert" before she giggled like Mary Kay Buck, a girl in my class at school.

"You expect I'm right about those horses she's got not liking her, huh, Mama?" I asked.

Mama finally turned to face me and firmly planted her hands on my knees. "I expect you're right."

I puffed proudly before she added: "But, young man, that doesn't mean we shouldn't feel sorry for the woman."

I wanted to protest, to remind my Mama that meanold-nasty Martha Snyder yelled at me something frightful, made me cry even though I was the "little man" of our house. But, as I listened to Mama speak, I realized she and I had it all far better in the world than Martha Snyder. Mama and I had each other.

"Okay," I sighed.

And so that December as I started off to make my rounds of the livery stables, I was armed with my Mama's wisdom that Old Lady Snyder, as I came to call her to myself but not to Mama, was an object of pity and nothing more.

With my wagon in tow, I walked up to Shram, Eden and Ricketts, the livery stable closest to home. I broke into a huge grin when I saw Winnie Shram standing at the door to the horse pens. Winnie Shram, I figured, was a thousand years old and, best of all, he had no teeth … not one.

"Well, I'll be pitched in a ditch," Winnie Shram said when he saw me coming.

"Howdy, Mr Winnie," I called out. Mama forbid me from calling any adult by his Christian name. Winnie Shram forbid me from calling him Mr Shram. So, Winnie Shram and I came up with a name-calling deal that would pass muster with Mama.

I pulled my Radio Flyer up to the wide entrance. In the background, I could hear horses neighing and the sound of a couple of workmen jabbering about a fight they saw the night before at a speakeasy called the Longhorn Club where the stable hands all passed their spare time.

"Is it that time of the month already, boy?" Mr Winnie asked. I grimaced at being called 'boy' because, after all, I was ten.

"Yes, sir, Mr Winnie."

"Well, I'll be then," he replied. I paid special attention to the inside of Mr Winnie's mouth when he spoke, never having seen anything quite like a completely toothless fellow.

"Do you have any?" I asked, trying to sound like a manly horse trader and not a boy in search of straw.

"I bet we do, boy," Mr Winnie said. "I reckon you better come on in and have a look around beforehand, don't ya know."

"Can I?" I replied, sounding all boy and happy at what I knew was an invitation to look at the horses.

"Well, I believe you should," Mr Winnie replied, sounding quite like my looking at the horses benefited the working of the livery company.

I scampered inside, going from enclosure to enclosure, sizing up the muscled animals, the strong horses, almost all of which had brown hair. I spent nearly an hour eyeing the animals and visiting with a couple of the stable hands, the two fellows I heard talking about the brawl at the Longhorn Club.

"I heard about the fight," I said to them, trying to sound mature and conspiratorial. The fellows went along and shared the blow by blow with me as we each chewed on a stick of hay.

By the time I finished my rounds, Mr Winnie had put a neat bundle of straw into my Radio Flyer. The wagon, because of the built-up sides, could hold just the amount of straw I needed to collect.

"See ya around, Mr Winnie," I called back to the oldster as I returned to the road in front of the stables.

"I'll be lookin' for ya," he hollered back, flashing a whopping large and totally toothless smile.

Next stop on my route was Denver Livery, the place's owners both standing just inside the entrance to their own stable area, keeping out of the cold. Jody O'Malley and James Cooney, both young and broad shouldered men in their twenties, each puffed on identical pipes.

"It be Dubliner," Mr Cooney declared as I walked over to where the man stood. The owners of Denver Livery always called me 'Dubliner' because of my Mama's folk and all.

"Why ain't you off to the school?" Mr O'Malley asked.

"Christmas," I replied.

"What you say?" Mr O'Malley asked.

"It ain't Christmas, Dubliner," Mr Cooney added.

"But it will be," I said, trying to speak with manly authority.

"And it'll be St Paddy's day, too," Mr O'Malley quipped.

"And Easter, Dubliner," Mr Cooney needled.

They waited for me to respond and I finally explained the school closed down for a couple weeks around Christmas time.

Quite like at Shram, Eden and Ricketts, the Irish owners of Denver Livery allowed me the run of the place. On that day, they had in their stables the all white horse I had seen a couple of times before.

"She be a Palomino," Mr Cooney reminded me.

I nodded, feeding the beauty fistfuls of crisp winter hay.

"Someday, Dubliner, I betcha you'll be owning a horse yerself as fine as this one here." "Me?" I marveled.

"Yep, I reckon so, Dubliner."

Looking back over to the majestic animal, I mumbled: "Maybe so … maybe so."

After finishing my roundabout of the horse pens, Mr O'Malley pitched several forks of clean straw into my Radio Flyer. The Irishman did not bother with neatly binding up a little bale for me with twine.

I wheeled my wagon back out onto the street, dreading what stood directly next on my route … Snyder Stables and Martha Snyder. I had no intention of stopping at Snyder's, but I still needed to roll past to reach Gitano, Tulareo and Puleo. I envisioned Martha Snyder pounding out of her pens like a gnarly spider plunging for prey.

I thought about dragging my wagon clear to the other side of the street, but I did not want the Irishmen or toothless Winnie Shram to think I was afraid of something like Martha Snyder.

Without knowing it at first, I had slowed my pace, apprehensive about my nearing approach to the frontage of the Snyder operation. At that moment, a gust of wintry wind blew from the direction of Martha Snyder and her horses. I even thought her stables smelled much worse than the other livery holds. I took some pleasure in imagining the particular foulness of the air around the Snyder Stables came because of Martha Snyder herself.

Gearing myself to pick up my speed and rush past Snyder's, I suddenly spotted a flurry and flash near the entrance to the offensive stable pens. And there she was, Martha Snyder pounding from her pens quite like I imagined only a moment earlier.

Her head was topped with frazzled orange hair that made her look as if a jagged bolt of lightning had zapped at her. Her expression, fierce and vicious, also looked to be the aftermath of a lightning strike.

Martha Snyder's face was patchy, a peculiar pasty white overlaid with crimson dots. On a holiday ornament the color combination might look festive, even pretty. But on a woman's face, particularly a beastly creature like Martha Snyder, the look was positively dismal, fiendish to boot.

"You there!" the frightful apparition bellowed. I nearly dropped the handle to my Radio Flyer. I quickly glanced around to see if someone else might be about, another person who was the target of Martha Snyder's shriek. As it turned out, I stood alone.

I said nothing. I stopped walking. I felt my heart pound almost as if it might rip through my shirt, sweater and wintertime jacket.

Martha Snyder, with her flying orange hair and surly scowl, barreled right for me. I felt certain that if she didn't break her pace she would careen right into me, or into my wagon half filled with straw.

In a seeming flash, Martha Snyder was on top of me, inches from my face.

"You there!" she yelled again, her sour, hot breath rushing at me. I cringed, from the rotten egg smell and the loudness of the creature's voice. "Beggin' are ya?" she cursed.

I remained frozen, feeling my stomach roll from the wicked odors coming from the frightening being hovering next to me on the street.

"Little beggar like ya should be kilt," she screeched. "Have your worthless heart cut right out … right out of ya, I say. Cut out and tossed to the dogs."

She laughed, a hysterical howl, after she spat out 'the dogs.'

"And your mammy, I'm sure she's a whore. A whore!"

I felt tears pool up in my eyes when the foul smelling, rotten looking woman went on about my mama.

"A whore and a bugging beggar," she screamed. "I should just have you kilt right now to put ya out of ya mis'ry."

I could take no more. I yanked my wagon and worked my shaky legs as best I could, aiming directly towards the Italians' stables. As my feet pounded on the frozen ground that made the street, I heard Martha Snyder behind me shrieking with demonic laughter.

I did not even see Paulo Gitano, the son of one of the owners, leaning against the doorframe as I dashed inside the seeming security of the Italians' horse pens.

Paulo Gitano was seventeen, had olive skin, black hair and green eyes that startled me every time I saw the young man.

"Hey, kiddo," Paulo said, still leaning against the board.

"Paulo!" I was almost breathless. I felt my face flush, instantly embarrassed to know that Paulo Gitano had seen me run off from Martha Snyder. I wondered how the tough looking fellow would have handled the likes of Martha Snyder.

Catching my breath, I looked up at Paulo. He seemed to be gazing into the street and had a thin grin on his lips.

'Brother,' I thought, ready to crawl into a pile of hay, 'Paulo saw me running, saw me running from an old lady.'

"Witch try 'n' get ya?" Paulo asked, still grinning and still looking out at the road.

"Huh?" I asked, directing my eyes to my shoes.

"Witch try 'n' get ya?" he asked again.

"Witch? What?"

"Da witch. Did she try 'n' get ya?"

Hesitating and glancing upward, slightly, I asked Paulo if he meant Martha Snyder.

"Uh-huh," he grunted. "Da witch."

Knowing I sounded beaten, I told Paulo: "Miss Snyder called my mama a whore." I choked up when I repeated the bad, nasty word I'd heard only moments earlier.

Paulo bent at his knees and positioned himself to

my low eye level. "That ain't right, little man. Ain't right."

I nodded, knowing what Paulo said was true.

"You know what we do with da witches?" Paulo asked.

"Do?" I replied.

He nodded. "Yeah, yeah. Do you know what we do with da witches?"

"Who?"

Paulo patted his chest. "Us."

Puzzled, I repeated: "Us."

"Us Italians," Paulo boasted, thumping his chest once again.

"Oh – What?" I whispered. "What do you do ... with the witches?"

I knew he spoke of Martha Snyder.

Paulo leaned in close and whispered, his hot breath against my ear: "We burn 'em. We burn 'em up."

My eyes popped open wide and I took a couple steps back, amazed.

"You burn them," I murmured.

The wry grin returned to Paulo's face as he nodded his head. He rose up to stand once more.

"Need some straw?" he asked, all business as if no secret was shared.

"What?" I asked, picturing nasty Martha Snyder in a bunch of fire, her orange hair flaming, and smoke puffing out of her cruel mouth.

"Need some straw, little man?"

I nodded. "Please."

Like at Shram, Eden and Ricketts, Paulo made up a neat, tight bundle of fresh straw for me to cart home.

"Thanks, Mr Gitano."

"Uh-huh," he replied. I didn't spend any time looking

at the Italians' horses. I wanted to get home, to check on Mama. I felt as if the horrible words spoken, screamed, by Martha Snyder had bruised my mama even though Mama didn't hear the nasty woman.

I hurried to Morgan and Humbert's Livery, retrieved a bundle of straw, and turned around to head back home. I froze, realizing I would have to pass by Martha Snyder's stables once more.

I decided I would begin moving as fast as I could, with my nearly full wagon in tow. I figured by the time I reached the front of the Snyder stables I would be moving at such a clip that old lady Snyder might not see me and certainly would not be able to stop me.

I crouched down low like I'd seen college boys from the University of Denver do at a track and field day I got to go to with my Aunt Ruth and my cousins Els and Carl a couple of years ago. The position was strange, awkward, because I still needed to clutch onto the cold, metal handle of my Radio Flyer and its precious load of straw.

Taking in a deep breath of freezing winter air, an inhale so fierce my lungs ached, I took off running down the dirt street. My wagon trundled behind as I picked up speed.

In what seemed like no time, I raced in front of Snyder Stables, the harsh chill of the season biting at my cheeks and causing my eyes to pool. Directly in front of the lair of the nasty, old woman, one of my sneaker-clad feet caught up in the front of my Radio Flyer. The wagon tilted as I stumbled and in a horsehair I lay flat out on the ground, my knees badly skinned, and my load of straw scattered over the roadway.

"The straw," I muttered, looking directly up into the cold blue December sky. And then I heard a ferocious cackle, the somehow inhuman howl of Martha Snyder standing at the entrance of her filthy stable pens pointing at me, laughing at me.

My eyes, which had only moments before merely puddled wet from the cold, poured. I sobbed miserably, a broken cry, as I twisted over to my knees and hands scurrying and scooping up stray straw like a starving field mouse snatching nips of cheese.

All the while I crawled about the dirt snatching pieces of straw, Martha Snyder carried on with her wicked, piercing laughter. And then, worst of all, Martha Snyder shouted at what must have been the top of her lungs: "Little begging bugger! Your mammy! Your mammy, she's a whore! A whore!"

Hearing her – the lying, cruel creature – my heart raced, blood pounded in my head and forming tears so blurred my eyes I could not see anything, not even bits of straw strewn inches from where I crawled.

So distraught was I that I did not even hear Paulo Gitano and Winnie Shram walk to where I frantically and blindly groped about for straw. When Winnie Shram put a hand to my shoulder I imagined at that instant that wicked Martha Snyder with her wild and kinky orange hair and foul breath had drawn upon me. Consequently, I cringed.

"Boy, boy," Mr Winnie soothed, patting my shoulder. Paulo crouched down to look me in the face as both of the Irishmen came over to the commotion. I no longer heard Martha Snyder. I did not know if she stopped laughing and slinked away or if the relief I felt with the older men coming to my aid caused me to stop paying attention to her heartless cackling.

In a couple of minutes, the good fellows righted my wagon, collected my straw and mopped up my tears. I finally glanced around, taking a look at Snyder Stables. The old, crooked woman was nowhere to be seen.

Starting once more on my path home to my mama, Paulo called after me and said: "Remember what we do to da witches."

I did and nodded. 'Burn 'em,' I thought, walking quietly to my mama's and my little house.

The very moment I walked through the door of my house, Mama caught sight of my skinned knees.

"What in the world?" she asked, quickly dropping to her own knees for a better look.

"I slipped, fell," I explained, sort of being truthful. "It's no big deal," I added, playing the part of her little man.

"Let's get you cleaned up," she said and did. Once I was tended to, Mama and I went out the door and began carrying the straw I collected inside. We spent the next half an hour scooping out old straw from the mattress in the solitary bed Mama and I shared and filling it back up with my fresh harvest.

By the time we finished our work, I forgot all about my spill and accident, and even Martha Snyder and her ugly words. While I was out, Mama made up a batch of a dozen sugar cookies, a most rare treat as the sweetener was so expensive and so hard to come by.

The remainder of the day and the whole of the evening proved uneventful. After supper, Mama and I curled up on the freshly stuffed mattress and she read to me from a poetry book by someone she called Lord

Byron. Sometime during a poem about a forest, I was fast asleep.

After midnight, Mama and I awoke at the same time to the sounds of men shouting and horse hooves clattering down the frost-frozen street. We both sprang out of bed and dashed to the door of our home. Opening up and stepping just outside in our nightclothes, we both looked up the street to the livery stables.

"Oh, my Lord!" Mama exclaimed, crossing herself.

"Should we go look?" I asked, wanting a better vantage point to see what was aflame.

Mama hemmed and hawed for a minute or so and then agreed that perhaps we should 'go take a look.' Quickly, we dressed and hurried down the street, joining our like-minded neighbors.

Drawing closer to the burning structure, I easily saw that I was Snyder's Stables in flames. I thought of Paulo Gitano and his parting words to me: "Remember what we do to da witches."

Reflexively, my right hand shot up to my mouth and I gasped. Mama merely and fortunately attributed my response to bearing witness to the fire. She naturally had no idea that I wasted no time in concluding Paulo Gitano had lit up a witch in the person of Martha Snyder.

I debated telling my mama on the spot of my suspicions and then I heard the familiar shriek of Martha Snyder, the old hag, bellowing at a beleaguered firefighter. While in most ways I was relieved that the rotten woman had not roasted crispy, a small part of me wished she were stuck in her flaming horse pens.

"The horses!" I exclaimed, realizing for the first time that no matter what I thought of old lady Snyder, her poor horses were innocent of any wrongdoing and likely the regular victims of the woman's ubiquitous viciousness.

A voice behind me, with an Irish brogue, responded: "Lad, they all got out quite right and just fine." James Cooney from Denver Livery stood directly behind where Mama and I stood.

"Hello, James," Mama greeted, with what I thought was a bit of an extra sparkle in her voice.

"Ma'am," James replied, kind of bowing and definitely shifting nervously from leg to leg.

"Isn't this awful?" Mama asked. I wanted to respond, now knowing the horses were safe, "Hell, no!"

But I knew the consequences would include a soapy mouth and a swat on my back end.

"'Tis," James replied.

"What happened?" Mama asked.

James responded by first mentioning Paulo Gitano's name. I felt instantly certain the Irish man was on the verge of reporting that Paulo Gitano took fire to Martha Snyder's stables. But, James actually said: "Paulo tells me a lantern fell over into a pile of straw."

And so Mama and me, James Cooney and our neighbors, watched old lady Snyder's stables burn to the ground. After the fire was put out, Mama walked back to our home with me, her arm around my shoulders.

We snuggled back into our warm bed, on our mattress, old and worn but freshly filled with clean straw.

The End

Biography of Mike Broemmel

Mike Broemmel began writing professionally in 2000 after spending much of his adult life in the political arena. He began his career working in the White House for President Ronald Reagan.

The Shadow Cast was the second collection of short fiction by Broemmel to be published, released through an independent label in the United Kingdom. He has since authored a number of other collections of short fiction as well as several novels.

In recent years, Broemmel has enjoyed success as a critically acclaimed, award-winning playwright. His accolades include receiving a grant for his work from the U.S. National Endowment for the Arts and the inclusion of his play *Stand Still & Look Stupid: The Life Story of Hedy Lamarr* in the 2019 Féile an Phobail (the largest arts festival in Northern Ireland).

Other award-winning plays by Mike Broemmel include *Goddess People*, *The Row*, *The Baptism*, *Taking Tea with the Ripper*, and *Call Me Mrs. Evers*.

The latest stage plays from Mike Broemmel are *The Wind is Us: The Death that Killed Capote,* about iconic author Truman Capote, which is slated to premiere in 2020. In addition, Mother! Is to premiere in 2020 as well and chronicles the life of hell-raising labor leader Mother Jones.

More information about Mike Broemmel and his work is available at www.mikebroemmel.com.

Made in the USA
Middletown, DE
01 August 2021